Viz
THE HANGMAN'S NOOSE

A SWINGING COMPILATION OF THE ROPIEST BITS FROM ISSUES 112-121

EDITED BY ALBERT PIERREPOINT

ANGRY LYNCH MOB
Alex Collier, Chris Donald, Simon Donald, Steve Donald, Graham Dury, Simon Ecob,
John Fardell, Wayne Gamble, Stevie Glover, Ian Iro, Davey Jones, Paul Palmer,
Lew Stringer, Cat Sullivan, Simon Thorp, Biscuit Tin and Brian Walker.

EXECUTIONER
The not particularly well-hung Will Watt.

Published by Dennis Publishing
The Old Gibbet House
30 Cleveland Street
London W1T 4JD

Tel: 0207 907 6000
(calls cost £.1.50/min at all times. Maximum call length
18 mins. Please ask bill payer's permission before calling)

ISBN 0752228102
First printing Autumn 2004

D1341762

To subscribe, call **0845 126 1053**, or log on to **www.viz.co.uk**
And may God have mercy on your soul.

Prinited in Grate Britian

Panel 1: CAPITAL NOTION, RAFFLES! A BANK HOLIDAY SOJOURN TO THE SEASIDE. AH! THE TANG OF THE OZONE, PERCHANCE A BRACING DIP IN THE BRINY — AND MAYHAP THE LILTING STRAINS OF MERRY PIERROTS IN THE PIER PAVILIONS.

TESTICLES TO ALL THAT, BUNNY. I FEEL LIKE MANDIBLING SOME FUCKER.

Panel 2: LET'S STOP FOR A BEVERAGE, BUNNY. I'M EXPECTORATING PLUMAGE.

Panel 3: I SAY, RAFFLES, WHAT GOOD FORTUNE. A FELLOW MOTOR-BICYCLIST MUST BE INSIDE!

THAT IS INDEED MOST FORTUITOUS.

Panel 4: TINKLE TINKLE ♪ PLINKY-PLONK! TWANG! ♪

Panel 5: SQUIRE'S 'TWILIGHT ON THE WATERS?' FORNICATE THIS ORDURE. LET'S GET SOME REAL MUSIC ON THE PANHARMONOPTICON.

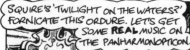

Panel 6: HERE WE GO. SOMETHING WITH A BIT OF A BEAT — KETTLEBY'S 'BELLS ACROSS THE MEADOW'!

EXCUSE ME. 'TWILIGHT ON THE WATERS' WAS MY SELECTION, SIR.

Panel 7: AND THIS, SIR, IS MY SELECTION. SO KINDLY TAKE YOUR SELECTION AND CALCITRATE IT UP YOUR FUNDAMENT.

I'M SORRY...!?

Panel 8: NOTWITHSTANDING, YOU WILL BE, PAL.

!?

Panel 9: THWANG!

Panel 10: WHAT ON EARTH..?

NO GENTLEMAN SCOOTERIST WORTH HIS SALT EVER VENTURES FORTH WITHOUT A SPARE LENGTH OF DRIVE CHAIN FOR HIS HILDEBRAND AND WOLFMÜLLER 1½HP EXCELSIOR.

GROAN

Panel 11: STOMP!

...ONE NEVER KNOWS WHEN IT MAY COME IN EXPEDIENT.

Panel 12: COME ON. LET'S FUCKING ABSQUATULATE BEFORE THE SCUFFERS TURN UP.

Panel 13: SHORTLY...

Messrs Osbert & Co of Brighton Purveyors of fine Tattoos to the Landed Gentry

BUZZ

Panel 14: THERE WE GO, YOUR GRACE. IT'S FINISHED.

TOPPING.

BUZZ BUZZ

Panel 15: A FINE EXAMPLE OF THE OEUVRE, DON'T YOU THINK, BUNNY?

INDEED RAFFLES.

IT LOOKS MOST SPLENDID.

Panel 16: I'M GOING TO GET 'AMITY' AND 'ENMITY' DONE ON MY KNUCKLES NEXT TIME.

Panel 17: LATER... I SAY, RAFFLES OLD BEAN! LOOK AT THAT COMMOTION ON THE BEACH!

HMM?

Panel 18: HUZZAH! IT'S CAPTAIN WEBB! HE'S COMPLETED HIS HEROIC NATATION OF THE ENGLISH CHANNEL! WE MUST GO AND PROFFER OUR HONORIFICATIONS.

INDEED, BUNNY. HE'S FUCKING ROCK.

Panel 19: HIP-HIP-HOORAH! HIP-HIP-HOORAH! HIP-HIP-HOORAH!

MRS. WEBB - KINDLY ALLOW ME TO BE THE FIRST TO CONGRATULATE YOU ON YOUR HUSBAND'S MOST MOMENTOUS ACHIEVEMENT...

WHY THANK YOU, LORD RAFFLES.

Panel 20: 'ERE. ARE YOU CHATTING UP MY BIRD?

SIR - REST ASSURED I WOULD NOT....

Panel 21: WHY? WHAT'S UP WITH HER?

Panel 22: PUNT-PUNT!

GO ON, MATTHEW! FUCKING LAPIDATE HIM IN THE FUCKING GENITALIA, MAN!

PUNT!

5

OH, LORDY IT'S THE FAT SLAGS

EEEH, TRAY... I THINK THE TELLY IS BUGGERED AGAIN... LOOK!

THAT BLOKE'S FACE IS ALL **PURPLE**

NO, THAT'S ALEX FERGUSON

THANK FUCK F' THAT. I THOUGHT WE WERE GOIN' TO 'AVE T' CALL THE BLOKE OUT AGAIN

AYUP THERE, GIRLS!... YER BACK DOOR WAS OPEN, SO I LET MYSELF IN, LIKE

MIND, Y' WANT TO WATCH OUT, Y' DO...

I MIGHT 'AVE BEEN A SEX MANIAC COME T' AVE ME WICKED WAY WITH YER!

WELL, YOU **ARE**, AREN'T YER?

ERM... AYE... I SUPPOSE SO

ANYWAY... WHAT D'Y' RECKON T' THIS?... TASTY OR WHAT?

HMM!... WHO IS IT?

IT'S **MY MISSUS**!!

THELMA? **NEVER**

IT IS!

'UNDRED QUID THAT COST ME... SHE GOT AN AFTERNOON'S PAMPERIN'- NAILS, HAIRDO, MAKE UP... ALL THAT SHIT, THEN A SESSION WI' A TOP GLAMOUR PHOTOGRAPHER.

EEH! THE LUCKY BITCH. WAS IT 'ER BIRTHDAY OR SUMMAT, BAZ?

NO! IT WAS A SWEETENER AFTER SHE FOUND YOUR KNICKERS IN THE FOOT-WELL OF ME SIDECAR

BUT WHAT 'AVE THEY DONE, BAZ?... SHE AINT THAT GOOD LOOKIN IN REAL LIFE, EVEN WI' ALL 'ER MAKE UP ON

SHE CLEANS UP A TREAT DOES THELMA. AN' THEY PUT VASELINE ON THE CAMERA LENS TO SOFTEN UP THE LINES A BIT AN' THAT.

STILL, SHE'S THE LIGHT OF ME LIFE... AN' I LOVE 'ER I DO.

AH! THAT'S REALLY LOVELY THAT IS, BAZ

AYE! D'Y' FANCY A BANG?

AYE, GO ON THEN. I'LL FUCK YUZ A BIT, BUT I CAN'T GO OFF, LIKE

EH!?

ME AN' THELMA ARE TRYIN' FORRA BABY, SO I'M SAVIN' IT F' HER

Y' CAN **FUCK RIGHT OFF** BARRY ASKWITH. YER NOT GOIN' T' LEAVE US HALF COCKED, Y' CHEEKY CUNT

OOOF!

PUNT!

SLAM!

SNIFF!

'OW ARE WE GOIN' T' WIN 'IM BACK, TRAY? 'OW CAN WE GET 'IM T' GO OFF UP US AGAIN?

'ELLO... FULCHESTER GLAMOUR STUDIOS?...

...I'D LIKE T' BOOK ME AN' ME MATE AN APPOINTMENT.

NEXT DAY...

DON'T FRET, SAN... WHEN BAZ SEES OUR GLAM SHOTS, HE'LL ONLY 'AVE KNACKERS FOR US

FULCHESTER Glamour STUDIOS

MISS BURKE? MISS TUNSTALL?

DO COME THROUGH FOR YOUR HAIR STYLINGS

CONTINUED OVER

Up the Arse Corner...

Sender: Stuart Wood, Leicester

Sender: Mel & Tim Pants, Burton on Trent

Sender: A. Rushmer, Wilmslow

Sender: Mr X, Atlantis

Sender: Vinnie Clark, e-mail

Sender: Deek, Daventry

&

Up the Arts Corner...

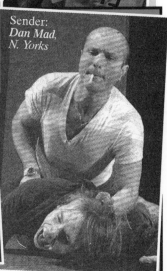

Sender: Dan Mad, N. Yorks

Sender: B. Sewell, Pudsey

Letterbocks

Letterbocks, Viz Comic, PO Box 1PT, Newcastle upon Tyne NE99 1PT

Star Letter

WOULD someone please tell my neighbour to stop licking my dog's testicles, it's putting me off my boiled eggs.

Ashley Foster
Warwickshire

I BOUGHT this savoury snack today, and imagine my dismay when, upon opening the packet, I found it to contain many small crisps as opposed to one large crisp. But I see the manufacturers had covered their backs.

Daniel
Newcastle

THE Big Issue would sell a lot more copies if they made their vendors smarten up a bit. Most of them look like tramps.

Tim Woods
e-mail

IF no one knows where Osama Bin Laden is, how come there are so many pictures of the old cunt?

Jim
e-mail

I RECENTLY read in the media that schizophrenia affects one in every hundred people. I beg to differ, as I work in a mental hospital where there are about ninety two people out of a hundred with it.

Nurse Joe Littleknow
e-mail

Carlos driving

RALLY driver Carlos Saintz ran through a crowd of 12 people at 100 mph and got a trophy. I ran through a bus queue and got 12 months, and I was only doing 65. It seems that there is one law for the foreigners and one for us.

J. Barnwell
London

I watched fat-tongued mockney Jamie Oliver on telly preparing a dish using 'the old chicken' with a dash of 'the old lemon' and a hint of 'the old tarragon'. You'd think with his money he'd be able to use fresh ingredients, not ones past their sell-by date.

Bobby Harrison
London

I AM not interested in the porn industry at all, and I wonder if Channel 5 are planning to show any documentaries not about the porn industry in the near future.

J. Sykes
Hull

SO it's our car, our flat and our money, but I notice it's always her tits. There's feminism for you.

Neil
e-mail

I AM planning to become a stalker of a major celebrity, but I can't decide between Britney Spears and Kylie Minogue. I wonder if your readers could offer any advice.

T. Woods
e-mail

* Who would you stalk? Would you bury yourself in Britney's bins and behold her bathtime baps through binoculars? Or would you rather wank yourself off through Kylie's letterbox? Write and tell us at the usual address.

IN issue 111 you printed a letter from someone in Australia who had just had a big shite only to find there was no toilet paper left. When this happened to a friend of mine many years ago, he swore blind that he got 4 good wipes out of a Spangle wrapper.

P. Clarke
Batley

LAST night, I dreamt I was shagging former Baywatch beauty Pamela Anderson. Imagine my disappointment when she turned out to be a flop in bed! Have any other readers dreamt of poking a celebrity who turned out to be shit in the sack?

The Hurricane
Salford

* Well, have you dreamt you were at it with a star? Were they any good? What did they ask you to do? Why not write and tell us. And remember that, because it's a dream, and you're not claiming it actually happened, under British law you can say anything you like.

I READ with anger that pop star Shakin' Stevens was charged with drink driving on New Year's Eve. How unfair. If they asked him to walk along a straight line in a steady manner, it's no wonder Shaky appeared to be under the influence.

T. Walsh
Burnley

I AM a lesbian trapped in a man's body. I am desperate to meet sympathetic women (preferably couples) who understand my plight, to see past the curse of penis affliction and initiate me into the joys of `lesbian love. Please, please reach out and help a sister in distress.

Paul Murphy (aka Ethel)
e-mail

ALTHOUGH I don't generally approve of these so-called suicide bombers, at least it gives people in utter despair something to live for.

Sally Ann
e-mail

Body double

AM I the only person who thinks that fanny mechanic Lord Robert Winston is moonlighting as 70s porn afficianado Pop Shot?

Eddie
Dunfermline

THE number 4 on my pocket calculator has stopped working. Are there any scientists out there with big calculations to do that do not include any 4s in them. If so, they can have it with pleasure.

Adrien Newth
e-mail

Survival of the shittest

HOW do people who subscribe to Darwin's theory of Evolution explain ginger people? People in hot countries have dark hair,

whilst people in cold countries have blond hair. In temperate climates, a mixture of hair colour is found. It can only be concluded that, in his wisdom, God made ginger people for a laugh and placed them randomly about the globe.

Rev. J. Porter
London

IF THE Americans can't find Osama Bin Laden, they should stop looking, sit down with a cup of tea and try to think where they saw him last. This always works when I can't find my car keys or glasses.

M. Ross
London

WHEN I make comments about the size of Britney Spears's tits and women not making good pilots, my girlfriend accuses me of being sexist. Yet when I punch her in the face she starts ranting and raving about it being wrong to hit a lass. The hypocrisy of it all dumbfounds me.

M. Hobson
Whitley Bay

EX-ARSENAL fan Osama Bin Laden has taken football hooliganism to new extremes with his attack on New York. It makes me hanker for the good old days when they just threw coins and darts at each other.

H. Monroe
Wigan

A NOTICE on the back of a tube of Colgate toothpaste says 'We do not make toothpaste for anyone else". Imagine my anger when my friend's tube of Colgate had exactly the same notice.

Danny Handley
West Midlands

I RECENTLY bought the December issue of GQ magazine with Natalie Imbruglia on the cover. She might have a nice face, but she's got knockers like dried up walnuts.

A. Beech
Gateshead

UP THE ARSE CORNER

Sender: David Pirie, Newcastle

Blue Peter fadge

ON A recent holiday in Somerset, our day a Wookey Hole caves was spoilt when we turned up to be told they were closed due to the BBC filming. Whilst disappointedly eating lunch at the picnic site, the crew turned up and took the table behind us.

We discovered that they were from Blue Peter, mainly because twat presenter Simon Thomas proceeded to spend the next hour shouting down his mobile phone, putting on ridiculous Welsh accents, taking the piss out of Blue Peter bring and buy sales, and generally behaving like a complete arsehole.

So thank you BBC for preventing us from seeing the caves, and a special thanks to Mr. Thomas for completing the job of ruining our day.

Simon King
e-mail

ARSENE Wenger said that Osama Bin Laden, an ex-Arsenal supporter, would not be welcome at Highbury again. Perhaps they should put a photograph of him on each turnstile, so that if he should attempt to get in he can be reported to the police.

J. Miles
London

LAST night, I wached a Premiership football match with disgust. The players were constantly blowing their noses by covering a nostril with a finger and snorting the mucus out. They should take a tip from my nan and always have a hankie poked up their sleeve when they take to the field.

Gary Warburton
e-mail

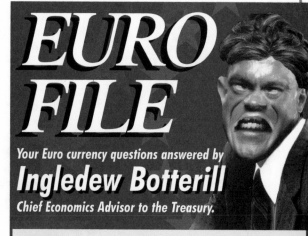

IDENTICAL twins. Use Morse code to cheat in exams by stabbing yourself in the arm with a sharp compass. The other twin, at home with a text book, can 'feel' the question and stab you back the answers.

W. Walker
Norwich

CHERYL from London. Stop your husband from shagging the readhead down the Coach and Horses by occasionally sucking his dick, you frigid cow.

T. Moss
London

NEWLYWEDS. Act in a surreptitious manner from the start of your marriage so as not to attract suspicion when you do have an affair.

Joel Young
Middlesbrough

POWER companies. After a blackout, wait until midnight before turning on the power again. That way, everybody's alarm clocks and videos will be automatically re-set.

Joe Leary
On fire in Australia

A USED condom filled with water and left on a radiator makes an ideal and inexpensive lava lamp.

T. Hogan
e-mail

MATHEMATICIANS. It is always easier to work with smaller numbers so when adding up big numbers, simply take one away from each figure and then add two onto your final number.

Tim Gibson
e-mail

RECENTLY defunct and apparently worthless European coins still work as legal tender for buskers, beggars, the honesty box in WHSmith and old ladies collecting for charities. Especially the RNIB.

Jamie Groves
e-mail

Massage parlour joke

Dear Sir,
I intend to holiday on the continent this year. Where do I get Euros from?

Euro notes and coins are widely available from banks, post offices and bureau de changes, although a commission will have to be paid when buying. You can of course avoid this commission by holidaying in Britain.

Dear Sir,
I'm driving through France to Spain this summer. Can I spend French Euros in Spain and vice versa?

Yes, of course, that is the whole point of the system. Any Euro can be spent in any country that has adopted the currency, regardless of where the actual notes or coins originated. You can use French Euros to buy as many straw donkeys and salmonella filled paellas as you like. Spanish Euros will likewise pay for antifreeze-filled French plonk and snails.

Dear Sir,
I recently returned from Rome where I bought a can of coke for 3 Euros. I paid with a 20 Euro note, and was given 50,000 lira change. Was I ripped off?

Confusions such as this will be commonplace whilst there is a period of changover. As a general rule, if you're buying a can of coke in Rome, you're being ripped off. Be careful of toddlers going through your pockets.

Dear Sir,
I'm going to Belfast for a conference in the Spring. Do I need to to buy Euros, as I hear the Irish have adopted the currency?

No, this is a common confusion. The Mick Irish are still using English pounds, it's the Bog Irish are trotting about with their pockets full of monopoly money.

Dear Sir,
My family have booked a villa in a rural part of mainland Greece. I am a little worried that being in such a rural place, the Euro may not be accepted. Should I take a mixture of currencies, Euros and Drachmas?

To be on the safe side, yes. In theory, every part of Greece should accept Euros, but in rural areas, the truth may be slightly different. Lets face it, when some oily, kebab-chomping copper with a gun is demanding 50 drachmas not to rape your wife and kids, you don't want to find yourself with a wallet full of bumwad from the Bank of Toyland.

Spew Your Bile... Spew
New Years Honours...

DOES anyone know why Sade got an OBE in the New Years Honours list? I can only think it's because 'Your Love is King' got to number 6 in 1984.

M. Turnbull, Leeds

ONCE again, the government have made a mockery of the Honours system. A knighthood for Yorkshire Ripper Peter Sutcliffe is a disgrace. As far as I can tell he has contributed nothing positive to society. Whetever next? A life peerage for Harold Shipman?

M. Geils, London

A LIFE peerage for Harold Shipman is a disgrace. What were the government thinking of? One can only presume that there has been some money changing hands. Whatever next? Dame Rose West?

F. Stanton, Rhyll

SO the BeeGees all got OBEs in the New Year's Honours list. In my opinion, gongs should have been given to Robin and Maurice, but not to Barry. Not for any particular reason, but the look on his face would have been an absolute treat.

M. Peg, Surrey

9

ROGER MELLIE

THE MAN ON THE TELLY

ONE DAY...

HELLO,.. ROGER MELLIE...

HI ROGER. SORRY TO CALL YOU ON YOUR MOBILE, ONLY I COULDN'T GET YOU AT HOME

NO PROBS TOM

LISTEN, ROGER... HAVE YOU SEEN THE PAPERS TODAY?

PAPERS?... NO!...

...BUT I'LL TELL YOU, TOM, SHE'S A FUCKIN' LYING *BITCH* THAT ONE... IT WAS *NEVER* RAPE. SHE WAS FUCKIN' *BEGGING FOR IT*

YOU KNOW WHAT THEY'RE LIKE, TOM...WHEN THEY SAY 'NO NO NO, DON'T' THEY MEAN 'YES!'..

THEY'RE ALL THE FUCKIN' SAME!!

WELL DON'T YOU FUCKIN' WORRY TOM! SHE'S FUCKIN' FINISHED! DRAGGIN MY NAME THROUGH THE SHIT, THE FUCKING WHORE!

I'LL FUCKIN' FINISH HER!..

...SHE'LL NEVER FUCKIN' WORK AGAIN, TOM... NEVER!

NO, IT'S NOT THAT, ROGER... BARGAIN HUNT PRESENTER DAVID DICKINSON HAS HAD A NASTY ACCIDENT... THE BEEB ARE LOOKING FOR A STAND IN. ARE YOU BUSY, ONLY I'VE GOT THE PRODUCER HERE NOW IF YOU CAN GET OVER?

SURE...

...WE'RE ABOUT 20 MINUTES INTO THE MATINEE, BUT I'LL MOTOR THROUGH IT AND WRAP IT UP AS FAST AS I CAN, OKAY?

10 MINUTES LATER...

WOTCHA TOM!

AH, ROGER...THIS IS PETER BARNYARD, PRODUCER OF "BARGAIN HUNT" I TAKE IT YOU'RE FAMILIAR WITH THE SHOW

SURE

THE ONE WITH THE SPIV WHO LOOKS LIKE THE BISTO KID

LISTEN, I'VE BEEN HAVING A THINK ON THE WAY OVER... I'VE GOT AN IDEA ABOUT HOW WE CAN SHAKE THE FORMAT UP A BIT...

ERM...WELL... THANKS, BUT...

FIRST OFF, YOU WANT TO DITCH ALL THAT BOLLOCKS ABOUT ANTIQUES AND RENAME THE SHOW *BARGAIN CUNT!*

OH... ERM...

THEN YOU GIVE A COUPLE OF UGLY BLOKES TWO HUNDRED QUID EACH AND SEND 'EM INTO A KNOCKING SHOP...

THE ONE WHO GETS THE MOST FUCKS FOR HIS MONEY IS THE WINNER. GREAT, EH?

WELL, PERHAPS IF THE RATINGS DROP, BUT I THINK WE'LL STICK WITH THE FORMAT WE'VE GOT AT THE MOMENT

OKAY, JUST REMEMBER IT'S MY IDEA

TOM, YOU'RE MY WITNESS

ANYWAY, ROGER, WE'RE FILMING AT AN ANTIQUES FAIR TOMORROW... THEY START VERY EARLY, SO COULD YOU BE THERE AT 7 A.M. SHARP...

TOM HAS ALL THE DETAILS

NO WORRIES, PETE... I'LL BE THERE!!

NEXT DAY...

ERM... I... DON'T KNOW

WHERE THE HELL IS HE, TOM!? IT'S HALF PAST BLOODY ONE!

...HE'S USUALLY SO PUNCTUAL

CONTINUED OVER

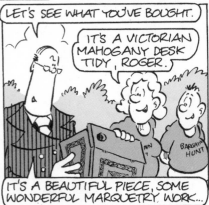

16

THE REAL ALE TWATS

NOW THIS IS A SAMPLE OF PEMBERTON'S AWLD TRADITIONAL

BEER TASTING TONIGHT

A MEMENTO OF MY SOJOURN TO THE PRIORY TAVERN IN PENMONSHIRE LAST MONTH

A MOST CONVIVIAL HOSTELRY

ASK IF IT'S CASK

ALE SAMPLES

DRIP DRIP DRIP

ROGER THE LANDLORD HAD AN IMPRESSIVE COLLECTION OF DRIP TRAYS ON DISPLAY IN THE SALOON BAR

SIP! SIP! SIP!

A FRUITY LIGHT ALE WITH A TANGY HOP ON THE NOSE

CLEAN-TASTING WITH A QUICK, DRY FINISH. 4.8% ABV.

NOW WE HAVE WHET OUR PALATES, LET US ADJOURN TO A SUITABLE ALEHOUSE

I'LL JUST SPRUCE MYSELF UP BEFORE WE VENTURE FORTH

SQUIRT SQUIRT

SPRAY-ON FOOD PARTICLES WITH SOUP

BEST FOOT FORWARD, FELLOW CASKETEERS

OHO! A NEWLY REFURBISHED WATERING HOLE

CLUB EXOTICA

STRIPPERS INSIDE

AND EVIDENTLY THEY ARE PURVEYORS OF "STRIPPERS" ALE

I BELIEVE I SAMPLED IT AT THE SWANSEA BEER FESTIVAL IN '82

HM. NO, STRIPPERS IS NOT IN THE GUIDE — MAYHAP IT IS THE PRODUCT OF A NEW LOCAL MICROBREWERY

LET US SUBJECT IT TO THE APPRAISAL OF OUR ALE-TUTORED TASTEBUDS

GOOD DAY, MINE HOST. WE WOULD LIKE TO SAMPLE THE STRIPPERS, IF YOU PLEASE

THEY'RE ON IN A FEW MINUTES

AH. A FRESH BARREL. THEN THERE IS NO HASTE

ONE SHOULD NEVER HURRY THE ALCHEMICAL PROCESS OF PREPARING A VIRGIN CASK

IF YOU'RE STAYING YOU'LL HAVE TO BUY DRINKS

THIS IS WHAT I AM ENDEAVOURING TO DO

KINDLY PAY ATTENTION. THREE BRIMMING PINTS TO BE BROUGHT TO US IN THE SNUG, PLEASE.

TSK. THE JUKEBOX MUSIC SEEMS UNNECESSARILY INTRUSIVE

ONE LONGS FOR NOTHING BUT THE CLICK-CLACK OF DOMINOES AND THE MERRY BANTER OF DRINKING FRIENDS

THREE BEERS. THAT'S TWENTY FIVE POUND.

DEAR OH DEAR. ACCORDING TO MY HYDROMETER, THE ABV OF THIS ALE IS MERELY 2.2%

GRIND BUMP

HARDLY A JUSTIFICATION FOR THE SOMEWHAT EXCESSIVE PRICE

AND LOOK! THIS IS UNBELIEVABLE!

PING PONG BALLS

POP! POP! POP!

MY CAMRA-ISSUED MEASUREMENT CARD INDICATES THAT IT IS FULLY 2ml SHORT OF A LIQUID PINT!

NOW THEN, BARMAN, YOU CAN'T EXPECT ME TO ACCEPT THIS SUBSTANDARD PINT, CAN YOU?

NOW, WHAT ARE YOU GOING TO DO TO RECTIFY MY DISSATISFACTION?

ONE SPECIAL TOP-UP COMING UP, SIR

TUG TUG TUG

AH. THAT'S MORE LIKE IT. A FULL-BODIED PINT WITH A GOOD CREAMY HEAD

NOTHING LIKE A FINE BEER PULLED STRAIGHT FROM THE WOOD

NEVERAGAI

IT'S THE WORLD'S most exclusive funfair! Entrance is strictly by invitation only, and once inside you're guaranteed the time of your life. It's Neverland, the private theme park built by pop superstar Michael Jackson in his back yard. The guest list reads like a who's who of the Hollywood entertainment industry, as A-list celebrities and their kids rub shoulders in the queues for the rollercoasters and helter skelters.

But behind the welcoming facade of flashing lights, candyfloss and merry-go-rounds, is a darker side which Jacko makes sure his guests never get to see.

One man who has glimpsed what goes on behind the scenes is Smethwick lavatory attendant Bob McNally. And now he's set to spill the beans on the seedy goings on he witnessed. And he sends this warning to any star invited to Neverland: "If you'd seen what I've seen, you wouldn't take your kids within a million miles of that place!"

One day last summer, Bob was surprised to be offered the job of attendant in the toilet block at Jackson's California fairground.

❝I'd just got in from work and my wife told me Michael Jackson had been on the phone, wanting me to fly out to the states to do some work at Neverland. I still don't know why he'd chosen me. I'd done a pretty good job unblocking the gents at Smethwick Community Centre the previous week, and I suppose the word must have got around.

stretch

"I didn't need asking twice. It was the opportunity of a lifetime. I just had time to pack my plunger, and next thing I knew I was in a stretch limousine on my way to Tipton airport, where Jacko's private jet was waiting to whisk me to America."

neil

Ten hours later McNally found himself at Neverland, and he couldn't believe his eyes.

"The place was packed with stars. Everyone there was a household name. The atmos-

by our entertainment correspondent **Clancey Beauregard**

phere was one of fun and frivolity, and there at the centre of it all was Michael Jackson himself. He was laughing and joking with all the children. It seemed very innocent at the time."

louis

But the reality of the pop star's funfair was far from innocent, as Bob was shortly to discover.

"That afternoon, I came out of the gents after fitting a new disinfectant cube in one of the urinals. I looked over and saw Home Alone child star **Macauley Culkin** walking towards the coconut shy. It was three balls for a dollar, and I clearly saw the innocent youngster hand Jackson a ten dollar bill. He gave him his three balls

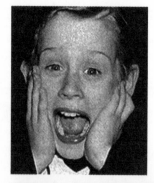

in return, but only FOUR dollars change. I couldn't believe my eyes. He'd diddled Culkin out of five dollars. That little boy went home alone, and five bucks down."

But, as Bob soon found out, it wasn't just kiddies that Jacko was diddling.

liston

"Later that day I was having a tea break when I spotted Dirty

Harry star **Clint Eastwood** eyeing up the prizes on the shooting gallery. He handed over a dollar bill and Jackson passed him his air rifle and three pellets. As he lifted the air gun, Clint looked confident - and with good reason. Over the years, he'd proved his sharpshooting skills picking off baddies in a fistful of spaghetti westerns.

"Three tin ducks should have

"Don't let your kids within a mile of the place"
~Bob McNally

proved no problem, but on this occasion, Eastwood was the man with no aim. That rifle was shooting every which way but straight. Clint couldn't believe it... but I could. For moments earlier I had seen Michael Jackson bending the sights on the gun with pliers. He can deny it till he's blue in the face, but I know what I saw. Michael Jackson owes Clint Eastwood an apology. And a goldfish."

ali

Another star who was conned out of a prize by the wacko singer is **Sir Elton John,** and this time it was a big Garfield. "Jackson was drumming up custom by moonwalking in front of a darts stall, grabbing

It's not Double Fair

McNally recalls the time he saw Michael Douglas and Catherine Zeta Jones heading towards the Toytown merrygoround with a pushchair. He watched as baby Dylan sat in the fire engine, and Jacko came round to take the money.

"Douglas gave him fifty cents, but Jackson insisted that the fire engine was a two seater, and single occupancy cost double. He refused to start the ride up unless the Fatal Attraction star coughed up another fifty cents. He said it was nothing to do with him, it was just a rule of his fairground.

"Douglas refused, and went to take the toddler, who was by now crying, out of the fire engine. Catherine Zeta Jones told him just to give Jackson the money."

A surly Douglas paid up and the ride started, but it was too late for Dylan, says Bob.

"His parents were so upset that they forgot to wave at him as he came past. By the end of the ride, he was crying his eyes out again. Jackson couldn't have cared less. He just stood by the controls in a vest, smoking and staring into the middle distance."

Lifting the lid - Lavatory attendant McNally yesterday

lowed by his entourage. In the words of his own song, which struggled up to 42 in 1981, nobody wins in Jackson's fairground."

heap

According to Bob, Jackson had hundreds of little scams for squeezing cash out of his star customers. Take the waltzers, for example. Thanks to Jacko, the people on it were being taken for a ride in more ways than one.

"I remember seeing **Nicole Kidman** and **Tom Cruise** on the waltzers. Jackson was spinning their car faster and faster and they were being tossed around like ragdolls. After the ride stopped, the wobbly-legged Hollywood couple staggered off laughing towards the hook-a-duck stall. Little did they realise that Jackson was in their waltzer helping himself to all the loose change which had fallen out of Cruise's trousers.

There must have been half a million dollars easy. Tom may have had his eyes wide shut, but his pockets were wide open, and he was easy prey for sneaky Jackson."

how

Bob himself avoided getting ripped off at Neverland until one day when he finished work early and went to get a bite to eat.

"I fancied a toffee apple and a drink, so I went to Jackson's refreshments stall, a dingy caravan parked in some long grass

next to a generator. My apple looked alright from the outside, but under the toffee it was a different story.

magpie

The skin was as wrinkled as a prune, and the inside was soft and mushy. It must have been three months old if it was a day. I threw it away in disgust after one bite. I asked for my money back, but Jacko looked me in the eye and told me I hadn't bought it from him."

blue peter

And McNally fared little better with his drink.

"I asked him for a big cup of coke, but I ended up with two dollars' worth of ice and just a slurp of cola. It was a complete

rip-off. Jackson may have had his head set alight during a Pepsi advert, but now it's his customers who are getting burnt."

jolly roger

A week into his contract, McNally was told his services were no longer needed.

"I'd been sacked. Officially it was because I'd been caught stealing forty rolls of toilet paper, but that's nonsense. The real reason was obvious; I knew what Jackson was up to, and he knew that I knew. I was dangerous, so he had to get rid of me.

"And anyway, I was only taking the toilet rolls so I could get the wrappers off at home and make an early start the next morning. **"**

his crotch and shouting: 'Score over six to win. Three darts for a dollar.'

John spotted a three foot toy Garfield on the stall and thought it would be lovely to win it for his partner David Furnish.

um

"Sir Elton handed over his cash and threw his darts. He did pretty well, scoring twenty-one, and confidently stepped forward to accept his prize. But Jackson simply pointed to a tiny sign fastened to the Garfield, reading: 'Take me home if you lose', and handed the singer a small gonk with cardboard eyes.

"Elton John was absolutely furious, and stormed off fol-

Carrie on Losing

SEX & the City star **Sarah Jessica-Parker** got more than she bargained for when she tried to hit the jackpot in the Neverland amusement arcade.

McNally tells how the 38 years old actress, who plays Carrie Bradshaw in the hit show lost over $60 in Jackson's amusement arcade.

pumping

"I stood and watched her pumping money into the penny waterfalls like it was going out of fashion. Every five minutes, she'd be off to get more coins, leaving **Ally McBeal** guarding her place. In his change booth Jackson, dressed in a threadbare knitted cardigan, would look up from his racing post, hand her a margerine tub full of nickels, and she would run back to the machine. Then she'd feed all her money back in, desperately trying to dislodge a huge overhang of coins.

any old

"Eventually, Parker's frustration got the better of her, and she started rocking and kicking the machine. Jackson was out of his change booth like a rat out of a trap. He told her to beat it, and she

did." But McNally doesn't know why he bothered.

"That machine was never going to pay out, no matter how hard she hit it. Earlier that day I'd seen Jackson gluing the coins in place with Araldite."

ROLLCALL of EVIL!

IF YOUR KIDS are invited to Neverland, then take care. Here are *Jackson's Five* favourite scams for getting his sticky fingers on their spondoolicks.

● The grip on the amusement arcade cranes is too weak to successfully pick up the packets of cigarettes with out of date fivers sellotaped to them.

● In order to win on the **hoop-la** stall, the hoop must go over both the bottle of pomagne AND the wooden base on which it stands. However, the diameter of the wooden base is about an eighth of an inch larger than the hoop.

● Jackson offers a prize if he guesses your weight and gets it wrong. What he doesn't tell you is your prize is worth twenty cents...and each guess costs you a dollar.

● Wacko readily demonstrates that the targets are not fixed to their stands on the **coconut shy**. But what he doesn't tell you they've been drilled and filled with lead shot, making them all but impossible to knock down.

● It's not unknown for the Billy Jean star to slip the occasional **foreign coin** in with your change, so check it carefully.

BROUGHT TO BOOK

JK ROWLING makes much of the fact that she was a single mum on benefits whilst writing her first Harry Potter book. Well, if she was receiving benefits whilst writing, she was technically working, as she was doing it with a view to making money from her quaint meanderings. It follows, therefore, that she is one of the benefit cheats that the government are so keen to crack down on. If anyone would like to report her, the number to call is 0800 854440.

G. Brandolani
e-mail

I SHOULD be on that Friends Reunited website but I'm playing truant.

Andrew Cartledge
e-mail

MY SISTER comes home from work, puts on my dad's overcoat, flat cap, hobnail boots and scarf. Then she goes to the pub with our greyhound, drinks six pints of bitter and staggers home after closing time. Am I am right to worry about this cross dressing behaviour, and should I get her to seek help?

C. Fantastic
Chelmsford

I WISH people would be more specific when talking about September the 11th. It's now 2002, so how the fuck do we know which September the 11th they are talking about?

RFN4
e-mail

WAKEY SHAKEY

I CAN'T see what the problem is with Shakin' Stevens drink driving. If he ran someone over whilst drunk, he could simply jump out of the car and sing them out of any coma that he'd just knocked them into.

T. Thorn
Northumberland

LAST week I read that another traffic warden was attacked whilst working. Motorists would do well to remember that while receiving a parking fine is inconvenient and annoying, parking inspectors are only doing their jobs. Mind you, it's a cunt's job and only cunts would want to do it.

Peter Owens
e-mail

HART ATTACK!

WHEN I was little, wizard of the charcoal sticks Tony Hart visited our school to do some pictures of elephants or whatever. Our teacher sent us out, as a welcoming gesture, to meet him as he parked his car. On a given signal from our teacher (out of view behind a wall), we walked towards him in an orderly fashion and said "Welcome, Mr. Hart". He grimmaced, wide-eyed and said "Monstrous, naughty children". Then he panicked, clutched his briefcase to his chest and shouted "Go away! Go away and leave me alone". He started gesticulating, pointing us to get away from him and swinging his briefcase as though his life was under threat from a few 3-foot tall infants. Our teacher poked his head around the wall, completely baffled by his behaviour. Us lads just started to play football in the yard.

Richard Hatfield
e-mail

YOU'VE GOT FE-MAIL

THE OTHER night, I dreamt I was boning Connie, the AOL girl. Imagine my delight when she took some speed and asked me to do bum games.

A. Skraga
e-mail

LAST NIGHT I drank 10 pints of Guinness, followed by 10 bottles of port which I rounded off with 10 bottles of Advocat. This morning I shat a perfect rolled up German flag.

Will Turnhill
Reigate

ACCORDING to Newton's law, energy cannot be destroyed or created, only changed from one form to another. So why are all these boffins predicting we will one day run out of power? If you ask me, it's just another con trick by the gas board trying to stick their prices up.

Gavin McKernan
Ballycastle

ARE YOU still doing Celebrity Cunts? Anyway, back in 1990 I was living in Manchester and was looking for someone to jumpstart my MK2 Escort. What unbelievable luck to see wavey mic monkey man Ian Brown out of the Stone Roses sitting in the passenger seat of a car in the traffic. Upon asking for help and saying how much of a fan I was, "Fuck off, you sad cunt, get a proper car, son" came the reply. What a tosser.

Oz
e-mail

Sorry, Oz, but as a baggy-trousered Madchester hell-raiser, Ian behaved exactly as he should have. Had he smiled, signed autographs and jump started your car, he would have been a complete cunt.

I'M SICK and tired of smokers having all the luck. It's about time someone thought of us

alcoholics and invented an alcohol patch which lets a steady stream of booze into the blood to keep us nicely topped up throughout the day.

B. Bollockhead
e-mail

ENCLOSED is a panel from The Beano dated 12th January 2002 that my son brought to my attention with the comment that it was the dirtiest thing he'd seen in print.

P. Armitstead
Liverpool

A RECENT report from the University of Chicago said that women are attracted to men that smell like their father. Well I'm not. My dad's been dead for three months and he must fucking ming.

Jane Harris
London

Letterbocks

E-mail letters@viz.co.uk

Letterbocks, Viz Comic, PO Box 1PT,
Newcastle upon Tyne NE99 1PT

RECENTLY DIVORCED MOUSE!

Ding-dong!

HI! WE WERE JUST OFF DOWN THE PUB AND WAS WONDERING IF YOU FANCIED GETTING OUT AT ALL FOR A WHILE?

NAH! NOT UP TO IT YET, THANKS!

MAYBE ANOTHER TIME, MATE, YEAH?

sigh! THE HOUSE JUST SEEMS SO BIG!

sniff!

Paul Palmer

TﬦP

WIFE beaters. When hitting your wife, get hold of a crocodile, a string of sausages and a policeman to recreate some of that seaside magic for the kids.

Michael Edwards, Stockton on Tees

OLD people. Prevent being beaten black and blue for paltry amounts of money by carrying large sums of cash with you at all times.

Frank Blofeld, Wales

DON'T fork out thousands of pounds on a jacuzzi-style bath. Make your own by placing a hairdryer in the bath.

Jack Plywood, Wiltshire

PLACING your penis in the bottom of your girlfriends popcorn box will give her a real shock at the cinema. Especially if you're at home watching football at the time.

Michael Edwards, Stockton on Tees

DON'T bother going to any trouble for loaded, elderly relatives. As their parting shot, they invariably leave the lot to someone who has never lifted a finger to help them.

Cecil Gaybody, Firkham

LADIES. Avoid premature widowhood by preventing your husband entering the bathroom with any electrical appliances.

Susan Plywood, Wiltshire

NURSING home staff. Modify a bathtub by attaching roller skates to the bottom, and next time you give an old man a bath, roll him down a country lane for some 'Last of the Summer Wine' style fun.

Michael Edwards, Stockton on Tees

TﬦPs

HOBO-EROTIC

I THINK that the Big Issue would be better off producing jazz mags. This would mean that if your wife discovered any of your 'specialist literature' you could merely claim that you were helping the homeless.

Luke Robson-Smith e-mail

FORGET about Pop Idol judge Simon and his high waist band, how about this for a contender for the 'Homer Simpson trousers up to the Throat' award? Can any readers beat that? And by the way, I've knobbed Ginger Spice and have pictures to prove it.

Chris Bilton Rotherham

* Well, readers, Chris Bilton has thrown down the gauntlet. Have you got any photographs of old codgers with their trousers round their armpits? Or maybe you've got pictures of yourself poking Ginger Spice. We'll be interested to see either. Send them to our usual address and mark your envelope High Trousers/ Ginger Shafting.

EVERY time I visit a big city, I get fed up with some scruffy bastard offering me a bigger shoe. I'm happy with the size I've already got.

Dave Oliver Hartlepool

ENCLOSED is a photograph of a Spoilt Bastard who accompanied us on a recent trip to the Alps.

Friends of Timmy Llandudno

I FOR one welcome reforms to the postal service. Private companies will be a boon as, currently, Royal Mail regulations prevent me from sending excrement through the post. Let us hope the new companies will be a bit more liberal.

Haig Paxton Ayrshire

I FEEL that Norway should join the EU without delay. Not for any political or economic reasons, just to stop Sweden and Finland from looking like a big cock and balls on the new euro coins.

Andy Dunn Stroud

I HAVE a part-time Saturday job and am unable to buy Viz as well as any decent porn mags, so I decided to continue just purchasing Viz. I do however feel that you need to compensate me, and I will reluctantly accept a picture of Britney Spears's arse printed in the forthcoming issue so that I can continue to wank.

Dave Blackwell Kent

* Here you go, Dave...

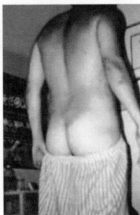

Sender: Dan Greenwood, Weston-Super-Mare

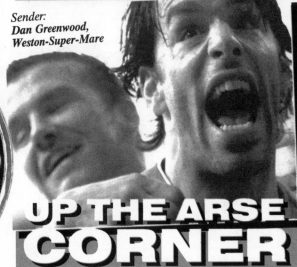

UP THE ARSE CORNER

25

Jack Black & his dog Silver

in the

MYSTERY OF THE SHORTBREAD & LONG TROUSERS

Jack Black and his dog Silver stepped onto the station platform near the remote Northumbrian village of Embleton-on-the-Wall. It was Spring half term at last, and they were going to spend it here with Aunt Meg in her converted Kentish oasthouse.

Hello, Aunt Meg!

Hello, young Jack!

Let's get you two home. You'll be wanting a nice hot bath after your long journey.

You can say that again

Shortly...

My, you have grown, Jack. Now, have you washed down on the farm?

Yes

Have you cleaned inside the farmer's hat?

Yes, Aunt Meg.

Come on then. Let's get you dry.

Wait a minute!...

...what are these little hairs around my tassel?

Bless you, Jack. They're called pubes. They're nothing to worry about, just a sign that you're turning from a boy into a young gentleman.

...and because of that, we'll go to the village in the morning and buy you your first pair of proper long trousers!

Gosh! Really!?

Woof!

That evening, Jack was so excited he found it hard to get to sleep, and spent the whole night tossing in his bed...

Bright and early the next morning, Meg, Jack and Silver arrived in Embleton-on-the-Wall.

E. W. POOLE GENTS OUTFITTERS

Hello Mr. Poole. I'd like some long trousers for my nephew, Jack. It's his first pair.

Goodness. Pubes around his dicky mint already is it, Meg?

That's right, Mr Poole.

Ah! Don't they grow up quickly these days...

But I'm afraid my entire stock of long trousers has been stolen....

What!?

I don't understand it, Meg, really I don't.

But who on earth would want so many trousers, Mr. Poole?

I don't know, Jack. PC Brown is baffled. The only clue he could find was a few biscuit crumbs by the broken window...

...it's all very mysterious!

It *was* all very mysterious, but as they left the shop, they saw something which puzzled them even more...

Morning, Meg. ...Jack.

P.C. Brown!! What the...!?

Ah, yes. I'm sorry about this rather unusual attire. I had to borrow some of my wife's clothing...

...only my police trousers have been stolen off the washing line at the station.

Well, what a funny old day it's turning out to be, Jack...

NORTHUMBERLAND LINGERIE

Trousers... crumbs... it doesn't add up!

REDPATH GROCERS

BROKEN SHORTBREAD -large tins- NOW HALF PRICE!!

...first of all there are no trousers in the shop and then the village bobby turns up in his wife's underwear... whatever next...?

His mind full of the day's events, jack once again tossed and tossed until the early hours, but he couldn't get to sleep.

Come on, boy. We've got to get to the bottom of this mystery...

...and I think we should start with that sinister grocer

Woof!

Jack and Silver dressed quickly and hurried down the darkened Northumbrian lanes into Embleton...

They hid by the grocers shop and watched, and waited for what seemed like hours, until...

Look, Silver ...a lorry!

And there's Mr. Redpath...

...he's signalling to the driver.

McTAVISH SHORTBREAD of SCOTLAND

REDPATH GROCERS

Careful, boy. Don't let them see you.

REDPATH

Och!

Hoots!

Crivens!

So that's his game...

...old Redpath is smuggling illegal Scotsmen across the border in tins of shortbread...

...they're stealing our trousers, taking them back to Scotland and no doubt selling them on the black market. I'm sure they'd fetch a pretty penny in the land of the kilt.

Silver crept forward for a better look, but...

HONK!

It's a dog!... And he's seen everything!

Grab him, quick!

27

As the evil Redpath grabbed hold of the dog detective, Jack ran for help...

...and it wasn't long before a breathless Jack arrived at Embleton Police House...

...where he woke PC Brown...

Puff! Pant! Puff! Pant! Puff! Pant!

What is it boy?...

...are you trying to tell me something?

Why...I do believe you want me to follow you

Puff! Pant!

Hang on, Jack... I'll get my coat

As they ran back, Jack told PC Brown all about Mr Redpath's dastardly plot...

Meanwhile, in the backroom of Mr. Redpath's shop...

Heh! Heh! Another braw nicht's trooser theft. These beauties'll hae a street value o' muckle bawbees back in Glasgae

Och aye! Yon slacks're worth up tae twa poond a pair.

Come on, hurry up! Your bus back to Scotland leaves at dawn.

Suddenly...

Hold it right there, Redpath! The game's up!

OUT!

Crivens!

Whit the hoots!?

Jings!

Help m'boab!

That's what you think, PC Brown...one step closer and the dog gets it.

I think he means it!

But the village bobby was not to be outdone so easily. With lightning agility, he reached into his pocket for his regulation Northumbrian Constabulary ninja death stars and threw them with deadly accuracy.

THUK! THUK! THUK!

WOOOOAAAAAA-WAH!

Then he finished the job with his samurai sword...

THWIT!

HIAAA-OOOO-WAAAAH!

Wow!! That was super, PC Brown. How exciting!

Thanks, Jack san. Just doing my job.

Later that afternoon...

I just popped round to say well done, Jack. Thanks to you, one of England's worst Scotsman smuggling rings has been broken.

What happened to all the illegal Scotsmen?

You've no need to worry about them, Meg. Our dog handling team chased them into the river Tweed. They were drowned.

Did you here that, Silver? They were all drowned, every man Jock of them

And as a reward, Jack... a pair of long trousers recovered from the shop.

I'm afraid Jack won't be needing those after all, PC Brown.

Eh!?!

You see, those weren't pubes I spotted under my bridge the other night...Silver was moulting, and he was in the bath with me. They were just a few of his stray hairs which clung to me as I stood up

But I'll keep these for when his balls do drop.

Still, you know what they say, PC Brown......pubic hair today, gone tomorrow!

Ha! Ha! Ha!

Ha! Ha! Ha!

The End

28

Royal College of SURGEONS

BRAIN SURGEON WANTED APPLY WITHIN

EXPERIMENTAL ROCKET PROPULSION RESEARCH ESTABLISHMENT

NOW HIRING SCIENTISTS

FULCHESTER PIG FARM

SHIT SHOVELLER REQUIRED

SHE'S REYT. A AM F-FF-FF-FFUCKIN' USELESS. A CAN'T DO OWT. A THOWT THEH'D BE A FFUCKIN' JOB AHT THEER FOH ME ....BUT THEH IN'T.

The FEDERATION BREWERY

ACE LAGER PRODUCTION LINE WORKER REQUIRED TO START IMMEDIATELY £300 per week APPLY WITHIN.

SHORTLY...

NOW, YOU SIT HERE, MR. ACE, AND WATCH THE TINS GO BY. YOUR JOB IS TO REMOVE ANY TINS WHICH ARE DENTED.

OBVIOUSLY, IT'S THIRSTY WORK, SO THE MANAGEMENT DON'T MIND IF YOU HELP YOURSELF TO THE OCCASIONAL TIN.

SO...

...OCCASIONAL...NOT ALL...OCCASIONAL...NOT ALL...OCCASIONAL...NOT ALL...NOT ALL...OCCASIONAL...

=GLUGE=

FRIDAY...

...HERE'S YOUR WAGES, MR. ACE. LET'S SEE... THAT'S £300 BASIC FOR THE WEEK...

=RATCH=

...PLUS SEVEN 16-HOUR NIGHT SHIFTS AT DOUBLE TIME... MAKING £1200...

=RATCH= =RATCH=

...SO THAT'S £1500 GROSS.

HOWEVER, WE'VE HAD TO DEDUCT THE TRADE VALUE OF YOUR =AHEM=....OCCASIONAL TINS OF ACE.......

=RATCH= =RATCH=

LEAVING YOU WITH...

...£1.49.

CHINKLE

WAGE PACKET £1.49

SHORTLY...

WELL, AT LEAST A'LL BE TEKKIN' A WAGE 'OME.

...A WURKIN' WAGE.

=MWAH!= A CAN'T WAIT FOH TER SEE 'ER FACE WENN A WALK IN WI........

PATEL'S 24 HOUR NEUTRINOMART

8 ACE £1.49

8 ACE £1.49

WAGE PACKET £1.49

PATEL'S 24 HOUR NEUTRINOMART

8 ACE £1.49

8 ACE.

31

33

34

Letterbocks

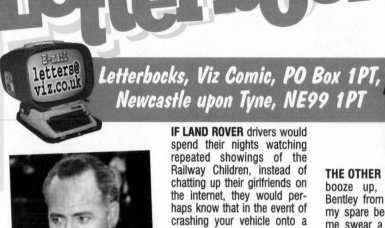

Letterbocks, Viz Comic, PO Box 1PT, Newcastle upon Tyne, NE99 1PT

E-mail letters@viz.co.uk

THE OTHER day at work, I stood fondling a woman's arse whilst all my mates stood around laughing. Then I made a playful grab at her tits. Fortunately, I'm Jonathan Ross and was doing the Mystery Celebrity round of 'They Think It's All Over', so I didn't get taken to a tribunal for sexual harassment.

J. Ross
London

Money rabbit

I FANCY having a bit of rabbit for my tea tonight. Could anyone tell me if it's cheaper from a butcher's or a pet shop?

J. Picklay
Worcester

MY HUSBAND constantly asks me to talk dirty to him in bed, but I just can't do it. I have a terrible stutter, particularly over the letter F.

G. Clamp
Rhyll

I WOULD just like to say good on Barrymore for bouncing back to our screens. Good riddence to the days when a troubled, alcoholic drug-addled, middle-aged homosexual would be banished from hosting a prime-time, family TV show merely for having a drugged, sexually injured corpse fished out of his swimming pool amid rumours of foul play.

Matthew Edwards & Mark Rowland
East Croydon

THEY SAY one swallow doesn't make a summer. That's bollocks. I got this great nosh off a bird last April and I was still smiling in December.

Jon Wainwright
Chester

IF LAND ROVER drivers would spend their nights watching repeated showings of the Railway Children, instead of chatting up their girlfriends on the internet, they would perhaps know that in the event of crashing your vehicle onto a railway line, the correct proceedure is to remove your pants and wave them at the oncoming train rather than imagining that your mobile phone will somehow help you.

Sparky
Birmingham

Robo-cop a look

LAST WEEK on Robot Wars, there was an unusual camera angle, looking down on horsefaced co-presenter Julia Reed. Had I been quick enough, I could have got my knob out and pressed it against the TV screen, which from the correct angle would have given the impression that she was sucking me off. However, I wasn't quick enough, and wonder if any of your readers happened to video it.

B.V. Greenback
Tadcaster

I WAS devastated the other day when my boss called me into his office and said he was going to fire me. I broke down in tears and begged him to reconsider. Imagine what a fool I felt when I suddenly remembered that I am the human cannon ball at the circus, and my boss was merely offering to help me practice. Do I win £5?

John Townsend
e-mail

THE OTHER night, after a booze up, my mate Paul Bentley from Bradford shat in my spare bed. He then made me swear a vow of secrecy, but I'm tempted to tell everyone. What do your readers think? Should I tell the lads or should I keep it shut?

Matthew Wainwright
e-mail

*What do YOU reckon? Should Matthew Wainwright tell all his mates that his pal Paul Bentley from Bradford shat himself in bed? Or is that kind of information no one else's business? Write and tell us what you think and we'll announce the results of our poll in the next issue.

MAD old people come out with the best insults. Today, this old tramp saw me riding my bike on the pavement and she shouted, "Lose the bike, you fucking infantile. You dirty white cock cunt!" That couldn't be bettered by any rational young mind.

J. Wiles
e-mail

No more heroes

I AM concerned with the recent fall in the number of 'Have-a-go-heroes'- these assistant shopkeepers or passers-by who are willing to risk serious injury or death to safeguard 40 B&H and £7.50 from the till. Come on, lads (and lasses), get stuck in.

D. Sherwood
e-mail

Bigg mistake

I HAD to write to point out a glaring mistake in issue 112 of Viz. I read it from cover to cover several times, but could find absolutely no reference to my restaurant, The World Famous Rupali, Bigg Market, Newcastle upon Tyne. However, to show that there are no hard feelings, I will buy a drink for anyone presenting this magazine whilst dining at my restaurant (offer excludes parties of 100 or more).

Abdul Latif, Lord of Harpole,
The Rupali Restaurant,
Bigg Market,
Newcastle upon Tyne

I HAVE been reading Viz now for approximately 15 years now, and I've nearly finished it. As you can see, I carted it to the top of Mount Kilimanjaro and pretended to read it, even though I was weaker than an EastEnders plot. Do I win a free subscription?

Jeff Noon, Keighley

* Sorry, Jeff. We've been so overwhelmed with mountaineers wanting free subscriptions, that we've had to limit them to those individuals pretending to read the comic at 6000m or more above sea level. At 5895m, you were 105m short. Close, but no cigar.

THE VIZ CRYPTIC CHESS-BRIDGE CROSSWORD

by Tiberius   No. 21,947

ACROSS
1 Knight to Queen's Rook (anag) (4)
3 Jack, Queen, King and Ace all come up trumps (3)
5 Dealer calls the suit, but is it a trick? (2,4)
8 Kt-Q6 (3)
9 White plays B-KB7 and the Queen is lost, we hear (3)
12 Spades are trumps, so finesse the hearts (3,3) Four of spades, five of clubs. Check! (3)
14 Black's second move threatens white
15 Queen's rook (4)

DOWN
1 The end of the rubber, so to speak (3)
2 Queen takes Kings Bishop 4 and mates? (4,2)
4 Black castles, and the game goes on (3)
6 Length is strength, but not when your partner is sitting on the ace (2)
7 Clubs are trumps (anag) (4,2)
10 Re-doubling made by confident declarer, oh Jack of diamonds (2)
11 Dummy plays hearts. Fools mate! (3)
13 P-K3. A well known gambit for the Queen's side (3)

Winner of No. 21,946: Mr. Bamber fucking Gascoigne, London.
The Viz Cryptic Chess-Bridge Crossword Book 8 is available from bookshops priced £4.99.

CHRIS Bilton's high-waist-banded old duffer was a truly magnificent sight in the last issue. As a tribute, I am pleased to present this shot of the late British composer Ralph Vaughan Williams. Judging by the look of him, it wasn't just the lark that was ascending - it was his trousers.

Jeremy Bines
London

IT APPEARS that Tesco are saving money on artwork. Viewed this way up, this logo is for strong onions. But turn it upside down and it's the logo for family sized hairy pie.

The Elves
Surrey

I HAVE lived in Hong Kong now for 5 years. I think it is wonderful that there is such a large and thriving local Chinatown, and that the Chinese community has integrated so well with the British. It's a lesson in racial harmony to us all.

D. Gow
e-mail

FOLLOWING a recent shopping trip to Ikea, I was pleased to hear that they are opening another 100,000 square foot store. That should create another two fucking jobs.

Noel Hogan
e-mail

TO THE gentleman advertising his requirement for '8 inch Locks' on the toilet wall at Corley Services southbound, may I recommend the Yellow Pages as an excellent source of local ironmongers.

Adrian Newth
e-mail

THE LEGEND of Bigfoot, a humanoid ape-like creature living in the Rocky Mountains of America was first told by the native Red Indians centuries ago. Due to the vastness of the terrain, it is quite possible that such a creature could live undiscovered. Obviously, however, it could not live for centuries, so it follows that there would have to be a breeding population. Based on my own field studies, I have calculated that the area where the bigfoot has been spotted could support around two hundred individuals. Just imagine if we captured all these magnificent beasts and trained them to perform Michael Flatley's Riverdance. What a show *that* would be!

T. Fletcher
University of Denver

I have a dream

THE OTHER night I dreamt I was shagging the blonde one out of ABBA. It was the worst experience I've ever had to endure. Why the fuck I couldn't have dreamt that I was shagging his gorgeous wife Agnetha instead, I'll never know.

Angry Bob
Blackpool

I DON'T think Delia Smith likes cooking very much. By the look of disgust on her face and the way she handles food, you'd think she was washing a tramp's dick.

Murph
e-mail

WHO SAYS flattery gets you nowhere? I've just been to my mum's in Flattery's Taxis.

Andrew Cartledge
e-mail

POP IDOL? *Bone* idle more like. What has Will ever done to deserve fame other than get a few votes on a Saturday night. There were no phone in polls in

my day. It was all down to hard work. If you wanted to make the big time you had to suck off half the judges and let the compere piss all over your face.

D. King (Miss Butlins, Skegness, 1976) e-mail

Wankabout

WHILST driving in the middle of nowhere in the Australian outback recently, one of my tyres blew out. Considering myself pretty much fucked, my mood was brightened when I discovered that my car had rolled to a halt right next to a discarded bongo mag. What are the chances of that, eh?

Westy
Australia

Hit and missus

A POSTER in my doctors surgery concerning wife beating read *'Don't suffer in Silence'*. Well, whenever I punch my missus on the jaw she screams like a fucking banshee. It makes me wonder if doctors know what they're talking about half the time.

R. Crumble
Northants

I THOUGHT all your readers might like the fact that the Prime Minister of India is called Hairy Vadge Pie, or something like that.

Ian MacKinnon
e-mail

I'VE ALWAYS disliked pubs and hated the idea of running one. When I was a boy, my father told

me that I must stand up to the things I feared, and only in that way would I overcome them. So I opened a pub. It was hell at first, but after five years I am coping quite well, taking one day at a time.

J. Fryer
Leeds

THEY SAY that a dog is a man's best friend. Rubbish! My best friend is Ken Finch.

Lee Prescot
Widnes

I'VE JUST been on a drinking binge that lasted for ten days. I hit levels of drunkeness that I have never achieved before, yet at no time during this marathon piss up did I find TV gardener Charlie Dimmock even vaguely attractive. I'm just curious to know if any readers have ever actually been so hammered that they fancy the ginger hyena.

Dieter Minogue
e-mail

I WAS surprised to see that stammering Pop Idol Gareth had signed a deal to advertise *Diet Pepsi*. Wouldn't he have been better off advertising *Penguins*.

Alex Oak
Newcastle upon Tyne

HE ALWAYS SAID HE'D LEAVE THIS PLACE IN A BOX

THIS WAY UP

AMAZING -BUT SHIT

Surely the most unusual celebration in the history of football was that performed in June 1966 by television variety star Bruce Forsyth. To celebrate England's famous World Cup victory over West Germany, all-round entertainer Forsyth sung and danced non-stop from Land's End to John O'Groats. During his marathon routine Brucey sunged 12,487 songs, wore out 157 pairs of tap dancing shoes, and lost 3 top hats in high winds on the Pennine Way.

During World War II German military chiefs experimented with 'human messenger pigeons' for delivering important documents on the field of battle. Volunteer soldiers carrying vital messages were fired towards their destination from a giant circus canon. In one week alone 67 men died from head injuries, and the experiment was later abandoned.

Despite its vast size - a full grown adult could weigh up to 25 tons and stand 12 metres in height - the mighty Tyrannosaurus Rex had quite a small cock. Yet they still managed to produce more smegma than any other dinosaur! The T Rex's small arms made washing its bell end impossible. Archeologists believe that as a result, from a foreskin no bigger than Pop Idol judge Simon Cowell's polo neck, the giant reptiles could produce three tons of knob cheese per day.

At the height of the Cold War Russian spymasters hatched a bizarre plot to kidnap Manchester United and England star Sir Bobby Charlton and replace him with a double. The agent they planned to use was said to be such a perfect likeness he would have fooled even Bobby's footballing brother Jack.

Y'AAL REET WOR KID?

DAH JACK. I AM GOOT!

In 1973 rock singer Rod Stewart called in paranormal investigators after he awoke one night to find a ghost giving him a blow job! But the spooky mystery was solved when Rod's 'ghost' turned out to be Britt Ekland underneath a blanket.

FELIX and his AMAZING UNDERPANTS

THE SIX WIVES of HENRY THE EIGHTH

IN THE COURT OF KING HENRY VIII

LET THIS BE PROCLAIMED THROUGHOUT ALL OF ENGLAND...

THAT I, KING HENRY, SHALT MARRY EACH OF THESE SIX FAIR LADIES

NOW AWAY WITH THEE ALL TO THY BEDCHAMBERS

THOU MUST PREPARE THYSELVES TO BE MY QUEENS

HENRY'S TRUSTED MINISTER CARDINAL WOLSEY STEPPED FORWARD

ONE MOMENT, MY LORD

'TIS THE LAW AND CUSTOM OF ENGLAND THAT BRIDES-TO-BE MUST HAVE A HEN-PARTY BEFORE THEY ARE UNITED IN HOLY WEDLOCK

SO BE IT. TONIGHT MY SIX BRIDES SHALT HAVE A GIRLS' NIGHT OUT

BUT ONLY FOR A FEW QUIET HALVES, MARK YOU ~ OR MY DISPLEASURE SHALL BE GREAT

6PM IN TOWN

AND THROUGH IT A-A-A-ALL SHE OFFERETH ME PROTECTION

LOTTA LOVE AND AFFECTION VERILY, I'M LOVING ANGELS INSTEAD

SIX BOTTLES OF MEAD BREEZER, SIRRAH

AND, I'FAITH, MY FRIEND HERE SAYS THOU HAST A MOST COMELY FUNDAMENT

'PON MY HONOUR I NEVER DID, THOU LYING COW

* MC MADRIGAL MASTER NIGHTLY!

DOTH WE HAVE A HEN PARTY HERE TONIGHT, LADIES AND GENTS?

VERILY, YAAAAY!

FORSOOTH, I CANNOT HEAR THEE

VERILY, YAAAAY!

9PM

HAD A GOOD LOOK, HAST THOU SIRE?

WHY DOST THOU NOT COMMISSION A FRIGGING PORTRAIT, 'TWILL LAST LONGER

CROMWELL'S BAR

WAHEY! SHOW US THY CHASTITY BELT, PRITHEE

CHILL OUT ROOM

IN FAITH, GOOD SIR, SHE IS NOT WEARING ONE

HEH HEH

HAST THOU ANY CHAMBER MUSIC BY SIR CHRISTOPHER DE BURGH?

BY MY TROTH, THAT ANNE OF CLEVES HATH THE APPEARANCE OF AN ELEPHANT IN THAT DRESS

SIR ROBBIE IS LUSH 4EVA

TRULY, SHE THINKETH THAT SHE IS ALL THAT, BUT SHE IS NOT

41

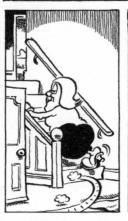

REVEREND RAMSDEN'S RINGPIECE CATHEDRAL

THE REV. RAMSDEN WAS THE MOST UNUSUAL VICAR IN BARNTON, FOR HE HAD A MAGNIFICENT GOTHIC CATHEDRAL... ...UP HIS ARSE!

ONE DAY...

PRINT-O-PRONTO

GOOD MORNING. I'M HERE TO PICK UP 2000 POSTCARDS OF MY CATHEDRAL, ST. MARY-IN-THE FIELDS

AH, YES!

HERE THEY ARE, REVEREND

EH? OH, DEAR. I THINK THERE'S BEEN A BIT OF A MIX-UP...

THIS IS 2000 CLOSE UPS OF A BIG, DIRTY RINGPIECE... TUT!

NO, NO. THESE ARE FINE. THIS IS A BEAUTIFUL VIEW OF THE SOUTH TRANSEPT

THE PORTICO DATES FROM 1655, YOU KNOW...

AT 25p EACH, THESE WILL RAISE ENOUGH CASH FOR THOSE MUCH-NEEDED REPAIRS TO THE STEEPLE

SHORTLY...

CATHEDRAL VIEWS 25p

EXCUSE US, REVEREND

YES. WOULD YOU LIKE TO BUY A POST-CARD?

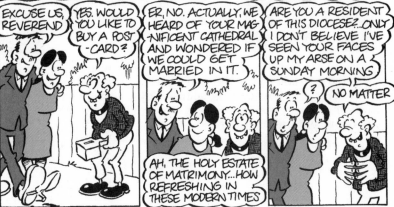

ER, NO. ACTUALLY, WE HEARD OF YOUR MAGNIFICENT CATHEDRAL AND WONDERED IF WE COULD GET MARRIED IN IT.

AH, THE HOLY ESTATE OF MATRIMONY... HOW REFRESHING IN THESE MODERN TIMES

ARE YOU A RESIDENT OF THIS DIOCESE?...ONLY I DON'T BELIEVE I'VE SEEN YOUR FACES UP MY ARSE ON A SUNDAY MORNING

NO MATTER

NOW, I EXPECT YOU'LL WANT THE FULL CHOIR WITH THE ORGAN PLAYING THE WEDDING MARCH?

OOH, YES...

...AND PLENTY OF FLOWERS BEHIND THE ALTAR.

OF COURSE

BUT IF I COULD REQUEST, NO CONFETTI!... THE VERGER HAS TO SWEEP IT UP, YOU SEE

...AND THE BRISTLES OF HIS BRUSH STICK IN MY PILES... LOOK!

COME ON, MURIAL... WE'LL GET MARRIED IN A REGISTRY OFFICE... **ECCLESIASTICAL RECTUMS INDEED!**

SHORTLY...

REV. RAMSDEN!

CATHEDRAL VIEWS 25p

WE'RE FROM THE BBC. WE CALLED YOU LAST WEEK IF YOU REMEMBER

INDEED I DO

BBC OUTSIDE BROADCAST UNIT

WELL, WOULD YOU LIKE TO SHOW US AROUND?

GOOD EVENING. THIS WEEK'S 'SONGS OF PRAISE' COMES FROM THE CATHEDRAL OF SAINT MARY IN THE FIELDS...

...BUILT HERE UP THE REV. RAMSDEN'S CRACK IN 1422 IT IS ONE OF THE FINEST EXAMPLES OF DIRTBOX ARCHITECTURE IN BRITAIN...

NEXT DAY..

RAMSDEN...YOU'VE BEEN UP TO YOUR TRICKS AGAIN... BRINGING DISGRACE ON THE DIOCESE WITH YOUR ARSEHOLE/CHURCH SHENANIGANS

...YOU LEAVE ME NO OPTION

I'M **DECONSECRATING** YOUR CHURCH!

THERE!

CERTIFICATE OF CHURCH CONSECRATION

R-R-RIP!

OH, WHAT AM I TO DO, NOW? STUCK HERE WITH THIS BIG DISUSED CHURCH UP MY ARSE

AHEM! I'M FROM THE PUB CHAIN 'WETHERSPOONS', AND I COULDN'T HELP BUT OVERHEAR

NEXT DAY...

DON'T WORRY, REVEREND. THESE THINGS ALWAYS TAKE TIME TO ESTABLISH THEMSELVES...

JUST WAIT TILL FRIDAY NIGHT

J.D. WETHERSPOONS 'CATHEDRAL ARMS' OPEN TONITE ALL PINTS £1 PUB GRUB

YOUR JACKSY WILL BE **HEAVING** WITH PUNTERS!

Who was... JACK the RIPPER?

Jury - set to crack the 114-year-old mystery

IN THE BLOODY anals of murder, only one criminal case has remained unsolved above all others; and that's the one about Jack the Ripper. For ten dreadful weeks in 1888, the east end of London was shocked by a series of grisly murders. Newspapers dubbed the killer *Jack the Ripper*, but no-one was ever tried for the gruesome crimes. Even today, 114 years later, Scotland Yard are no nearer to solving the case.

In an attempt to finally bring the killer to justice, we've enlisted the help of one of Britain's most experienced detectives to weigh up the evidence against four prime suspects.

For forty years Jack Jury has worked as a front line crimefighter in some of Britain's toughest supermarkets. Starting as an ordinary beat store detective in the 60s, Terry worked his way up through the ranks to become head of undercover surveillance (chilled foods) at Morrisons supermarket in Whitley Bay.

Here, he takes time out from looking into people's bags for frozen sausages to look into this case for fresh evidence and so casts new light on one of the most unsolved series of murders in the history of crime. *Each suspect is scored out of 10 on Motive, Means & Opportunity.*

> *When you've been in this business as long as I have, you develop a sixth sense when it comes to criminals. I can spot a lifter, as we call them, a mile off.*
>
> *It's hard to explain, but when I'm watching somebody by the freezers, I seem to know that they're going to steal something, even before they do. It's a feeling in my bones, and I get that exact same feeling when I look at photographs of all 4 suspects.*
>
> *When somebody steals a chicken, they need motive, means and opportunity. It's exactly the same when murdering women, so let's see how our suspects fit Jack the Ripper's profile.*

Suspect	Motive	Means	Opportunity
Merrick, John  **Alias:** *The Elephant Man* **Occupation:** *Freak*	As a hideously deformed elephant man, Merrick would almost certainly have suffered rejection by females from an early age. Cruel taunts from Victorian girls at the school disco may well have left their mark on his psyche. And elephants never forget. Who can say for certain whether his bubbling resentment of women didn't later boil over into an orgy of sickening violence in the dark back streets of old London town. **10/10**	Merrick was given free range of Whitechapel hospital by Dr Frederick Treves, and would therefore have had easy access to a bewildering array of sharp knives from the kitchen and doctors' bags from the staff room. Who knows what uses his twisted mind could find for these implements of death, as he skulked amongst the shadows of the back streets of old London town. **10/10**	The window of opportunity was certainly open for Merrick. His rooms were situated only yards from where the victims met their fates. However, Jack the Ripper was known to disappear into the crowd after perpetrating his foul deeds, and it is doubtful whether a trumpeting fifteen ton bull elephant with a sack over its head would find it easy to merge into the bustling night-time crowds of Victorian Whitechapel. **7/10**
Hawking, Steven  **Alias:** *Professor Steven Hawking.* **Occupation:** *Boffin*	On the surface, happily married scientist Hawking seems to have no especial hatred for women. Who can say why a leading intellectual with a balanced, stable personality should choose to murder at least five prostitutes - possibly more - in the most gruesome way imaginable over a century ago. Only Hawking knows the truth of what he did or did not do in the foggy shadows of nineteenth century London. **6/10**	No-one knows more about the time/space continuum than Hawking. Appearing on Star Trek five hundred years in the future proves that the Cambridge egghead has already mastered the technology necessary to travel through time. He can flit between the past and future as easily as he can hop on a bus, and a murderous trip to the smoky maze of Victorian London's back streets would be no problem. **10/10**	Hawking would only have to be out of his nurse's sight for a split second to accomplish the Ripper's killings. With his time machine, he could spend an hour murdering a nineteenth century London prostitute, and arrive back in twenty-first century Cambridge ten minutes before he set off! And because he's read the history books, he knows that he was never brought to justice for his dreadful deeds in the gaslit back streets of England's capital. **10/10**
Nightingale, Flo.  **Alias:** *The Lady with the Lamp, Forces Sweetheart.* **Occupation:** *Retired nurse*	After a career spent looking at men's innards, Nightingale may have been curious to find out what was inside a woman. The sight of pox-ridden soldiers and may have encouraged her to rid the streets of good-time girls. At the same time, virgin Florence would have felt envious of the prostitutes, who had sex up to ten times every day. Who can say whether this envy finally spilled over into a sickening murder spree amongst the smoggy back streets of old London. **10/10**	With or without a knife, it's doubtful whether a 68 year-old former nurse would have been a match for a gin-soaked toothless prostitute who would have thought nothing of brawling in the cobbled gutters outside the smoky alehouses of the East End's notorious red light district. Her trademark lamp also counts against her, as it is well known that Jack the Ripper relied on the smoky dark gloominess of old London town to accomplish his dark deeds undisturbed. **8/10**	When the first murder was committed, Nightingale had spent the three decades since the end of the Crimean War in bed, giving her ample opportunity to plan such a series of grisly killings down to the last tiny detail. And her meticulous planning certainly paid off, for the deceptively frail old nurse never stood trial for the murders of Mary Nichols, Annie Chapman, Elizabeth Stride, Catherine Eddowes and Mary Kelly. **10/10**
Holmes, Sherlock  **Alias:** *Basil Rathbone, Conan the Barbarian.* **Occupation:** *Consulting detective.*	Sherlock Holmes's only relationship with a woman ended when she met a violent death. Perhaps, by carrying out the Jack the Ripper killings, he was wreaking a sick revenge on all the women of Victorian London who hadn't met a violent death by making them meet one. More simply, the murders may have been motivated by greed. Addicted to opium, Holmes may have robbed the prostitutes of their money to pay for drugs and violin lessons. **10/10**	Highly intelligent Holmes would have run rings around the feeble-minded police of olden times. Access to scalpels would also have proved no problem; it's certain that Dr Watson, played by Nigel Bruce, would have trusted Holmes with his medical bag. His lodgings at 221b Baker Street were suspiciously near to the scenes of the Whitechapel killings; a matter of just 4 stops on the Bakerloo Line, changing at Embankment, and then a mere 8 stops on the District Line. **10/10**	As a self-employed detective, no-one would have been surprised to see Holmes slipping unseen in and out of his lodgings in the middle of the night. His network of street urchins - *the Baker Street Irregulars* - would have informed him of the whereabouts of potential victims. A master of disguise, Holmes could have dragged a victim up a back lane dressed as a one-legged pirate, murdered her as a circus ringmaster, then made his escape in a Chinese washerwoman costume. **9/10**

"I was MURDERED by Jack the Ripper... but I'll NEVER reveal his identity!" ~ Nichols

Mary Nichols was the Ripper's first victim. She was discovered dead at 3.30am on 31st August 1888. Her throat had been cut and her body mutilated. Now, for the first time since her savage murder she speaks to columnist Lynda Lee Stokes... and reveals that she KNEW HER KILLER!

EXCLUSIVE INTERVIEW!

I WAS A YOUNG PROSTITUTE new in London and with stars in my eyes. One foggy night in August 1888 I was soliciting in Whitechapel when I was approached by a tall young man wearing a cloak and hat, and carrying a Gladstone bag. He had a scottish accent and I thought I recognised him from the television, but I couldn't be sure in the atmospheric gaslight.

He asked me if I was doing business and I said yes. He offered me a shilling and we went into a narrow passageway.

razor

He said he wanted to murder me, but I told him no. He told me: "You know you want it really." The next thing I knew he'd pushed me up against a wall and started murdering me with a cut-throat razor. I kept telling him to stop, but he wouldn't take no for an answer. He just kept on murdering me.

wheely big cheese

Before I knew what was going on, he'd cut my throat and mutilated my body. He stepped over my corpse and made his escape, vanishing swiftly into Victorian London's maze of back streets in the direction of the GMTV studios.

I never said anything at the time, because I knew no-one would believe me, and I was also dead. However, since then I've spoken to at least four other dead prostitutes who have also been murdered by the same household name.

Nichols - in 1888 yesterday

114 years later, I am still adamant that I will never name my killer. I took his secret with me to the grave, and I'm going to keep it there. But the memory of being murdered will stay with me for the rest of my life. These days, whenever I see Jack the Ripper fronting daytime television programmes, sitting next to Fern Britton and smiling like butter wouldn't melt, my blood runs cold. "

copyright the Daily Mail 2002

No one ever knew his identity... And here's

10 MORE THINGS YOU NEVER KNEW about JACK the RIPPER

1 THE Whitechapel murderer is believed by many to have been a member of the Freemasons, a secret club of corrupt coppers, businessmen and councillors. To this day, each new member of the society is entrusted with three secrets: a super club handshake and password, the names of the eleven herbs and spices that go into the batter for Colonel Sanders's Kentucky Fried Chicken, and the true identity of Jack the Ripper.

2 THE smallest ever man to be suspected of being Jack the Ripper

was Calvin Phillips. American crime author Patricia Cornwell accused the four-inch high New Yorker of carrying out the slayings using a darning needle as a dagger, a thimble as a top hat and half an After Eight wrapper as a cloak. And making his escape in a hansom cab made from a roller skate...pulled by a mouse!

3 THE legend of Jack the Ripper has inspired many films. The most recent one, 'From Hell', took over £100,000 at the box office and starred Hollywood heartthrob Johnny Depp as the killer.

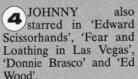

4 JOHNNY also starred in 'Edward Scissorhands', 'Fear and Loathing in Las Vegas', 'Donnie Brasco' and 'Ed Wood'.

5 HE was also in 'Sleepy Hollow' but it wasn't very good.

6 JOHNNY recently married Jennifer

Aniston, who plays Rachel in 'Friends'.

7 SORRY. That was Brad Pitt.

8 BRAD Pitt starred in 'Seven', 'Twelve Monkeys', 'Fight Club' and 'Meet Joe Black'

9 HE was also in 'Ocean's Eleven' but it wasn't very good.

10 BRAD recently married Jennifer Anniston, who plays Rachel in 'Friends'.

FINBARR SAUNDERS & HIS DOUBLE ENTENDRES

MILLIE TANT
& HER RADICAL CONSCIENCE

FOR YOUR THIGHS ONLY

OPENS TONITE! LAPDANCING CLUB

HUNH! THIS IS DISGUSTING! PRO-POSITIVE FEMINACTION IS CALLED FOR!

SO... RIGHT. THIS IS OUR PLAN TO BRING DOWN THE PHALLOCRATIC MIND-RAPISTS...WE STAND AND WE PHOTOGRAPH EVERY SINGLE MAN WHO ENTERS THE CLUB!

WE THEN PUBLISH THEIR FACES ON THE INTERNET. THIS WILL RESULT IN THEIR *ABSOLUTE SHAME* IN THE EYES OF ALL THEIR *FEMALE* FAMILY MEMBERS...ERM, IF THEY SOMEHOW HAPPEN TO LOOK AT THE WEBSITE...

...ANYWAY, YOU CAN SORT OUT THOSE SORT OF LITTLE DETAILS LATER, SISTERS. OKAY, DOES EVERYONE KNOW WHAT THEY HAVE TO DO?

ANTI LAPDANCING DEMO-MEET 12:30

?

SHORTLY... AH-HAH!

TONITE LAPDANCIN CLUB

CAN YOU JUST WAIT A BIT, I THINK I HAVEN'T TURNED IT ON. HOLD ON. *HEE-HEE!*... SILLY ME... HOW DO YOU MAKE THE FLASH WORK? ...

I THINK YOU PUSH THAT ORANGE ONE THERE, THEN YOU'LL HAVE TO WAIT FOR IT TO WARM UP.

BAH! IT WAS NO DOUBT A MAN WHO DESIGNED THIS CAMERA! HE HAS PLAYED A DELIBERATE PART IN THE PENIS-WEILDING CONSPIRACY, DELIBERATELY PREVENTING THE PROGRESS OF THE WIMMINSTRUGGLE.

SHORTLY... AH-HA! TESTOSTOCRATIC RAPE-INDUCER! I WILL POST YOUR FACE ON THE INTERNET FOR YOUR WIFE AND CHILDREN TO SEE!

FLASH!

OH, THANKS. THAT'S REALLY NICE.

STOP THE POTENTIAL RAPE OF WIMMIN!

I THINK THERE MUST BE SOME MISTAKE HERE.

HAH!... MISTAKE!... YOUR MISTAKE IS TO WORK AT AN ESTABLISHMENT THAT MAKES IT'S BUSINESS THE FANTASY OF *RAPING WOMEN!*

NO, YOU SEE TONIGHT IS A WOMEN'S NIGHT. ALL THESE MEN YOU'RE PHOTOGRAPHING ARE THE DANCERS.

COME AAAAN!!

GET YA FUCKIN' COCK OUT!

Letterbocks

Letterbocks, Viz Comic, PO Box 1PT, Newcastle-upon-Tyne, NE99 1PT.

letters@viz.co.uk

IT COMES as no surprise that Ulrika Jonsonn has broken yet another marriage. She wrecked mine back in the eighties. It was in the days when the blond hornbag used to read the weather. I didn't have an affair with her, my wife caught me spannering one off in front of the telly whilst she was on, and she went back to her mother's.

T. Hope
London

WHOEVER says that mobile phones will one day completely replaced the telephone kiosk is talking utter nonsense. Have they ever tried to piss into a Nokia 8210, or smear an unwanted kebab on the inside of an Ericsson T65?

A. Tern
Fulham

Sender: Jim, e-mail

UP THE ARSE CORNER

DOES THIS bloke look like Roger Mellie or what?

Hugh Fardon
Lichfield

IN CONTRAST to the jubilation during Princess Diana's funeral, I was saddened by the lack of clapping at the Queen Mother's send off. We all applauded her death in our house, we even cheered.

Paddy Patterson
e-mail

WE HAVE heard many tributes to the Queen Mother, saying how above all, she had time for people. Well she never had any time for me. I was her dentist.

Graeme Kenna
Wallasey

I THINK Viz and some of its readers are a bit hard on truck drivers. Just recently, a kind trucker who was delivering to my work sold me a backpack jammed full of clothes, footwear and toiletries for £5. Fair enough, most of the contents won't suit me, but it'll make ideal Christmas and birthday presents for my sister. Top bloke.

Stuart Wilson
Scotland

THE QUEEN Mum's funeral showed Britain at its best and was a fantastic spectacle for visitors to London. I think we should have a Royal Funeral every year, it would certainly keep tourist board coffers full after recent heavy losses. How about Prince Edward for the week before Wimbledon 2003, and Fergie for the slack September period 2004.

SJ Cawood

LIKE MANY of your readers, I regularly masturbate whilst driving, but being public spirited, would like to reduce the risk of accidents to other road users. Does anyone know if any hands free kits are available on the market?

Bluey
Bromsgrove

I WAS saddened to learn of the death of the Queen Mum, whose remarkable life was one dedicated to the service of her country and her family. Her galvanising devotion to duty put the other freeloading, layabout royals to shame. Imagine my disappointment then, when I learned that she died peacefully in her sleep at 3.15 on a Saturday afternoon. What the hell was she doing in bed on a Saturday afternoon? The lazy bitch.

U. Helmet
e-mail

LAST NIGHT I dreamt I was being chased by a load of Frankensteins. Imagine my surprise at discovering on waking up that I had shit the bed.

Matt Hindle,
Sheffield.

PS. To any pedantic twats out there, yes I *DO* know that Frankenstein was the doctor, not the monster. In my dream I was being chased by a load of Doctor Frankensteins who wanted my various body parts for unholy creations they were planning on making.

IS IT just me, or does everyone like to 'christen' a new pair of underpants?

M. Clarke
Newark

WITH REGARDS to the letter from Richard Hatfield (issue 113) regarding Tony Hart's bizarre behaviour, I would like to reveal that as a child I used to live next door to him, and he had a 10 foot concrete fence with fierce dogs behind it. He used to burst our footballs if they went over, and he never opened his curtains. He was a right weirdo.
Looking back, I think his name might have been Tom Hart, but he was definitely a painter as he did my mate's dad's lounge.

Mick Laird
Stourbridge

I ALWAYS thought women golfers were lesbians until I chanced upon this picture of LPGA tour winner Cristie Kerr. Phwoooor!

Hellpass
e-mail

WHILST THERE will inevitably be those who attempt to get a 'cheap laugh' out of the death of the Queen Mother, we should remember her tremendous contribution to the war effort. As the BBC pointed out, she "bravely remained in London beside her husband" during the war. This contrasts sharply with the actions of my own grandfather who on the declaration of war immediately left his wife and children and pissed off, first to France, then North Africa, Italy, France (again) and finally Germany. The shame will always be with me.

George Nisbet
e-mail

DOES ANYONE know where David Beckham lives? I heard on the radio that he sells thousands of newspapers a day, and I wouldn't mind popping over for a quick one with Posh whilst he's out on his paper round.

Natty Bimmel
e-mail

WITH REFERENCE to Matthew Wainwright's e-mail in issue 114; He should definitely keep quiet about his friend Paul Bentley's 'accident'. I have been in a similar situation, and was sworn to secrecy when my mate Big Daz Rowe soiled his mother's bed after a particularly heavy night. I have never told another living soul and will take his secret to the grave with me.

J. Lugg
Paignton

I WAS walking through a car park in Newcastle, and happened to pass regional news presenter Carol Malia as she loaded her car. It became apparent that she didn't know I was passing, as she let the biggest undergarment stainer I've heard a woman produce. Her face was a picture as she noticed me giggling behind her. Do I win a tenner?

Stu Holt
South Shields

I WAS shocked to hear that after her death, the Queen Mother's coffin was in turd at Windsor Castle. Surely it would have been more respectful to bury her in soil.

R. Savage
Berwick

THERE ARE always winners and losers in a budget, and this one is no exception. The Chancellor put 6p on a packet of fags, but took 14p off a pint in a country pub. I used to enjoy a pint or two at my local, but now I find if I drive to a little pub in the middle of nowhere and have 12 pints every night, after a week I've saved enough to cancel out the rise on my 60-a-day fag habit.

C Dibbs
e-mail

I RECENTLY had to use a public phone box in London, and was shocked to see a card advertising advertising a 'Spanking by a naughty nurse, any time'. No wonder my mother has been waiting for a hip operation for 18 months when these so-called healthcare professional are willing to abandon their patients at the

drop of a hat in order to attend to someone's sexual lustings.

Matthew Eve
e-mail

I HAD four shits yesterday. *Four!* Can any of your readers beat that?

James Millar
e-mail

THE FUNERAL of Her Majesty the Queen Mother was indeed a sad and sombre occasion. The BBC, by using David Dimbleby as the commentator, added to the sombreness and added to the nation's grief. If they had asked Murray Walker to do the commentary, his fast talking would have made the funeral exciting, and his humourous gaffes would have kept us laughing through our tears.

Martin
Yorkshire

WE WERE all greatly saddened by the death of the Queen Mother, but let's look on the bright side. With the clocks going forward the night after she popped her clogs, she has already 'lost' an hour of being dead.

Guy
Nottingham

ISN'T IT about time that the late Princess Margaret stopped leeching off society and got

herself a proper job? I for one am fed up of paying taxes so she can sit about in an urn on the Queen's mantlepiece all day doing fuck all.

Andrew McKinnon
Dundee

SO PRINCE Charles thinks the Queen Mum was a 'truly magical grandmother' does he? Well, I'd have thought my granny was pretty magical too, if she lived in a big fairytale castle and travelled everywhere in a gold coach with a platoon of her very own living toy soldiers to guard her.

Madra
e-mail

LIKE THE Queen Mum, my grandfather was a frequent visitor to the East End during the dark days of the blitz, but he was never hailed as a hero by the people of London. That's because he flew Heinkel bombers for the Luftwaffe.

Werner Hoffmann
Munich

IT'S NO wonder celebrity chefs like Gordon Ramsey are always stressed. I would be if I was caught on TV doing a woman's job.

Tim Woods
e-mail

IF HOMELESS people are so poor, how can some of them afford to keep two dogs? My old Gran only has one Springer Spaniel, and after she's forked out for its Bonio, she's hardly got any change left for the Bingo.

Mark Hewitson
London

Top Tips

THAT LITTLE bald-headed bloke off the Benny Hill show. Next time Benny Hill slaps you rapidly on the head, hit the fat fucker back. Bullies don't pick on people who stand up to them

Fat Al White, Wrenthorpe

SAVE time by only ever watching one Bruce Willis movie.

Zed, e-mail

AMERICAN High School teachers. Increase your efficiency by announcing which chapters to read from the textbook for next class some time before that fucking annoying bell rings.

Justin Deegan, e-mail

BUYING chain or wire at B&Q? Cut off the length you want and abandon it elsewhere in the store. Next day, buy it from the reduced bucket for half price.

Edd Hillman, e-mail

THRIFTY shoppers. Save cash when buying apples in the supermarket by removing the stalks to reduce the weight. You'll be smiling all the way to the checkout on your 176th visit as you effectively claim your free apple.

Will Mayes, e-mail

IF A member of your family suffers with Parkinson's disease, increase their self esteem and sense of worth by making sure they are the first to handle a new bottle of sauce at mealtimes.

D. Lee, e-mail

GIVE yourself the impression of being 'high' by lying down in a really hot bath whilst smoking a fag, then standing up as if the Queen had just walked in.

Glenn Wild, Rotherham

MAKE delayed train journeys fly for everyone by tutting and sighing as much as you can down the closest person's earhole.

Keren Kehoe, e-mail

GERMAN perverts. Go to a beach in California and shout "Help! I've been stung by a jellyfish!" As the most natural remedy for this is dousing the sting in urine, you're almost guaranteed a golden shower from a gaggle of Baywatch beauties.

Brian Eggo, e-mail

E-mail
toptips@viz.co.uk

Have *Your* Say

We went on the streets to ask your views on whether, in the wake of the Queen Mum's death, Prince Charles should marry Camilla Parker-Bowles.

...I THINK Charles and Camilla should have married before the Queen Mother died. She would have loved to see her favourite grandson happy, and we could have seen some great camcorder footage of the old girl flashing he bloomers whilst dancing and falling over at the reception.

...I WOULD love it if they got married, just so I could see the Queen pull that fucking face she pulls, the one as if someone has just farted.

...CHARLES WOULD be the first to admit that he made mistakes in his marriage to Lady Di, mistakes that he would not make again. If he married Camilla, he certainly couldn't sneak off and poke someone uglier that his wife.

...I HOPE they don't get married. If they had a son, with his ears and her teeth, the next in line to the throne could be a fucking rabbit.

...I THINK they should get married. Let's not forget that Camilla's cousin is 'Who Wants To Be A Millionaire' winner Judith Keppel, and she'd buy them a fantastic present like a diamond encrusted toaster or a solid gold fondue set.

...PRINCE CHARLES is 54 and he still lives at home with his mum. He should get married straight away before people start to think that he's a lifter like his brother.

ANOTHER TUESDAY NIGHT IN NIAGARA

HAROLD! HAVE YOU DONE THE WASHING-UP?

SIGH... YES DEAR.

HAVE YOU TAKEN THE BINS OUT?

YES DEAR.

HAVE YOU GONE OVER THE FALLS IN A BARREL?

... IN A MINUTE.

HAROLD!

I SAID IN A MINUTE!!

YOU KNOW, MRS MULROONEY ACROSS THE WAY NEVER HAS TO ASK HER PHILIP TWICE TO GO OVER NIAGARA FALLS IN A BARREL!

I SAW HIM GO OVER FIRST THING THIS MORNING!

FIRST OF ALL, THAT'S TOTALLY DIFFERENT, ISN'T IT! HE DIDN'T USE A BARREL— THAT WERE JUST A BARREL-LIKE DEVICE!

WHOLE DIFFERENT GAME, THAT IS!

OH YES? AND WHAT ABOUT MRS. TRUDEAU FROM UP THE ROAD? HER KENNETH WENT OVER THURSDAY LAST— BROKE SEVEN RIBS AND HE WERE IN A COMA FOR A WEEK.

IT WERE FIVE RIBS, WOMAN, AND THAT WAS NEVER A COMA — JUST A LIFE-THREATENING CONCUSSION!

GOT AN ANSWER FOR EVERYTHING, YOU HA— BLOODY HELL! THAT'S EDINA DIEFENBAKER'S DENNIS GOING OVER NOW!

LOOK AT THAT! THEY'RE AIRLIFTING THE TWISTED WRECKAGE OF HIS BODY TO HOSPITAL! I'LL NEVER HEAR THE END OF THIS!

IT'LL BE AIRLIFTED DENNIS THIS AND AIRLIFTED DENNIS THAT— AND WHAT CAN I SAY?

EH?

IT'S NOT AS IF I ASK FOR THE MOON AROUND HERE... I MEAN—

WELL HALLELUJAH— HE'S OFF HIS ARSE! IT'S A BLEEDIN' MIRACLE!

RIGHT— HERE'S YOUR THERMOS AND SANDWICHES. NOW GET A MOVE ON— IT'S ALMOST TIME FOR CORRIE.

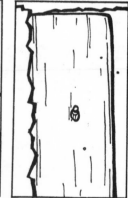

... SO I SAYS TO VIVIAN, I SAYS NO DEAR! YOUR ALAN IS ONLY PRESUMED DEAD. MY HAROLD WAS PRONOUNCED DEAD FOR TWENTY-TWO MINUTES ON THE OPERATING TABLE!

AND YOU SHOULD HAVE SEEN HER FACE—

GOSH, ROGER! WAIT TIL I TELL THE GIRLS YOU LOST YOUR ENTIRE BODY TO FROSTBITE IN YOUR ATTEMPT TO REACH THE NORTH POLE BY HOT-AIR BALLOON!

YOU'RE THE BEST HUSBAND EVER!

I'VE PACKED YOU SOME SAUSAGE ROLLS, AND HERE'S YOUR 'TIMES'...

RH '02

I'M OFF TO VISIT MY GRANDMA, READERS

AND THIS **DE-MUSTYFIER** I'VE INVENTED WILL PROTECT ME FROM THE SMELL OF STALE URINE, BODILY DECAY AND DESPERATE LONELINESS

OOH — MY POOR OLD HIP GIVES ME MERRY HELL WHEN I USE THE STAIRS, GILBERT

PERHAPS I SHOULD BUY ONE OF THOSE STAIR LIFTS THAT THORA HIRD ADVERTISES

THORA HIRD, SHMORA HIRD

I'LL BUILD YOU A SUPER STAIR LIFT OUT OF THIS LENGTH OF INDUSTRIAL STRENGTH ELASTIC

THERE. YOU SIMPLY PULL THE LEVER, AND MY **ELASTO-LIFT** WILL CATAPAULT YOU GRACEFULLY INTO THOSE CUSHIONS ON THE LANDING

SOUNDS FOOLPROOF, GILBERT. HERE GOES...

AND — GROAN... DON'T WORRY, GRANDMA

MY 'NINE-NINE-NINE-O-MATIC' WILL PHONE YOU AN AMBULANCE IN NEXT TO NO TIME

CLICK WHIRRR
CLICK WHIRRR

AT THE HOSPITAL QUITE APART FROM THE HEAD INJURIES, YOUR GRANDMOTHER REALLY NEEDS A HIP OPERATION

BUT IT'LL COST YOU £200 IF YOU WANT ME TO MAKE A DECENT JOB OF IT

CRIKEY

WARDS

OPERATING THEATRE

WHERE AM I GOING TO GET 200 QUID FOR GRANDMA'S HIP OPERATION?

BAH! I'M SICK OF MY PATIENTS HAVING OUT-OF-BODY EXPERIENCES WHEN I'M OPERATING ON THEM

SWAT SWAT

THEIR DISEMBODIED SPIRITS KEEP FLOATING UP TO THE CEILING AND PEERING OVER MY SHOULDER WHILE I'M TRYING TO WORK.

DON'T DESPAIR, DOC

I'LL MAKE A **PSYCHIC SPOOK CATCHER** OUT OF THIS OLD VACUUM CLEANER

C'MERE, YOU ASTRALLY PROJECTED PEST!

HMMMMMMMMM

GO GETTIM, GILBERT!

OOPS! SHLURRP!

!

I'VE ACCIDENTALLY SUCKED ALL THE PATIENT'S INTESTINES OUT, INSTEAD

GUT MY PATIENT, WOULD YOU?

OPERATING THEATRE

BOOT

CLEAR OFF!

GOLLY

CLANK CLANK

LOOK AT ALL THE SURGICAL EQUIPMENT THAT'S BEEN ACCIDENTALLY LEFT IN THAT PATIENT'S GUTS

I'M A SCRAP METAL DEALER AND I'LL GIVE YOU £200 AND A BALLOON FOR THAT STUFF

GREAT!

SO HERE'S THE £200 FOR MY GRANDMA'S HIP OPERATION, MR DOCTOR

I'LL PERFORM IT RIGHT AWAY, GILBERT

BUT YO SKANKY BITCH GRANDMA YOU BETTER LISTEN GOOD I'M THE GREATEST FUCKIN DOCTOR IN THIS BAD-ASS NEIGHBOURHOOD...

BIG SPEECH TODAY

THUMP THUMP THUMP

OH NO! HE'S GIVING HER **THAT** SORT OF "HIP HOP ORATION"!

VIZ 114

PUNCHLINE COURTESY OF STEVE

Beast attacks toddler in own house

PARENTS in the West Midlands were warned to be on their guard yesterday after the Loch Ness monster punched a toddler in the eye.

Two-year-old Tyrone Champignon was watching television on the sofa at his home in Walsall when the 200 foot cryptozoological beast crept in through patio doors and gave the tot a shiner.

Mum Doreen Turpentine rushed in to find her young son howling in pain, nursing a black eye. She said: "I couldn't see what was going on. Then I saw three big humps sticking up from behind the sofa. I just screamed."

fence

Dad Baxter Champignon heard her cries and rushed into the lounge. He threw empty beer cans at the animal and chased it into the garden where it jumped over the fence and disappeared.

"We were too shocked to take in what had happened at first," said Baxter. "But thinking about it now, Tyrone is lucky to be alive." he added.

dance

The RSPCA said: "The Loch Ness Monster, if it exists, is normally a placid animal and it is unusual to hear of it being sighted in a house as far south as Walsall." And they dismissed claims that the animal meant to hurt Tyrone.

"We certainly don't think the animal meant the child any harm. It was probably looking for somewhere to

Little Tyrone yesterday, and (above) the beast that blacked his eye

sleep, and the boy startled it," they added.

fish

But Nicholas Witchell from the National Anti Loch Ness Monster Society disagreed.

He said: "Frankly, the Loch Ness monster, if it exists, would be a menace. Unlike the cuddly toy wearing a Tam O'Shanter you see in Scottish souvenir shops, it would be a savage predator. I've imagined the damage it could cause to a shoal of krill, and it's not a pretty sight, believe me."

And he issued a warning. "If it does exist, now it has punched one child in the eye it will have a taste for it. None of our children is safe."

swallow

However, a more cautious note was sounded by David Sutton, managing editor of crackpot nutrag Fortean Times.

He said: "Clearly, something gave Tyrone a black eye but we shouldn't jump to conclusions. It could have simply been a large seal, a piece of floating wood, or perhaps silver-suited space creatures from another space-time continuum in search of fuel for a crashed flying saucer."

spit

A spokesman for Walsall Hospital said: "We can confirm that the boy had been punched in the eye, and cannot rule out the possibility that the Loch Ness monster did it."

HAIR APPARENT - Young's toupée at the ceremony with Prince Charles yesterday

ARISE, SIR-RUP
Gong for Radio Two-pée

BY CHORLTON WHEELIE · our Royal Correspondent

Housewives' favourite toupée, Jimmy Young's wig was knighted yesterday, and then cracked a joke about its Radio 2 arch rival - Wogan's weave.

"Terry's syrup will be tearing its pretend hair out with jealousy when it hears about this!" it quipped.

The hairpiece, 52, received the award in the New Year's Honours list for services to the 78-year-old broadcaster's pate, which it joined from new in 1950.

The wig said that the short ceremony, conducted by Prince Charles at Buckingham Palace, was a nerve-wracking experience.

It told reporters afterwards: "I haven't been this nervous since Jimmy did a live broadcast from the rear seat of a Tiger Moth at the Farnborough Airshow in 1976."

MICKEY'S MINIATURE GRANDPA

YOUNG MICKEY MARSTON'S GRANDPA WAS CONVINCED THAT A GYPSY'S CURSE HAD SHRUNK HIM TO A REMARKABLE FOUR INCHES IN HEIGHT

HI MICKEY. I'M JUST HAVING MY TEA

AND THIS MATCHBOX AND COTTONREEL MAKE AN IDEAL DINING TABLE AND CHAIR FOR SOMEONE OF MY TINY STATURE. MUNCH!

I'M SCARED, MUM. MAKE GRANDPA STOP TALKING TO ME

DON'T BE SILLY, MICKEY. IT'S NOT DAD'S FAULT THAT SHELL EXPLODED NEAR HIM DURING THE WAR. AND WE ONLY COME TO THE HOSPITAL TO SEE HIM ONCE A MONTH.

NOW YOU STAY THERE AND KEEP YOUR GRANDPA COMPANY WHILE I SPEAK TO THE WARD NURSE ABOUT HIS MEDICATION.

NOW'S OUR CHANCE TO SNEAK OUT OF HERE AND FIND SOME ADVENTURES, MICKEY

I'LL SIT IN THE FRONT OF YOUR HAT LIKE THE LITTLE MOUSE IN 'DUMBO'

THEN YOU CAN SMUGGLE ME OUT OF THE DAY ROOM WITHOUT ANYONE NOTICING

OW! STOP IT, GRANDPA!

OH DEAR. COME ON, DAD, LET'S HAVE YOU BACK IN YOUR CHAIR

GET HIM OFF ME, MUM!

BAH! I'VE BEEN SPOTTED, MICKEY ~ SHE MUST HAVE EYES LIKE A HAWK

WE'LL SEE YOU THE SAME TIME NEXT MONTH THEN, DAD

>PSST< DON'T WORRY, MICKEY ~ I'LL MEET YOU OUTSIDE IN A COUPLE OF MINUTES

POOR MICKEY WILL BE SO DISAPPOINTED IF HE DOESN'T GET TO PLAY WITH HIS INCREDIBLE MIDGET-SIZED GRANDPA

I'VE GOT TO FIND A WAY TO GET OUT OF HERE — BUT HOW?

>GRUNT, WHEEZE< IF I CAN JUST DRAG THIS FEATHER OVER TO THE WINDOWSILL

THEN I COULD USE IT AS A HANG-GLIDER, AND FLOAT DOWN OFF THE WINDOW LEDGE AND LAND ON THE LAWN.

WOW! I'VE GOT CAUGHT IN A SPIDER'S WEB

AND I THINK THAT HUNGRY-LOOKING SPIDER HAS MISTAKEN ME FOR A JUICY FLY

SHRIEK! GET OFF ME, YOU GREAT HAIRY BRUTE!

>GASP< IF IT OVERPOWERS ME, I'M DONE FOR

PHEW! I'VE DRIVEN IT AWAY

HOLD ON, MICKEY — I'M ON MY WAY!

I'VE TIED MYSELF TO THE FEATHER WITH SOME STRANDS OF COTTON — AND OFF I GO!

LET'S JUST HOPE A LIGHT BREEZE DOESN'T BLOW ME INTO THE BRANCHES OF THAT TREE

CRUMP!

LATER

I'M AFRAID HE SUFFERED TRAUMATIC HEAD INJURIES, MRS MARSTON

YOU SHOULD PREPARE YOURSELF FOR THE FACT THAT YOUR FATHER WILL NOT BE THE SAME PERSON THAT HE USED TO BE

HI MICKEY ~ WE'LL HAVE SUPER ADVENTURES TOGETHER NOW THAT I'M AN EIGHTY-FOOT-TALL GIANT

BUT BE CAREFUL! I MIGHT ACCIDENTALLY CRUSH YOU LIKE AN ANT BENEATH MY GARGANTUAN FOOT!

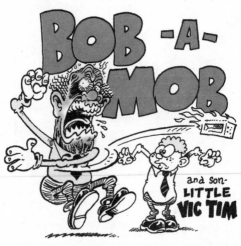

BOB -A- MOB

and son- LITTLE VIC TIM

BREAKFAST TIME...

LOOK AT **THIS!** IT SAYS HERE YOU ARE NEVER MORE THAN 4ft AWAY FROM AN **EVIL BASTARD SCUM PERVERT** — THEY MUST BE **EVERYWHERE!**

BOB, DEAR— COULD YOU TAKE LITTLE VIC INTO SCHOOL TODAY...?

... I HAVE A BIT OF A COLD ~ SNIFFF

WAAAAGHHH!!! AN EVIL SUSPECT BASTARD PERVERT— IN MY OWN HOME!!

PELT! PELT!

YOU WICKED MONSTER SCUM! THIS IS FOR THE KIDS!!

SMACK!!

OOH- SHOT!!

IT'S A DISGRACE. KIDS SHOULDN'T EVEN BE EXPOSED TO THOSE BEASTS EXISTENCE AT THEIR AGE.

COME ON DAD— WE HAVE TO CROSS WITH THE LOLLYPOP LADY TO GET TO THE MINIBUS TO SCHOOL

WHAT?!

AARGH!! YOU INHUMAN SCUM!! LURING INNOCENT KIDS ACROSS ROADS WITH GIANT CONFECTIONARY!

STOT!

YOU CAN ROT IN HELL FOREVER YOU EVIL BITCH WHORE— AND I'LL PULL THE LEVER!

THERE. THE KIDS ARE MUCH SAFER NOW.

CRUNCH!

SHORTLY...

HERE'S THE MINI-BUS NOW, DAD

HMMN?

BASTARD!! EVIL WICKED PEEDO MONSTER SCUM!! DRIVING OFF WITH LITTLE KIDS! COME OUT LIKE THE MAN YOU AREN'T FOR THE BEATING THAT'S TOO GOOD FOR YOU!

BANG! BANG! BANG!

LET ME OVER THIS BARRIER— I'LL RIP YOUR GUTS OUT AND HANG YOU SLOWLY WITH THEM, YOU CRUEL, CALCULATING **MONSTER!**

LATER... WELL WE HAD A BIT OF A DETOUR TO AVOID THE LOCAL SCOUT HUTS, CATHOLIC SEMINARIES, SWIMMIN' POOLS & CHOIR SCHOOLS, BUT IT'S ALL FOR YOUR OWN GOOD...

...AND THERE'S STILL FIVE MINUTES OF LESSONS LEFT!

AH- HELLO LITTLE VIC'S DAD. YOU'RE JUST IN TIME. WE HAVE ONE SCHOOL PHOTO LEFT.

OOH!

AS YOU CAN SEE, I'M AFRAID LITTLE VIC WAS STOOD IN THE FAT KIDS SHADOW AND HE'S COME OUT A LITTLE GRAINY. NEVER MIND. I CAN EASILY TOUCH HIM UP ON MY COMPUTER AT HOME.

WHAT?!!

KILL THE PEEDO

FOR THE KIDS

KILL MERCKEL KILL

V12 120

58

IT'S LAURIE DRIVER

8 am... ≡SNORE!≡ ...WIFFLE WAFFLE... ≡SNORE!≡ WIFFLE...

DING-A-LING-A-LING-A-LING!

EH!? WHASSA...!?

YAWN!

≥BLINK≤ ≥BLINK≤

PLAP! PLAP! PLAP!

EEH. ANOTHER DAY ON THE ROAD... NOW, WHERE AM I?

OOH. I'M ON THE M6. I MUST'VE MADE BETTER PROGRESS THAN I THOUGHT.

I MAY AS WELL HAVE ANOTHER 40 WINKS.

≡SNORE!≡ ...WIFFLE WAFFLE...≡SNORE!≡ ...WIFFLE WAFFLE...

SHORTLY...

WHAT'S THE PROBLEM MATE?

I THINK THE ENGINE'S MISFIRING. IT'S MAKING A TERRIBLE NOISE IN THE CAB.

WHAT LIKE?

IT SOUNDS LIKE GOD SAYING THE WORDS "BELL RINGING" OVER AND OVER AGAIN.

IT MIGHT BE YOUR TIMING. I'LL HAVE A QUICK FIDDLE.

SO.. V.V.VROOM! V.V.VROOM!

HOW'S THAT?

NAH. HE'S SAYING "BILL SWIMMING" NOW.

V.V.V.VROOM! VOOM!

WHAT ABOUT NOW?

"KILL WOMEN" "KILL WOMEN" YEP. SPOT ON. CHEERS.

SHORTLY...

KILL WOMEN KILL WOMEN...

BINGO!

SCREEECH!

TSSSCHH!

FANCY A LIFT, LUV?

THANKS. CAN YOU DROP ME OFF JUST OUTSIDE DERBY?

2 HOURS LATER...

DERBY 4m

BUT...

WOOOOOOO! WOOOOOOOO! WOOOOOOO!

AW, BOLLOCKS.

HOW CAN I HELP YOU, OFFICER? WHAT SEEMS TO BE THE PROBLEM?

YOU'RE LOSING YOUR LOAD, MATE.

DEAD WOMAN IN A CARPET FELL OUT ABOUT A MILE BACK.

HOW MANY BODIES YOU GOT IN THERE ANYWAY?

ERM... ABOUT FORTY.

WELL, YOU WANT TO KEEP 'EM A BIT MORE SECURE. WE WOULDN'T WANT 'EM SPILLING OUT ALL OVER THE CARRIAGEWAY.

I'LL JUST CHECK YOUR TACHOMETER WHILE I'M AT IT, MATE.

TSK. SAYS 'ERE YOU MURDERED 4 WOMEN IN THE PAST 8 HOURS. IS THAT RIGHT?

AYE.

YOU DO KNOW, DON'T YOU, THAT YOU'RE SUPPOSED TO HAVE A 30 MINUTE BREAK EVERY TWO MURDERS?

YES, SORRY.

YOU'LL TIRE YOURSELF OUT. I'LL OVERLOOK IT THIS TIME, BUT YOU JUST MAKE SURE YOU HAVE A NAP.

YES, OFFICER. I'LL HAVE ONE STRAIGHT AWAY.

SO... ≡SNORE!≡ ...WIFFLE WAFFLE...≡SNORE!≡ ...WIFFLE WAFFLE...

HURTLE!

CAUTION ROAD WORKS & FOG

THE MODERN PARENTS

© John Fardell 2002

We're running a bit late.

Don't worry, there's no queue at our check-in desk, look... Just that one family.

AIR 10 BRITISH AIRWAYS CHECK IN

We need to check in for the 10.40 flight to Mauritius.

That's fine. If you could just put your luggage on the..

Actually, could I just check one thing?.. Your aircraft do run on **environmentally sustainable fuel**, don't they?

Er.. I'm not really sure... Now if you could just..

Well, you should be better informed about the practices of the company you work for!.. You wouldn't want your salary to be paid for by the **blood of endangered species** killed by global warming, would you?

I think you'd be better taking up such questions with your holiday company, sir.

We're not with a **holiday company**! We're not **tourists** you know!.. We're independent travellers.

Our consciences wouldn't allow us to deprive the local population of land and resources by staying at a luxury resort for rich westerners.

We're going to travel from village to village by ox cart, interfacing with the real Mauritian people in a meaningful, non-patronising way, aren't we Tarquin?

We wanted to go to EuroDisney.

Of course, we'll be careful to respect all the local customs...

Except for the **food**, obviously...They actually slaughter pigs, you know... It's **barbaric!**

So we're taking all our own ingredients with us to prepare wholesome vegan meals around the village camp fires.

I'm sure the Mauritians will all become vegetarians once they've tasted my Lentil Bake Surprise.

I'm sure, sir, but I've got a lot of other people to check in... If you could just..

Just a minute... I also want to make sure our flight path doesn't take us under any holes in the ozone layer... We don't want to catch skin cancer...

20 minutes later...

...and furthermore we want a guarantee that all coffee served on the flight will be made from Fair Trade, GM free coffee beans and..

Look- Here are your boarding passes. Just **go**!

What a **rude** woman! These multinational airlines treat their customers like sheep.

Put your bags on the X-ray conveyor belt, please. And put any keys and metal objects into the tray before walking through the gate.

Tsk! It's like living in a **police state**!

BEEEEEEP

If you could step over here please, sir.

Get your hands off me! This is a **violation** of my human rights!

Calm down, sir... I expect you just forgot to take some keys out of your pocket...

You only picked me out because I've got a **beard**, didn't you?

Ah, could I ask you to remove this metal neck pendant and walk through again, sir?

This isn't a **pendant**... It's my **Sacred Tribal Arrowhead**... I made it last week at our Rainforest Craft Workshop. I never take it off.

I'm afraid we have to confiscate all sharp objects, sir.

That's outrageous! This arrowhead is part of my cultural identity and anyway, I'm an internationally renowned pacifist!

You'd let me through if I was an **arms dealer**! Just because I signed a petition supporting the Palestinians last week, you're treating me like some kind of terrorist!

Well let me tell you, a lot of people think that your political masters in America brought September the 11th on themselves...

I mean, if I **was** a Palestinian refugee whose family had been **butchered** by your CIA death squads, I'd be morally justified in hijacking a plane and crashing it into the White House!

Security!.. We've got a nutter with a **knife**!

On our way!

Quick, Guin, grab our tickets and passports and the holiday money..

Get away from me, you imperialist fascists! No-one's going to stop me getting on that plane!

Let's go!

2 days later...

How long have you been members of al-Queda for?

Who else helped you plan this attempted hijacking?

Do you know the whereabouts of Osama bin Laden?

Let us out of here! Tarquin and Guinevere will be sick with worry!

MAURITIUS HILTON
★★★★★

Your Coca Colas and Ice Cream Sundaes, sir.

Ta!

JF 2002

61

TRANNY MAGNET

HULLO, READERS! I'VE DECIDED TO STOP WALLOWING IN SELF-PITY ABOUT MY CURSE OF ATTRACTING TRANSVESTITES AND TRANSSEXUALS! I'VE GOTTEN MYSELF A LITTLE JOB...

...AS A TV REPAIR MAN.

DING DONG!

OOH, I'M SO GLAD YOU'RE HERE. MY SILICON TITS NEED ADJUSTING!

AAGGHH! IT'S *THAT* KIND OF "TV REPAIR"!

FIVE SECONDS LATER...

GLOOM

WALLOW

OH HOW I PITY ME.

STOP FEELING SORRY FOR YOURSELF, WILLIE! THERE ARE OTHER JOBS.

:Sniffle: I SUPPOSE YOU'RE RIGHT, MUM. LET'S HAVE A LOOK IN THE FULCHESTER JOB RAG.

LOOK! HERE'S A GOOD ONE IN A MUSIC SHOP.

SOUNDS LIKE MY TRUE VOCATION!

SITUATIONS VACANT

WANTED:
Assistant to work in Virgin CD Store. Good rates of pay. The ideal applicant would be stumpy, fat and bald with a big nose and buck teeth.

TWATS! Earn up to £25 a week by being an annoying cunt who rings people up to sell them finance deals on double glazing

IN THE SHIT? Call Nosher's Debt...

NEXT DAY...

HO-HO! I WALKED THE JOB INTERVIEW! I START TODAY!

VIRGIN CD Shop

WOO! LOOK BOYS! THIS MUST BE THE NEW ASSISTANT!

MMMM... I WOULDN'T MIND LOSING MY CHERRY TO HIM!

DOES MY BUM LOOK BIG IN THIS, GORGEOUS?

YIKES! IT'S A *VIRGIN* CROSS-DRESSERS SHOP!

GERROFF!

LATER. AGAIN.

I NEED TO GET AWAY FROM IT ALL, MUM. I'VE BOOKED MYSELF A HOLIDAY ON A DESERT ISLAND.

LOVELY.

IF YOU HAVE A HOLIDAY ROMANCE, DON'T FORGET TO BE CAREFUL. I DON'T WANT YOU SURPRISING ME WITH ANY GRANDCHILDREN! HEH-HEH.

AW, MUUUM! YOU'RE EMBARRASSING ME!

...SO PLAY IT SAFE AND GIVE HER ONE UP THE ARSE.

LATER...

HERE I AM ON A DESERT ISLAND. THE PERFECT PLACE TO FORGET ALL MY TROUBLES.

5-STAR HOTEL

I'M SORRY TO TELL YOU THAT YOUR HOTEL WAS WASHED AWAY IN A TROPICAL STORM LAST NIGHT.

OH NO!

...BUT WE HAVE FOUND YOU ALTERNATIVE ACCOMODATION.

CHANNEL 4 ARE ON THIS VERY ISLAND FILMING A NEW SERIES OF "I'M A CELEBRITY, GET ME THE FUCK OUT OF HERE" AND THE STARS HAVE AGREED FOR YOU TO SHARE THEIR SLEEPING ARRANGEMENTS. IT'S BASIC, BUT--

SHARE WITH THE LIKES OF TARA PALMER-TOMKINSON AND NELL McANDREW? YES PLEASE!

GREAT. YOUR HOUSEMATES FOR THIS SERIES ARE LILY SAVAGE, EDDIE IZZARD, DAME EDNA EVERAGE, DANNY LARUE AND THE GHOST OF J. EDGAR HOOVER.

© LEW STRINGER 2002

ROBIN HOOD and RICHARD LITTLEJOHN

BE OF GOOD CHEER, MY MERRY BAND OF MEN

I SHALL COOK UP A HEARTY MEAL OF MINCE AND POTATOES TO FILL OUR BELLIES

AND THAT'S NOT THE ONLY KIND OF "MINCING" GOING ON IN THIS KINGDOM. YOU CAN'T RIDE THROUGH THE GLEN WITHOUT BEING EXPOSED TO GAYS ENGAGING IN ILLEGAL HOMOSEXUAL PRACTICES.

YET THE SHERIFF OF NOTTINGHAM AND HIS LEFT-WING CRONIES TURN A BLIND EYE. AND WHY? FOR FEAR OF "OFFENDING THE MINORITIES" **YOU COULDN'T MAKE IT UP.**

GADZOOKS! 'TIS FRIAR TUCK — HE HAS TAKEN AN ARROW IN THE BACK!

AND IT'S NOT THE FIRST TIME A FRIAR HAS BEEN "TAKEN FROM BEHIND." THE TRENDY MEDIEVAL CHURCH IS A HOTBED OF GAY SEX.

WELL PARDON ME FOR BEING POLITICALLY INCORRECT. BUT I THOUGHT THE BIBLE TAUGHT US ABOUT ADAM AND EVE — **NOT ADAM AND STEVE.**

>CHOKE< HURRY, ROBIN ~ MAID MARION HAS BEEN TAKEN PRISONER IN THE SHERIFF'S CASTLE!

COME, LITTLEJOHN — THE TWO OF US SHALL RESCUE MAID MARION FROM THE SHERIFF OF NOTTINGHAM

MORE A CASE OF THE SHERIFF OF **BOTTINGHAM.** HE AND HIS LOONY-LEFT CRONIES ARE OBSESSED WITH PROMOTING THE SO-CALLED "GAY LIFESTYLE"

IF THE SELF-APPOINTED GUARDIANISTA LIBERAL ELITE HAVE THEIR WAY, HOMOSEXUALITY WON'T JUST BE LEGAL. IT'LL BE **COMPULSORY.**

YOU COULDN'T MAKE IT UP.

YES, YES, WE MUST MAKE HASTE TO THE CASTLE, LITTLEJOHN.

QUIETLY, NOW. WE SHALL SLIP PAST THE GUARDS IN THROUGH THE BACK ENTRANCE

AND THAT WON'T BE THE ONLY KIND OF "SLIPPING INTO BACK ENTRANCES" GOING ON.

THE MUESLI-MUNCHING METROPOLITAN INTELLIGENTSIA WANT TO PUT ANAL SEX AND FISTING ON THE SCHOOL CURRICULUM

IF YOU OBJECT, THEY'LL BRAND YOU A "HOMOPHOBIC NAZI"

HUNH?

WE ARE ALL GOING TO HELL IN A TUMBRIL CART

IT'S ROBIN HOOD!

QUICKLY, LITTLEJOHN — WHILE I HOLD THESE TWO OFF, CLIMB UP AND RESCUE MARION

TAKE HER TO THE OLD WOODCUTTER'S COTTAGE IN THE FOREST

THAT'S NOT THE ONLY KIND OF "COTTAGING" TO BE FOUND IN THE WOODS.

SHERWOOD FOREST? **QUEERWOOD** FOREST IS MORE LIKE IT.

ZOUNDS! HERE COMES THE SHERIFF

HA HA! AT LAST I HAVE YOU, ROBIN HOOD

YOU AND YOUR OUTLAW FRIEND SHALL HANG FROM THE GIBBET, TOMORROW MORNING AT COCK-CROW

AND SO NEVER MIND COCKS CROWING, IT'S MORE A CASE OF COCKS **GROWING**

GAY MEN'S COCKS, THAT IS. GROWING ERECT AND COMMITTING SODOMY ON TAXPAYER'S MONEY. YOU COULDN'T MAKE IT UP

STOP! RELEASE THOSE TWO MEN AT ONCE!

HUZZAH! 'TIS GOOD KING RICHARD, RETURNED FROM THE CRUSADES

YES! AND I AM BANISHING YOU, SHERIFF OF NOTTINGHAM, TO THE TOWER OF LONDON

THERE ARE GOING TO BE SOME BIG CHANGES ROUND HERE

..I MEAN JUST **LOOK** AT THE MUCK IN THIS KINGDOM

EEEH! IT LOOKS LIKE YOU HAVEN'T FLICKED A DUSTER ROUND FOR MONTHS

AND SO

FREE STATE-FUNDED KY JELLY FOR GAY ASYLUM SEEKERS

QUEERWOOD FOREST

PUBLIC COTTAGING AREA

STRICTLY NO HETEROSEXUALITY ALLOWED! £500 FINE

"BAH! YOU COULDN'T MAKE IT UP

FAMILY VALUES NOT PERMITTED BY ROYAL ORDER

Letterbocks

Letterbocks, Viz Comic, PO Box 1PT, Newcastle-upon-Tyne, NE99 1PT.

E-mail letters@viz.co.uk

ON A recent trip to Edinburgh, I bet my mate Purple Elvis that he couldn't eat 50 Chicken McNuggets in an hour and keep them down. He not only managed to eat all 50, but he also licked the box, and all in a time of 39 minutes 2 seconds. Do any other readers know any similar big fat cunts?

Ollie Scull
e-mail

THESE NEW 'Gentlemen's Clubs' are a complete con. I went in one the other night and it was full of women. To add insult to injury, most of them were practically naked.

Robert Warren
e-mail

WITH REGARDS to Hellpass's letter (issue 115) about the LPGA tour winner photograph. How does her kissing a foot long glass dildo make you think she's *not* a lesbian?

Stuart Eagles
e-mail

EVERYONE IS always very quick to point the finger at paedophile priests. But in all fairness, surely half the blame should be on the ten-year-old boys for being just so damned sexy.

Ronald Lilycropp
Canada

I AM a good doctor about to be struck off, just for having sex with one of my patients - ten fucking years training down the drain. The British Veterinary Council are cunts.

Paul Murphy
e-mail

UTILISING THE 'law of averages', I've just calculated that at her current shagging rate, Ulrika Jonsson should be slotting me in for a session on or around June 7th 2005. I can't wait.

Adrian Newth
e-mail

I SEE that in the latest Sainsbury's advert, Jamie Oliver is complaining that his mum bought him a load of ready-made sauces, which he doesn't need because he's "a chef, for Pete's sake." Perhaps in future she should stick to buying him tampons.

Dick
e-mail

AN ENGLISHMAN'S home is his castle? Nonsense. I'm Scotch.

Billy Connolly
My Castle in Scotland

AND WHEN YOU WENT OUT YOU LEFT THE DOOR OPEN ALL MORNING

SORRY LOVE. I'M NOT THINKING STRAIGHT TODAY

ELTON JOHN has been moaning on about strangers feeling they can come up and talk to him just because he's famous. So when I passed him in Harrods the other day, I thought I'd let him make the first move for once. Was he grateful? The flabby dung-shover didn't say a dickie bird.

Mike Barman
e-mail

A BIG thank-you to my local Big Issue sellers for extending my life. Since the loveable scroungers have taken up position blocking my access to the local shops and bus station, I have no option but to take a walk the long way round in order to avoid their witless dirge. Consequently, I have lost two stone and relieved considerable pressure on my heart.

Wolfgang Liebbfraumilch
Stalingrad

ARE YOU still doing Celebrity Cunts? If so, a barman mate of mine was told to "just get the fucking drinks in" when he asked pint-sized singer Van Morrison for his autograph.

Gavin McKernan
e-mail

I READ with incredulity that lorry drivers, in conjunction with the Missing Persons Bureau, will now be travelling the length of the country with hoardings on the sides of their lorries advertising missing persons. Surely this is giving them a licence to boast about their exploits.

Louise Matthews
Leytonstone

I AM writing to warn any morris dancers that I recently bought a high-powered air rifle from some guy in a pub in Birmingham. I have also secured several vantage points in most of the towns located around the river Severn. If any of you bastards dare to wake me up at 7am clacking your sticks and jangling your bells during any folk festival I will shoot the ceremonial tankards off your belts. That goes for anyone who owns a squeeze-box too.

V.B. Hangover
e-mail

I HAD the misfortune to be in Port Stanley recently whilst the *Ground Force* team were doing their stuff at the local hospital garden. I went along for a gawp at Charlie Dimmock's norks, which were well worth a look, much better than the webbed-footed inbred Falklanders. Charlie was grafting for real, pushing a barrow around and shifting loads of shit. But Alan Titchmarsh was just the opposite. The idle twat just stood there with a hosepipe and only did any work when the cameras were filming, the lazy fucker.

Dave Carter
e-mail

WITH ALL the problems in the NHS, the staff could increase efficency at a stroke. When nurses move patients from beds in pairs, instead of lifting on the count of three, they should do it on the count of two, thereby speeding up the process by 33%.

Gabriel Vogt
e-mail

WITH IT being 20 years since the Falklands War, I see Simon Weston is raising his head again, milking the anniversary for all it's worth. I burnt my hand on the oven last Tuesday, and you don't see me kicking up a fuss.

Benjamin Toast
e-mail

DURING THE height of the war against terror, me and my mates had a few beers and watched the Rambo trilogy to take our minds off the bloodshed. Imagine our surprise when during the closing credits of *Rambo 3*, the words *"This film is dedicated to the gallant people of Afghanistan"* popped up on the screen. My, how times change.

Patrick Bateman
Gateshead

I WAS shocked to hear recently in the news that the Queen is set to receive a £50 million fortune in her dear old mother's will. What gets me is the fact that, unlike everyone else in the country, she will not be paying any inheritance tax thanks to a fucking 'special deal' with the government. What special fucking deal? I mean any other person would be forking out about 20 fucking million. Just who the fuck does she think she is? Still, she does a marvellous job and we shouldn't knock her.

Jamie Farr
Herts

THE Opera Babes? 'Opera', yes. But whilst I wouldn't climb over them to get to Luciano Pavarotti, I think the term 'Babes' is stretching it a bit, especially the one on the right.

T. Harris
Wolverhampton

THERE DON'T appear to be any celebrities with cancer at the moment. John Thaw gave up at the drop of a hat, not like your man Roy Castle. At least he made a game of it.

D.J. Furse
e-mail

IF THE Queen Mum (God bless her) really was the nation's favourite grandmother, why aren't we seeing any of her cash? She left ninety-odd million, and as far as I'm aware, us adopted grandchildren are getting fuck all in her will.

John Paul O'Kane
e-mail

HAS ANYONE done the exact maths about this yet? King George VI died in 1952 and Diana went toes up about four years ago. Then Margaret cakes it earlier this year, followed in the blinking of an eye by the Queen Mum. At this rate of acceleration of the Royals pegging it, we should be shot of the lot of them by the time the next football season starts, so no need for those annoying 2-minute silences before every match.

Iain Purdie
Bradford

TUBBY comedienne Dawn French is a complete hypocrite. If she really thinks that fat people are so attractive, why didn't she marry Barry White?

A. Forster
Wolverhampton

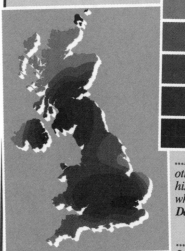

HEATHER MILLS is a complete hypocrite. Everyone in Britain knows she has only got one leg, so why does she go around with a plastic one, pretending she's got two?

J. Stoppard
Leeds

THE OTHER day I bought a copy of *Men Only* from my newsagent. Imagine my dismay when I got it home to discover it was full of pictures of women. To make matters worse, most of them weren't wearing a stitch.

Robert Warren
e-mail

I WENT to see a clairvoyant in 1999. She told me that on September 11th 2001, two passenger jets would crash into the World Trade Centre. I didn't take her seriously at the time, but now I can't forgive myself. If only I had listened I could have sold all my US stocks and shares before that date. But unfortunately I can't turn back time, and I must live with the fact that I lost nearly £280.

Conrad Fitblatt
Kippax

Sporting Supercunts

I BUMPED into Republic of Ireland manager Mick McCarthy after the Holland game at Lansdowne Road. I asked him for an autograph and he told me to fuck off. Have any other readers been abused by sporting personalities?

Mark Doyle
e-mail

THAT'S nothing. In my time I've been told to piss or fuck off by Les Cocker (Leeds United coach), Peter May (England and Surrey cricket captain) and Peter Bonetti (Chelsea and England goalkeeper).

Ian Iro
e-mail

Map of the Poo-shited Kingdom

In our last issue, James Millar threw down a shitty gauntlet by informing our readers that he had four shits in a day. Since then we've been swamped with unwanted information about the frequency of your motions. So much so, that we've been able to compile a map of the nation's bowel habits.

▮	1 shit every 3 weeks
▮	1 shit a week
▮	1 shit a day
▮	3-10 shits a day
▮	10+ shits a day

...I HAD six shits the other day, so that beats his measly effort. And what's more I'm a bird.
Daniela Gatto Ronchieri, *e-mail*

...TELL THAT puff James Millar I layed 3 cables in 1 hour 55 minutes last Thursday. And I'm talking Swiss rolls. Consider him shat on.
David Holmes, e-mail

...FOUR SHITS in a day, eh? Well if I have less than 4 every day there's something wrong. On average, it's 6 and my record is 8. And I'm not talking little plops or botty soup here, either, I mean full on king-sized Snicker bars. My nipsy is the healthiest muscle in my body.
Paul Mills, Sussex.

...FOUR SHITS in one day? As if that's a proud boast. I do more than that before I get out of bed in the morning.
Alex Thompson, East Lothian

Drive-by Bummings claim New Victim

A MANCHESTER man was last night said to be in a comfortable chair after becoming the lastest victim of a series of drive-by bummings.

Michael Fibreboard, 18, is the tenth man to be turked in the city since Christmas, and residents fear that the neighourhood is rapidly becoming a no-go area.

crack

The Moss Side resident was walking to his local crack-house last Saturday to buy a bag of smack when he was bummed three times in the arse by youths driving a stolen car.

Detective Constable George Oldspot who is leading the hunt for the botters commented: "We believe the intended targets of the bumming saw the car approaching and ran off. Mr Fibre-board was simply in the wrong place at the wrong time."

An anonymous local resident expressed concern and anger. "I don't know what this place is coming to. It's reaching the stage where the kids can't play out on the street with their guns any more," he said.

Top Tips

THE FAMOUS FIVE OF SUNSET LODGE

Albert, Dolly, Edna, and Frank, and Timmy The Budgie

Sunset Lodge
Residential Home
for
Retired Gentlefolk
Propietor:
Mrs. E. Robinson

THE FAMOUS FIVE WERE UP LATE AS USUAL, CHATTING AWAY ABOUT THE EXCITING EVENTS OF THE DAY...

IT WAS A SMASHING BIT OF HAM, THAT

SUPER, YES

TWEET!

PERHAPS THE MOST SUPER BIT OF HAM I'VE EVER EATEN

COME ALONG, YOU RASCALS. IT'S SEVEN O'CLOCK AND TIME YOU WERE IN BED. YOU'VE ALL GOT BUSY DAYS AHEAD OF YOU

YOU'RE GOING FOR A WALK TO THE END OF THE DRIVE, DOLLY. WITH EDNA

GOSH, HOW EXCITING!

AND FRANK AND ALBERT ARE GOING TO SIT UNDER TARTAN RUGS IN THE DAY ROOM

ARE WE REALLY, MRS. ROBINSON? THANKS AWFULLY

I SAY, SUPER!

OFF YOU GO, NOW. AND DON'T FORGET TO GET YOUR TABLETS FROM MATRON. LAST ONE IN BED IS A ROTTEN EGG

THE FAMOUS FIVE DRIFTED OFF TO SLEEP, BUT JUST BEFORE MIDNIGHT, FRANK WAS AWOKEN BY A SOUND...

SCREECH!

EH!? WHAT THE DICKENS...

QUICKRY NOW! CHOP! CHOP! WE GET VELLY VELLY GOOD PLICE FOR MRS. LOBINSON ON SLAVE MARKET

OOOOOOMPH! OOOOOOOOOOOMPH!

WAKE UP YOU CHAPS. MRS. ROBINSON IS BEING KIDNAPPED BY ORIENTAL SLAVE TRADERS.

GOSH!

WE'VE GOT TO STOP THEM!

LADIES' ROOM

COME ON! THERE'S NOT A MOMENT TO LOSE!

WAIT A TICK. I'VE JUST GOT TO GO TO SPEND A PENNY

I THINK WE'D BETTER ALL GO

OOH! A GOOD IDEA

YES

ABANDONED AIRFIELD 1 MILE

SORRY TO KEEP YOU WAITING, CHAPS, I NEED THE TOILET, BUT I CAN'T GO WHEN I GET THERE

COME ON! THERE'S NOT A MOMENT TO LOSE. DOWN THE STAIRS AT THE DOUBLE

COME ON, EDNA, YOU FIRST

CLUNK! HMMMMMMMMMMMMMMMMMM!

TWEET!

HMMMMM
MMMMM
MMMMMM
MMMMMM
MMMMM
MMMMMM!

OOOOOOOMPH!

HMMMMMMM
MMMMMM
MMMMMM
MM!

CLUNK!

CLUNK! HMM
MMMMMMMM
MMMMMMMM
MM!

PRESS!

HMMMMMM
MMMMMM
MMMMM
MMMMM!

IN YOU GET, DOLLY, QUICKLY...

...I'VE JUST GOT TO NIP FOR ANOTHER JIMMY RIDDLE

HMMMM
MMMM
MMMMMM
MMMM!
CLUNK!

PRESS! CLUNK!

HMMM
MMMMM
MMMMM
MMMMM
MMMMMM!

HMMMMMMM
MMMMMMMM
MMMM
MMM
MMM!

EVERYTHING'S A YEN

2/11   3/6

NOW... WHAT DID WE COME DOWN HERE FOR AGAIN?

ERM! OOH, WHAT WAS IT?

...IT WAS DEFINITELY SOMETHING

ERM!

TWEET!

EVENTUALLY...

HMMMM
MMMMM
MMMMMM
MMMMMMM
MMMMM!
CLUNK!

RIGHT! THERE'S NOT A MOMENT TO LOSE!

NEXT WEEK:
The Famous Five of Sunset Lodge are in pursuit as a gang of diamond smugglers attempt a getaway in souped up dragsters!

LEONARDO DA VINCI
THE ITALIAN RENAISSANCE SMUT-PEDDLER

O SOLE MIO!

MONA LISAS - 50p

I HAVEN'T-A SOLD A SEENGLE MONA LISA FORRA WEEKS

I KNOW! I'LL-A DO SOME PAINTINGS OFFA DA NAKED LADY HAVING-A RUMPY-PUMPY WIDDA SWAN, INSTEAD.

ALL MA PATRONS WILL WANNA BUY DA PEECTURES OFFA DA BIG BARE BOOBIES.

HOLY PEPPERONI! A COACH-LOAD OF CLERGYMEN WIDDA BONE-ONS!

VATICAN SUNSHINE BUS

MY NUDIE PEECTURES WEEL SELL LIKE-A HOT-CAKES

BUT..

GIRLS! GIRLS! GIRLS!

ADULT PIX

HOT GIRL ON SWAN ACTION

GALILEO GALILEI!

HUNH? THEY'RE ALL-A GOING INTO GALILEO'S PLACE NEXTA DOOR!

ROLL-A UP! ROLL-A UP! TEN-A PENCE A LOOK

GALILEO'S ALL NUDE

LIVE PEEP SHOW

SEX! SEX! SEX!

BAH!

GALILEO HAS-A EENVENTED DA **TELESCOPE** FORRA PEEKING AT MRS BORGIA OVER DA ROAD

SHOW

SEX! SE

NOW, WHO'S-A NEXT?

HEH HEH! I FIXA HIM WIDDA DAB OF PAINT ONNA END OFFA HIS TELESCOPE..!

HEY! THATSA NOT A NUDE LADY — SHE'S-A WEARING A BRA!

HUNH? B-BUT..

TSSH! EETSA SOFT-CORE RUBBISH. LETSA GO.

BAH! LEONARDO HAS-A PAINTED A BRA ONNA THE LENS!

I'VE EENVENTED A MACHINE FORRA PAINTING MA SAUCY PEECTURES.

SEX PORN

NUDE LADY COLOUR PAINT

SWAN COLOUR PAINT

HERE-A YOU GO, CARDINAL. HAVE A NICE-A WANK.

WHIRR

CLANK

HEH HEH!

JESUS & DISCIPLE COLOUR PAINT

NUDE LADY COLOUR PAINT

SWAN COLOUR PAINT

I CHANGE-A DA PAINT IN LEONARDO'S MACHINE WHEN HE'S-A NOT LOOKING

WHATSA DA MEANING OFFA THEES?! EETSA NOT A SEXY PEECTURE — EETSA JUST A LAST SUPPER WIDDA JESUS AND STUFF!

HO! HO!

NUDE LADY COLOUR PAINT

SWAN COLOUR PAINT

JESUS & DISCIPLE COLOUR PAINT

I'M-A NOT BUYING THEES

GRRR! I TEACHA YOU TO STEAL MY PUNTERS!

WHATSA MATTER YOU, HEY? GOTTA NO RESPECT?

LIVE PEEP SHOW

SEX! SEX! SEX!

WAIT A MINUTE - WHERE'S-A ALL DA PUNTERS GONE?

THEY'VE-A DEESAPPEARED

LIVE PEEP SHOW

SEX! SEX!

I THINK I CAN ANSWER THAT QUESTION, CHAPS...

HUH? EETSA SIR ISAAC NEWTON, DA ENGLISH PHYSICIST

MY **GRAVITY MACHINE** FOR MAKING WOMEN'S KNICKERS FALL DOWN IS DOING A ROARING TRADE!

SEXY AMATEURS

GRAVITY-O-MATIC 50p A GO

LIVE XXX ACTION

GRAVITY FORCE

Q HERE

HAW! HAW!

BAH!

GPD. ST. DJ. V113

69

Old Wives Tales Have Soap Stars in a Lather

EXCLUSIVE

Soap-

STAN AND DELIVER: Marjorie delivers vinegar onto Stan's chips

They never utter the title of 'The Scottish Play', they never whistle in the dressing rooms, they never say 'Macbeth' and they never perform with children or animals. Actors are notoriously superstitious, but according to a new book by a mobile caterer who has provided on-set food for all of Britain's leading serial dramas, when it comes to superstitions, the stars of our soaps take the biscuit.

In a 30-year career spanning three decades, Marjorie Bibby has dished out tea, sandwiches, soup, burgers (with or without onions) and advice to all of Britain's best known soap stars. And in her new book *'Soaperstitions'* (Croissant Books, £12.99), she lifts the lid on the old wives' tales which rule the behind-the-scenes world of our favourite TV shows.

Directors

"You might think that the writers and directors control who and what we see on our soaps, but you'd be wrong. The actors superstitions play a lot bigger part than anyone realises. Most people believe that Ross Kemp left EastEnders when he signed a million pound deal with ITV drama. But that's simply not the case, I can tell you. The truth is that he was hounded out of the thrice-weekly London soap by his fellow actors after their superstitions got the better of them.

"One rainy day, Kemp was filming a scene with Sharon Watts. The script called for him to leave the Queen Vic, open his umbrella and walk into that little park bit in the middle. But Kemp fluffed the shot, and opened his brolly whilst he was still inside the Vic.

"The cast and crew were clearly upset, and shooting was halted. Barbara Windsor

■ **by TRAFFORD LOVETHING**

maintained that the bad luck could be reversed if the actor simply turned round three times and spat. However, Kemp was having none of it, growling that it wasn't in his contract."

And according to Marjorie, things went from bad to worse. Over the coming months Kemp...

• *Dropped a knife in the Fowlers' kitchen, and then refused to tap it on the table leg, whilst saying: "Sharp surprise - tap it on wood, sure to be good"*

• *Put his hat on Phil Mitchell's bed without then placing it upside down on the windowsill overnight to let the devil out of it*

• *Placed his shoes on the table in Kathy Beale's cafe, and then refused to bury a piece of meat in the garden.*

"Eventually the cast got so scared that they petitioned the BBC to axe Kemp before his actions led to a jinx on the soap. Station bosses agreed, and the actor was given his marching orders.

"Chillingly, in his career since EastEnders, Kemp has been dogged by four pieces of terrible fortune; In Defence, Hero of the Hour, Without Motive and Ultimate Force."

Gladiator

Sometimes, there's simply no way for the soap stars to reverse their bad luck. Marjorie remembers being called onto the set of EastEnders on New Years Day a few years ago. The tea urn had gone on the blink over Christmas and the cast needed hot drinks.

"When I arrived, they were filming a scene in the launderette. Dot Cotton was going to have an argument with Pauline whilst doing a service wash for Dr Legg. The scene was going really well until Dot Cotton suddenly stopped. I thought she'd forgotten her lines until I saw her face. She looked like she'd seen a ghost. Then she started screaming.

"I'm washing on new year's

SUPERSTITIOUS: Armstrong & Cotton

day! I'm washing on new year's day!" she cried. The set fell silent. We all knew what that meant; Dot Cotton was washing someone out of her family. Dot was inconsolable, it's one of the few bad lucks to which there is no effective antidote. As a result, no-one was surprised when, a few months later, she opened her script to find out that her husband Charlie Cotton had been tragically killed in a lorry crash."

Pedigree

Not everybody in soaps is superstitious. But those who write it off as mumbo jumbo could be making the worst mistakes of their acting careers.

"I remember one occasion when I was serving food to the cast and crew of Brookside. At the time, the popular Liverpool soap was riding high in the ratings, with exciting storylines and entertaining characters. During the commercial break, producer Phil Redmond came to my van for a bacon sandwich, but whilst seasoning

SHARP SURPRISE: The EastEnders set where Kemp dropped his knife

Our Number's Up

Spoonbender's sinister warning to the world

We're all scared of the number thirteen, but top mystic conjuror Uri Geller, who rose to fame in the 1970s bending spoons using only the strength of his mind and hands, has recently begun to fear another number. The number **ELEVEN**.

❝ The number eleven will bring about the destruction of the world," he says. "Look at the evidence and you will see I am correct. The Twin Towers looked a bit like an eleven, and fell down on the **ELEVENTH** of September. 9-11 - add the three digits up, and it makes eleven. September is only **TWO** months before the eleventh month, and the Roman for two is eleven. Where were the twin towers? **NEW YORK CITY** - eleven letters. Which district? **IN MANHATTAN** -

eleven letters again. What crashed into the towers? **2 AEROPLANES** - eleven letters (if you count the number 2 as a letter) and where was the atrocity planned? in **AFGHANISTAN**. Eleven letters again.

Who was the attack perpetrated against? **GEORGE W BUSH** and **TONY BLAIR MP** - surprise, surprise, eleven letters each. And who was the evil terrorist who planned the outrage? **MR O. BIN LADEN, OSAMA B. LADEN, MISTER LADEN, MR. OSAMA BIN L., BIN LADEN ESQ.** However you spell his name, you come up with the same answer. Yes, that's right. **ELEVEN LETTERS.**

Some people would dismiss these bizarre coincidences as mere bizarre coincidences, but these coincidences are simply too bizarre to be written off as mere bizarre coincidences. ❞

it, he spilt some salt on the counter. I told him he ought to throw some over his shoulder to hit the devil in the eye, but he just laughed and walked off.

"However, the consequences of his hasty actions soon became clear. As the second half of the show began, a mystery virus broke out in the Close, the plots became farcical and Brookside got axed. Redmond should think twice next time he spills salt on the set of Hollyoaks."

Bum

Soaps work to tight schedules and even tighter budgets, and none more so than Emmerdale Farm. Marjorie recalls an incident where a star's refusal to tempt fate cost his soap bosses a fortune. Quite literally.

"I was on location in the Yorkshire Dales providing a finger buffet for the cast and crew of Emmerdale farm. They were about to film a scene where Annie Sugden was up a ladder cleaning the Woolpack windows. The script called for Seth Armstrong to walk under the ladder, look up her skirt and wolf whistle.

"But Seth was having none of it. He flatly refused to walk under the ladder, saying bad luck would visit his house three times if he did. The producers tried to persuade him, but he wouldn't listen. In the end, tempers frayed and he threatened to leave the series".

So Marjorie couldn't believe her eyes when she tuned in that night to see Seth walking under the ladder, as plain as day. She later found out that Yorkshire

SMASH! Broken mirror brought 7 years bad luck for Albert

In the hot summer of 1977, the Granada TV canteen failed a routine health and hygiene inspection, and Marjorie was called in to do a bit of emergency catering on the Coronation Street set.

"One of my first jobs was to take a cup of tea and a slice of black pudding to the dressing room of Rovers Return regular Albert Tatlock. He was getting ready for a scene, carefully applying purple greasepaint to the end of his nose, and as he reached for his cuppa he accidentally knocked his shaving mirror into the sink, where it shattered.

Albert froze with horror. I tried to make light of it, but deep down we both knew what the broken mirror meant."

And Albert didn't have long to wait. His 7

Albert Tatlock: Unbelievably bad actor

years of bad luck started the very next day.

Tatlock's catalogue of misfortune:

1977 Albert's real-life car fails its MOT due to a faulty brake light.

1978 While out shopping in Salford, Tatlock kicks a really big dog turd, and some of it goes all on the front and top of his shoe.

1979 The street veteran's real-life brother Sid mysteriously dies of natural causes at the age of 93.

1980 Tatlock leaves his trademark cap on a bus. It is never handed in, leaving the actor little choice but to buy a new one.

1981 Albert's nephew Ken Barlow's marriage to Dierdre Rashid flounders.

1982 While out shopping in Didsbury, Tatlock steps right into a dog turd, this time coating his heel and instep in foul-smelling orange excreta.

1983 Albert places a £5 each way bet on the Grand National, and his horse comes in fourth.

Finally, in **1984,** exactly seven years and a few months to the day since he broke his mirror, Tatlock suffers his biggest stroke of bad luck, when he dies in real life.

TV had ended up getting Pixar Studios in Hollywood - the creators of Toy Story and Shrek - to produce a special computer animated Seth for the 2 second shot. Apparently, just animating the whiskers on the veteran rubbish actor's face had taken over a year, at a cost of over £10 million. Ironically, the shot ended up on the cutting room floor and was never used.

'Soaperstitions' by Marjorie Bibby is available in publisher's outlets, supermarket tills and all-night garages from November 10th.

Why Do We...?

Have you ever wondered why we cross our fingers for luck, or are scared when a black cat crosses our path? Dr Boris Fäckt, professor of everything at the University of Wisconsin explains the origins of a few of the Soapstars superstitions.

• **Why is it unlucky to whistle on a Sunday?**

Ken Barlow out of Coronation Street
In Victorian times, whistling was said to be the sound of the devil's flute, and that anyone who could whistle was in league with Satan. These people were burned as witches on a Sunday after their dinner. That's why, although people are no longer burned at the stake, it is still considered bad luck to whistle on a Sunday.

• **Why is the number 13 considered unlucky?**

Benny out of Crossroads
This goes back to Victorian times when formal education was only available to the very rich. Consequently, bakers often had difficulty counting to twelve, and would often put 13 buns in a bag and charge only for twelve, losing money on the sale. As a result, many bakers ended up in debtors prison, put there by the number 13.

• **Why do we say 'White Rabbits' on the first day of the month, unless that month has an 'R' in it.**
Lofty Watts, EastEnders
This tradition dates back to times past when rabbits, especially white ones, were regarded as bringers of good fortune on the first day of the month, particularly if the month had an 'R' in it.

Sporting Superstartions

Paul Ince never puts his shirt on before stepping on the pitch, Tim Henman always laces up his left shoe first and Sally Gunnell never shaves on the morning of a race. Many of our favourite sports stars have secret rituals which they swear bring them luck. Here's a few of the more unusual ones.

• Olympic oarsman **Steven Redgrave** insists on always wearing his lucky underpants in every competition. "They're the pair I was wearing when I won my first rowing race at the age of six," he told us. "Obviously, they're far too small for me now, so for comfort I wear them over a normal sized pair."

• Leeds Rhinos rugby star Barrie McDermott's **superstition** has cost him more than £100,000 during his career. "On the day of my first professional match, I was so nervous whilst driving to the ground that I ran into the back of a taxi at a roundabout. However, during the game I played a blinder, and we won 64-12. I don't like to tempt fate and ever since that day I have to run into the back of a taxi on my way to a match." Barry's insurance premiums have gone through the roof and he is often beaten up by cabbies. "It's worth it, though," he adds. "Because we always win 64-12."

• World hop, skip and jump champion **Jonathan Edwards** goes through a special superstitious ritual at every athletics meeting he attends. "Before I leave the changing rooms, I kneel down, put my hands together and have a chat with an invisible bearded man who lives on a cloud," he says. "I ask him to help me win so I can have all the prize money and the big shiny cups for myself. He's only let me down a few times, like at the Atlanta Olympics when I only come second."

• **Top flight darts player** Jocky Wilson has won the Embassy World Darts Championship more times than any other player. And the hunky Scot attributes his success to having a lucky pre-match ritual. "All the players on the darts circuit share dressing rooms. Before each match, I'll sit and relax in the dressing room for ten minutes. Then, when my opponent isn't looking, I'll do a lucky shit in one of his shoes', he says.

• England goalie **David Seaman** offers himself up to Beelzebub at a stone altar in the Highbury dressing room before every match. "Dressed in black robes, I sacrifice six virgins by slitting their throats with a special curved dagger. Then I remove and eat their wombs and bathe in their still warm blood," he says. "The boss and the other lads think I'm daft as a brush, and deep down I know it's silly, but it keeps me focused before a game."

JACK BLACK
AND HIS DOG
SILVER

JACK BLACK AND HIS DOG SILVER WERE STAYING AT AUNT MEG'S COTSWOLD GUEST HOUSE IN THE VILLAGE OF NETHERDUCKFORD-ON-THE-WATER.

AUNT MEGS GUEST HOUSE
NO
DSS
PETS
BLACKS

OH FATHERLAND, FATHERLAND, SHOW US THE SIGN, YOUR CHILDREN HAVE WAITED TO SEE. THE MORNING WILL COME, WHEN THE WORLD IS MINE, TOMORROW BELONGS TO ME!

HOWWLL! HOWWLL!

THERE, AUNT MEG! DID YOU LIKE OUR SONG!

YES, JACK. IT WAS VERY NICE...

...BUT I THINK IT'S ABOUT TIME I GOT THAT OLD PIANO TUNED.

THERE'S A NEW PIANO TUNER SET UP IN THE VILLAGE. I SAW HIS ADVERT IN THE PAPER...

I'LL RING HIM STRAIGHT AWAY.

THE NETHERDUCKFORD ENQUIRER
LOCAL MAN CLIPS HEDGE EXCLUSIVE! WOMAN, 28, WASHES CAR

TEN MINUTES LATER...

THE PIANO TUNER IS HERE, AUNT MEG, AND GUESS WHAT...

...HE'S BLIND AS A BAT!

IT'S THIS WAY, MR BYRNES. FOLLOW ME AND TRY NOT TO KNOCK INTO ANYTHING.

RIGHT-HO! LEAD THE WAY.

JACK AND SILVER WATCHED FASCINATED AS MR. BYRNES SET TO WORK.

CLANG

HOW LONG TIL YOU FINISH, MR. BYRNES?

WELL, I THINK I'M JUST ABOUT DONE.

WHAT DO YOU SAY WE TEST IT WITH A LITTLE TUNE. EH JACK?

MR. BYRNES SOON HAD THE OLD PIANO SOUNDING LIKE NEW AND WAS PUTTING IT THROUGH IT'S PACES.

THOSE MAGNIFICENT MEN IN THEIR FLYING MACHINES, THEY GO UP-TIDDLY-UP-UP, THEY GO DOWN-TIDDLY-OWN-DOWN...

OH STAY AND PLAY ANOTHER SONG, DO, MR. BYRNES

SORRY, YOUNG MAN. I'VE GOT LOTS OF OTHER PIANOS TO TUNE TODAY.

WELL, I DON'T THINK I'VE EVER HEARD THAT OLD PIANO SOUNDING SO GOOD...

...AND AFTER ALL THAT SINGING, I THINK I'LL HAVE TO GO AND CHANGE MY TAMPON.

THAT'S ODD! I COULD HAVE SWORN I LEFT A BRAND NEW PACKET OF CUNT MICE IN THIS DRAWER. RIGHT NEXT TO YOUR SCHOOL CAP...

WAIT A MINUTE... THAT'S MISSING TOO. HOW ODD.

HERE, JACK. BE A LOVE AND POP INTO THE VILLAGE FOR SOME HEAVY FLOW JAM RAGS. I'M MENSTRUATING LIKE A STUCK PIG.

YES, AUNT MEG.

AND GET YOURSELF A NEW CAP WHILST YOU'RE THERE.

JACK AND SILVER WALKED INTO THE VILLAGE ON THEIR ERRAND.

CAPS 'n' TAMPONS

COME ON, SILVER. LET'S TRY IN HERE.

BUT...

SORRY, JACK. EVERYONE IN THE VILLAGE AS BEEN IN FOR SCHOOL CAPS AND TAMPONS TODAY. WE'RE COMPLETELY SOLD OUT.

WHAT ARE WE GOING TO DO?

I DON'T KNOW, JACK. YOU COULD TRY ACROSS THE ROAD

74

RICHARD E. GRANT SAYS ~ HEY MAN! THIS CARTOON IS JUST FOR FUN, YEAH? ARGOS IS A COOL PLACE TO SHOP DUDES!!"

75

THE 3 TENORS

DO RAY MEE

READER'S VOICE

SOUNDS LIKE THE TENORS ARE PRACTISING THEIR SCALES

NO — THAT'S JUST MY TUMMY RUMBLING

FA SO LA

WE'RE FAMISHED AS USUAL

COME ON FAMILY — WE'LL RAID HANK MARVIN'S STORE

HE'S HAD A NEW CONSIGNMENT OF FOOD DELIVERED

BAH! HANK'S STANDING GUARD

HANK MARVIN'S STORE

I'M KEEPING A CLOSE EYE ON YOU PESKY TENORS

I'VE AN IDEA! LUCIANO, PUT ON LITTLE JOSÉ'S UNDERPANTS AND THEN SING A LOUD OPERA

EH?

BUT THESE PANTS ARE MUCH TOO SMALL FOR ME

JUST ONE CORNETTO...

VERY HIGH-PITCHED

HEH HEH! THOSE TIGHT UNDERPANTS HAVE TURNED LUCIANO INTO A SOPRANO!

GIVE IT TO MEEE...

TINKLE   DOGGONE IT!   SMASH

THAT HIGH NOTE HAS SHATTERED MY GLASSES

GRR! I CAN'T SEE A THING!

HANK MARVIN'S STORE

BUNS

HO HO! GOOD THINKING, PLACIDO ~ THAT WAS ONE IN THE EYE FOR HANK MARVIN!

 # MEDDLESOME RATBAG

EXCELLENT! THERE WILL BE ONE MINUTE'S SILENCE HELD AT NOON TODAY TO COMMEMORATE THE ANNIVERSARY OF SOME TERRIBLE TRAGEDY OR OTHER

Daily Neb
PLAY TRAGEDY BINGO

I CAN HARDLY WAIT

IT'S NEARLY 12 O'CLOCK

NOW TO SEEK OUT PEOPLE FAILING TO OBSERVE THE MINUTE'S SILENCE, AND GIVE THEM A PIECE OF MY MIND

HUNH? I CAN'T FIND ANY TRANSGRESSORS

EVERYONE IS REMAINING PERFECTLY QUIET AND STILL

BAH! NO WONDER!

STREET EXHIBITION OF MANNEQUINS

THEY WEREN'T REAL PEOPLE, JUST SHOP WINDOW DISPLAY DUMMIES

ONLY 30 SECONDS LEFT, AND I'VE NOT FOUND ANYONE BREAKING THE ONE MINUTE'S SILENCE

FULCHESTER MATERNITY HOSPITAL

WAHHH!

AHA!

AT LAST

WELL, REALLY! CAN'T YOU KEEP THAT CHILD QUIET FOR JUST ONE MINUTE? I AM TRYING TO TAKE A MOMENT TO PAY MY RESPECTS AND HONOUR THOSE WHO DIED IN THAT TERRIBLE, TERRIBLE TRAGEDY

WAHHHH!

AND I FIND IT DEEPLY OFFENSIVE THAT MY THOUGHTS SHOULD BE DISTURBED BY ROWDY BEHAVIOUR OF YOUR ILL-MANNERED CHILDREN

IS IT A BIRD? IS IT A FELLA? NO! IT'S...

WOMAN-MAN!

Paul Palmer

SORRY IF I'M A BIT AGGRESSIVE!

I'M PRE-MENSTRUAL!

LOVELY BIT OF FISH THAT, PET!

CAN I WATCH THE FOOTBALL TONIGHT?

NO, LOVE! IT'S MY SOAPS TONIGHT, REMEMBER?

OH YES!

RIGHT YOU ARE THEN, LOVE!

ER... I MIGHT JUST NIP TO THE SHED, THEN!

SORT OUT MY POTS!

THAT'S NICE, DEAR!

AND, ONCE INSIDE

WHIRR!

CLICK!

WOMAN-MAN! THANK GOD YOU'RE THERE! LADIES-MAN IS ON THE LOOSE! WE THINK HE'S AFTER YOUR SUPER-POWERED UNDERWEAR AGAIN!

BY THE POWER OF PANTIES!

DO YOU THINK YOU CAN HANDLE HIM?

DON'T WORRY, CHIEF! THIS IS ONE LADY WHO WON'T FALL FOR HIS CHARMS! HE WON'T GET ANYWHERE NEAR MY KNICKERS! AND IF HE DOES HE'LL GET A NASTY SURPRISE!

HURRY, WM! THERE'S NO TIME TO LOSE!

DON'T WORRY! I'LL BE FIVE MINUTES!!

AND

IT'S RAINING MEN! HALLELUJAH! IT'S RAINING MEN...

RIP!

WAX

TCH! BLOODY HELL!! NOT ANOTHER LADDER!

TUF!

HOIST!

HMMM!

BAD BREASTS

STEALTH BREASTS

GAS BREASTS

HYPNO-BREASTS

DISTRACTO-BREASTS

TO THE BIRD-MOBILE!

SHRIEK!

I AM SO NOT GOING OUT WITH MY HAIR LIKE THIS!

SO

WHIRR!

EVENTUALLY

TO THE BIRD-MOBILE!

AS SOON AS I FIND MY KEYS!

I'M AT THE SPEED LIMIT, THANK YOU!

I'M NOT BREAKING THE LAW FOR YOU, MR. SPEEDY!

COMPENSATING ARE WE?

HONK! PARP! BEEP!

put! put!!

AND HAD A QUICK WEE!

World of SHOES

World of SHOES

World of SHOES

SALE

SALE

SALE

SHRIEK!

TUT! STUPID ROADS ARE ALL WRONG! I BET THIS MAP WAS WRITTEN BY A BLOODY MAN!

FUME!

FINALLY, AT THE LOVE-SHACK (SECRET HQ OF LADIES-MAN)

CREEP!

WOMAN-MAN! WELCOME!! I WAS WONDERING WHEN YOU'D FINALLY SHOW UP!

TIP TOE!

I'VE BEEN READY FOR HOURS!

HOW DID YOU KNOW I WAS HERE?

PEEK!

LET'S JUST SAY THAT THE BIRD MOBILE STANDS OUT, SHALL WE?

HONESTLY, LADIES-MAN! WILL YOU LOOK AT THE STATE OF THIS PLACE? HOW CAN YOU LIVE LIKE THIS? WOULD IT KILL YOU TO RUN A VACUUM AROUND HERE ONCE IN A WHILE? AND I'M NOT EVEN GOING NEAR THAT FRIDGE!

TYPICAL WOMAN! YOU'LL NEVER CHANGE ME! I - HAVE YOU LOST WEIGHT?

DON'T TRY THAT WITH ME! I -

WAG! WAG!

REALLY?!? DO YOU THINK SO? I'M NOT SURE! MY COSTUME FEELS LOOSER BUT I SWEAR I HAVEN'T BEEN TRYING!

BLUSH!

BY THE POWER OF CELLULITE! WHAT SORT OF FOOL DO YOU TAKE ME FOR? YOU'LL NEVER GET INSIDE MY KNICKERS!

TOO LATE, WOMAN-MAN! YOU'RE TRAPPED NOW! YOU'VE MESSED WITH MY EVIL MAN-PLANS FOR THE LAST TIME!!

PRESS!

SLAM!

NOW...

...TO CHARM THE PANTS OFF YOU! HA! HA! HA!

THINGS-LOOKING-BAD! ONLY-ONE-THING-TO-DO!!

MUST-OFFER-COMMITMENT!!

YOU'RE... ER... SPECIAL! YOU KNOW THAT, LADIES-MAN, DON'T YOU? I'M NOT SAYING I WANT TO MARRY YOU TOMORROW! GOD KNOWS, I'M NOT READY MYSELF!! I JUST WANT TO KNOW THAT THIS RELATIONSHIP IS GOING SOMEWHERE!

WHAT?

WHAT ARE YOU DOING?

STOP IT!

AND YOU DON'T NEED TO WORRY ABOUT ME WANTING BABIES! BABIES ARE A LONG WAY OFF! IF AT ALL!! I JUST KNOW YOU'D MAKE A BRILLIANT FATHER, THAT'S ALL!

NO! NO!! STOP IT, DAMN YOU!!

MY PARENTS WOULD LOVE YOU! I KNOW THEY WOULD! THEY'VE BEEN WAITING FOR ME TO MEET SOMEONE LIKE YOU!

ARGH!

CURSE YOU, WOMAN-MAN! YOU MAY HAVE SCARED ME OFF FOR NOW BUT I'LL BE BACK! YOU HAVEN'T SEEN THE LAST OF ME!

BLAST!

I JUST NEED A LITTLE SPACE RIGHT NOW!

ONCE AGAIN FEMININE GUILE TRIUMPHS OVER LADDISH SELFISHNESS! FOR WHEREVER MAN MISSES TOILET, WHEREVER TV REMOTES ARE HOGGED, WHEREVER A FELLA INSISTS ON DRIVING UNLESS HE WANTS TO GET RAT-ARSED, THERE WILL BE...

WOMAN-MAN!

SHIT! I BROKE A NAIL!!

IT's every boy's dream to become a Premiership footballer, walking out onto the turf as 50,000 voices sing his name. But to make it, he will need skill, dedication, team spirit, fitness and at least 110% commitment. Even then, most who set out on the road to glory will fall by the wayside before getting the chance to kick a ball in anger. For many, the disappointment can be hard to bear. Are you destined to join David Beckham and Michael Owen as a footballing hero? Or are you set to follow the likes of Eddie Large and the Pope and become a failed zero. Take our test, answering the questions a, b or c, and tot up your score. Do YOU have what it takes to become a...

PREMIER LEAGUE FOOTBALLER?

1 You go on a romantic weekend to Paris with your girlfriend. How do you show her a good time?
a. *Take her to the top of the Eiffel Tower, and surprise her with a bottle of Champagne.*
b. *Take her for a candlelit meal at a cosy bistro, and afterwards to a show at the Moulin Rouge.*
c. *Take her to a bar and kick her fucking head in.*

2 How many hours work could you manage in a week?
a. *35-39*
b. *40-65*
c. *1¹/₂*

3 You've been out partying all night, and you pop into a fast food outlet for a burger, only to be told that you have to choose from the breakfast menu. What do you do?
a. *Order anything that's available, you're so hungry you're not fussy.*
b. *Make your way to another fast food outlet in the hope that burgers are being served.*
c. *Scream that you want a burger cooked by a white man, then start kicking the place to bits.*

4 You are convicted of an appalling racist crime that disgusts the nation. How would you attempt to make amends and win back the respect of your community?
a. *Issue a heartfelt statement expressing deep regret and abject shame at your appalling behaviour, and hope that in time people will forgive your actions.*
b. *Attempt to undo some of the damage by committing yourself to a programme of voluntary work in the ethnic minority community.*
c. *Wrong foot a defender and slot one in at the keeper's near post.*

5 It's your son's birthday. How do you celebrate?
a. *Have a small party with a little cake, inviting his grandparents, cousins and a few friends from school.*
b. *Take him and a small group of friends to the Wacky Warehouse, or for a day out at the Sea Life Centre.*
c. *Have his stupid name tattooed across your arse in Ye Olde English capital letters.*

6 How big are your girlfriend's tits and what are they made of?
a. *Small to medium and made of flesh, skin and milk.*
b. *Medium to large and made of flesh, skin and milk.*
c. *The size of spacehoppers and made of something out of a vat from ICI.*

7 What would be your dream home?
a. *A brand new dull, nondescript two-bedroom Wimpy house.*
b. *An imposing forty-bedroom, Georgian stately home in its own grounds.*
c. *A brand new, dull, nondescript forty-bedroom Wimpy house in its own grounds.*

8 You find yourself out of work in your mid-thirties. What do you do?
a. *Get on your bike and look around your area for any work that's going.*
b. *Go back to college and retrain for a different career.*
c. *Sell crisps.*

9 You are queuing for stamps in the post office when an old lady accidentally nudges into you and catches your shin with her walking stick. How do you react?
a. *Smile and apologise, even though you were blameless.*
b. *Tut under your breath, turn to the person next to you and roll your eyes.*
c. *Hit the ground like a sack of spuds, roll over and over clutching your shin and lie groaning for a couple of minutes before standing up, taking a few tentative 'test' steps and limping theatrically back to the queue.*

10 What did you do on your last holiday?
a. *Spend a gentle week meandering along Britain's Inland Waterways on a rented canal boat.*
b. *Have a traditional seaside holiday, eating ice-cream and building sandcastles on the beach.*
c. *Go to a Spanish hotel and make a hard core porn video featuring you and your mates up to the apricots in impressionable teenage muff.*

11 It's Christmas, and you are doing food shopping in a supermarket. The place is packed, and when you get to the checkouts you find there is a large queue. How do you react?
a. *Stand patiently and wait your turn, it's only like this once a year.*
b. *Abandon your trolley, go home and return when it's less busy.*
c. *Send your wife to the front of the queue to screech "Do you know who we are?" at the unfortunate girl on the till, receiving a ban from every Tescos in Britain?*

HOW DID YOU DO?

Mainly a: Oh dear, you are no footballer, professional or otherwise. With your two left feet, you probably can't even kick a ball straight. Limit your footballing ambitions to a knockabout on the beach, or occasionally passing the ball back to some kids in the park. Better luck next time.

Mainly b: Close, but no orange at half time. You'd probably make a pretty good Sunday league player. You might even get the odd game for a half decent team of part timers like Blyth Spartans, Accrington Stanley or Southampton. But let's face it, you haven't got what it takes to make it as a top-flight pro.

Mainly c: Congratulations. The Premiership and a pair of poncy silver boots await. You must be over the moon and all credit to you because at the end of the day, it's the score that counts. You set your stall out early doors, gave it 110% over the full eleven questions and let your answers do the talking.

Christie: Sutcliffe injury 'no cause for panic'

Ford Open: 1
Broadmoor: 3

Broadmoor manager Reg Christie, the Rillington Place murderer, said he would not be forced into emergency transfer activity despite striker Peter Sutcliffe pulling a hamstring and being doubtful for the opening game of the season against Wakefield High Security Prison at the beginning of March.

Sutcliffe has been on great form since the Broadmoor players reported back for duty, scoring 5 goals in 3 games.

hamstring

The multiple rapist and murdering Yorkshireman was on target against Ford Open, opening the scoring against the category B side. But he pulled up sharply in the 61st minute after receiving a pinpoint cross from Fred West and was forced to go off. Sutcliffe will undergo scans today to assess the damage to his hamstring, but Christie believes he has enough quality back-up in the squad to take over if he is forced to miss the start of the season.

Christie said: "I will not risk Peter at Wakefield if it means he could break down again.

"We have to be patient with him. If we can get him back within the next two weeks, he will still have seven days to get match fit. If he isn't, I will not be rushed into the transfer market. I still have train-spotting murderer Michael Sams who's got the best right foot in the game."

quimstring

Whilst on the pitch, Sutcliffe caused havoc in the Ford defence, slotting one in after 14 minutes. The equaliser came just three minutes later with a forty yard pass from Tory liar Jeffrey Archer to Jonathan King, who met the ball with the sweetest of volleys into the top left corner of the Broadmoor goal.

The away side went back on top early in the second half with a goal out of the top drawer from Dennis Neilsen. Ford's defence were caught square following a neat through ball from Sutcliffe which found the gay cannibal unmarked on the edge of the 6 yard box for the simplest of touch-ins.

farting string

Broadmoor were far from comfortable for the rest of the game and were left cursing their luck after fluffing a series of chances. But in the 83rd minute the Ripper put the game beyond doubt after taking advantage of a dreadful backpass by sword of truth perjurer Jonathan Aitken.

Tin Man Tops Fantasy Poll

MOST WOMEN yearn to bed the Tin Man from the Wizard of Oz, with a funnel on his head and creaking metal joints.

The rusty romeo with his chopper in his hand came out top of dream fellas internet survey of UK women. Hunky firemen were runners up, followed by cheesemongers, elephant men and wombles.

But internet polsters said: "Nothing eclipses women's fascination with the heartless, mechanical heartthrob". *Reuters.*

LEATHER FORECAST

TODAY: The west of England will be calfskin and nubuck, becoming patent by evening. Eastern parts of the UK will start off chamois but will become suede later. Pigskin is expected in Northern Ireland and the west of Scotland as the patches of buffalo hide move east.

OUTLOOK: Patent and chamois everywhere tomorrow, dying away to leave the weekend mainly suede.

THREE DAY OUTLOOK

Saturday: Nubuck over South Western England and Wales	**Sunday:** Outbreaks of patent moving in from the North east	**Monday:** Mainly nubuck, turning to suede and chamois later

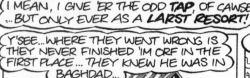

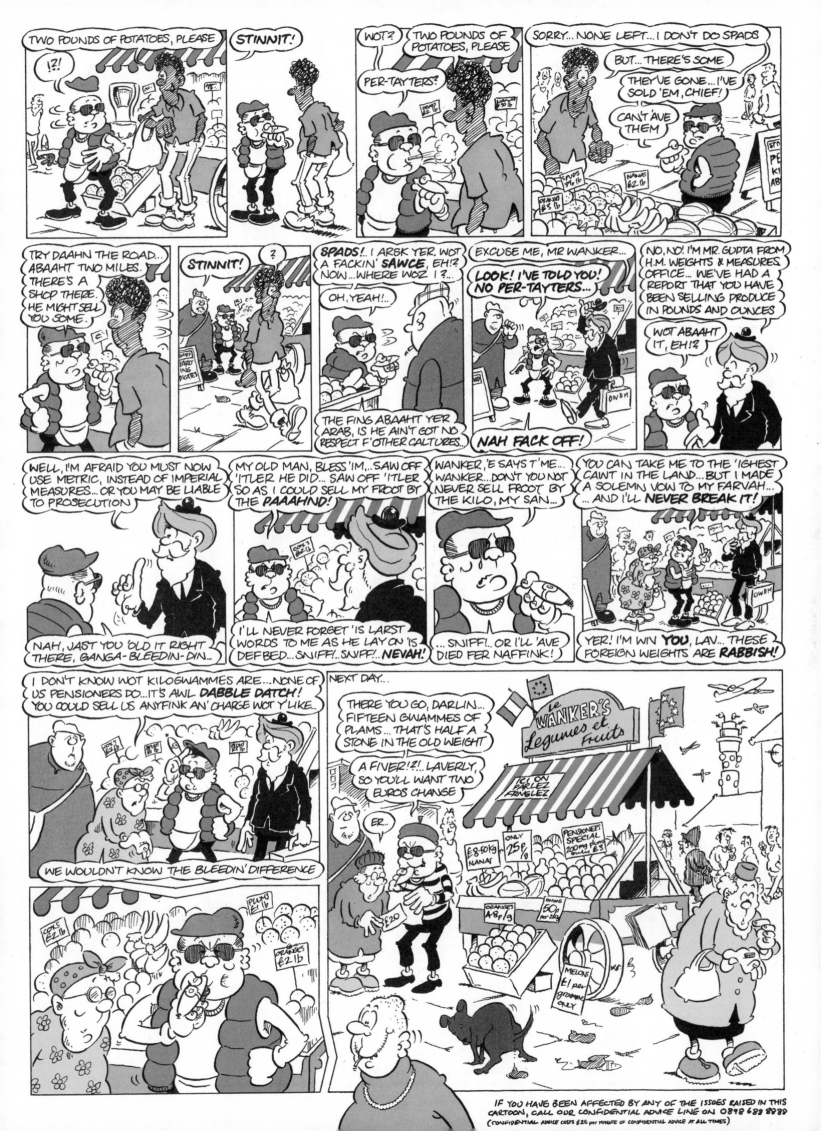

SEGS SECRE
HOLLYWOOD

EVERYONE has sat in the cinema and gazed up at the glamorous figures on the silver screen, wondering what it would be like to be in their shoes. But have you ever stopped to wonder what it would be like to *repair* those shoes that you're wondering what it would be like to be in?

One man who knows is Hollywood heelbar owner **Harold Brayson**. In a career spanning over 50 years, he has cobbled for everyone who is anyone in Tinseltown's hall of fame. From Humphrey Bogart and Marilyn Monroe to Uma Thurman and Toby Maguire ~ they've all been through the door of *Harry's Heel-U-Kwik* just off Sunset Boulevard, wanting their shoes repaired.

In his new book, *'That's Sole, Folks ~ The story of Harold Brayson'* (Welsh Rarebit Books, £19.99), he reveals all about his remarkable half century as cobbler to the stars.

Brayson says that in the celebrity cobbling business, you get to know a few things the public never finds out. A regular visitor in the fifties was Hollywood heart-throb **Rock Hudson**.

❝*I knew as early as '52 that Rock was a faggot. In June of that year he came in the shop to buy a pair of laces. Nothing strange about that, you may think. But get*

"Rock was dressing up as a dame and probably going with sailors"

this - they were blue laces, and I knew for a fact that Rock only had a pair of brown shoes. What's more, they were 16 inch, a size usually associated with women's shoes.

Now Hudson was married, but I knew his wife only wore slip-ons,

because I'd put her some segs in only that week. It could only add up to one thing - the hunky matinee idol was living a double life, dressing up as a dame and probably going with sailors.

I could've made millions if I'd gone to the press with what I'd found out, but I knew Hudson trusted me, so I kept quiet. Like doctors and lawyers, cobblers take a sacred oath to respect the confidentiality of their clients. And Rock Hudson's twisted perversion is a secret I'll take with me to the grave. ❞

My Instinct

BY HIS own admission, Harold basically a mender of the star shoes. But as **Sharon Stone** found out, he ocasionally makes slightly bigger impact on the film world

❝*We've all seen 'Basic Instinct', an everyone remembers the leg-crossing sequence. Well, what you probabl don't know is, if it wasn't for Harry Heel-U-Kwik that famous scene simpl wouldn't have been in the movie!*

bunion

Sharon Stone came in my shop on th morning they were going to start shoot ing. It turned out she had a bunion, an wanted me to cut a hole in the side o one of her nubuck T-bar court shoes t stop it chaffing.

Papa don't breach

BRAYSON is not only a master cobbler. His talent also extends to cutting keys, and the rollcall of stars who have stepped into his shop requiring duplicates reads like a Who's Who of Hollywood.

❝*Whether these keys are for their wives or mistresses isn't for me to ask. And if I know, I sure ain't telling!*

Frank Sinatra, Michael Douglas, Woody Allen and Errol Flynn have all taken advantage of my 2-for-1 offer, and had keys cut in the course of their affairs. But I tell you what I told them - Their adulterous secrets are safe with me. Wild horses wouldn't drag it out of me.

People often ask if I've ever cut a star's key for myself. Of course the temptation's there, but I've never given in to it. Apart for once or twice. And I'd certainly never use my privileged access to take anything from the houses of the

Shoe Suede Blues

IN his half century of cobbling, Bryson has seen many stars come and go. Most aspiring starlets who come into his shop never make the grade. But some go all the way.

❝*In '56 a good-looking young kid came in the shop for a can of Scotchguard. He told me he*

needed it because some jerk had just stepped on his shoes in the street outside.

I looked down to see he was wearing a pair of brothel creepers in navy suede.

leather

I explained to him how he ought to look after his footwear more carefully, because although suede is similar to leather, it doesn't share its hardwearing surface properties.

I told him: 'You shouldn't let anyone step on those shoes. The nap will be spoiled. You can do anything

that you want to do, but lay off of those blue suede shoes, and they'll last you a lifetime.' Those were my exact words.

suede

The kid didn't say anything, he just nodded thoughtfully and left the shop.

I guess I don't need to tell you who that kid was. He was Elvis Presley. And I sure don't need to tell you what song he went away and wrote. It was 'Blue Suede Shoes.'

scotchguard

They say Elvis made over 60 million dollars from that song. I got just 60 cents for the Scotchguard. ~ but that's shoe business. ❞

TS of the STARS

roved Right

I cut the hole and then she sat in a chair so I could try it on her for size. As far as I was concerned it was just a routine part of the job. However, as I knelt down she sparked up a cigarette and crossed her legs. I could see that she wasn't wearing any intimate apparel. My view left nothing to the imagination, I can tell you.

dubbin

I said to her: 'Hey, Miss Stone. You know what? That would make a great scene in your new movie.' She just smiled and left the shop, but I knew I'd set her thinking.

Thanks to my idea, 'Basic Instinct' grossed over 90 million dollars at the box office. I made just 90 cents, but Sharon didn't forget me; she sent me a ticket for the premiere. Unfortunately I couldn't attend because I

was expecting a delivery of 8 tins of dubbin and I didn't want the man to leave them on the step. **"**

stars. Apart from once or twice.

Madonna came into the shop for a duplicate key for her Beverly Hills mansion shortly before embarking on her Blonde Ambition tour. While she was away, I decided to let myself in for a look around.

In her closet I found dozens of pointy bras. They must have been worth thousands of dollars each, and it would have been easy for me to steal the lot. But it would have been wrong to betray my position of trust in that way, so I just took three or four.

My brother is a great Madonna fan, so I took him round the next day and he helped himself to a couple. After that, I destroyed my duplicate key in case it fell into the hands of anyone dishonest. **"**

AS you might expect, Brayson has had a lot of ups and downs in half a century of cobbling. Perhaps his lowest point came in 1955 when he was inadvertently responsible for the death of one of Tinseltown's brightest young stars.

"On the morning of September 30th, an up-and-coming actor by the name of James Dean called in, wearing a pair of patent leather winkle-pickers. He told me he'd just bought them, but was finding the soles a little slippy. In fact, he fell on his fanny twice inside my shop.

He asked me to roughen the soles up with a bit with some sandpaper. It was a routine job that would have taken me just minutes, but I was up to my eyes with work that day. I had to welt the uppers back onto Steve McQueen's baseball boots for the final scene of 'The Great Escape'. It was a big Hollywood production, and the

studio had offered me $4 - double my usual rate.

I told Dean to come back the next day, but he never showed.

That night I switched on the news and heard that he was dead. It seemed he'd been driving along

Rebel Without a Head

in his new shoes when his foot had slipped off the brake onto the gas pedal. His car had left the road, somersaulted twice and his head had come off.

If only I'd taken the time to scuff the soles of Dean's shoes, he'd still be with us today. My greed cost that young man his life.

I've never been able to spend the $4 I got for welting McQueen's shoes. It's still there in the till of Harry's Heel-U-Kwik, 304th Avenue, just off Sunset Boulevard, Hollywood. **"**

Extracts from *'That's Sole, Folks'* ~ *The Harold Brayson Story.'* ©Harold Brayson and Lonnie Donnegan 2002. Welsh Rarebit Books £19.99

NEXT WEEK: 'I Shod the Sheriff' ~ FF width feet in E-fitting cowboy boots - the secret of the Duke's walk.
& 'The Seven Year Itch' ~ The day Marilyn Monroe came in for athlete's foot powder.

Letterbocks

Letterbocks, Viz Comic, PO Box 1PT, Newcastle-upon-Tyne, NE99 1PT.

E-mail letters@viz.co.uk

SO what if the Royal Family costs each of us 58p a year? I'd rather it go to them than bloody asylum seekers. These foreigners come over here with all their relations, we give them houses, and they never do a stroke of work, just sponge off the state. They do a marvellous job. God bless 'em.

J. Froud
London

THE Queen gets 58p per year off every man, woman and child in Britain, does she? Well my three-year-old son gets 10p a week pocket money, which means she takes all his pocket money for 6 weeks. The thieving bitch.

J. Cursitor
Bristol

WHAT'S wrong with having Identity Cards? Anyone who objects is obviously a paedophile, and should be chemically castrated.

T. Stomer
Northampton

MAMA Cass choked on a sandwich. Jimi Hendrix choked on his own vomit. John Entwhistle, on the other hand, choked on a stripper. What a way to go.

T. Burnside
Leigh

I THINK getting free identity cards is a great idea. I'm going to apply for gas board, electricity board and social services home help ones. And a crime prevention officer one, so the old ladies will let me see their burglar alarms.

Spider Boy
Byker

IF THE makers of Oil of Ulay are so convinced that their spunk-like cream works, why don't they prove it by trying it out on Thora Hird? After a fortnight we'd all know one way or the other.

Mike Thomas
Mid Glamorgan

I'VE heard that supermarkets waft bakery smells around the store to subconsciously encourage customers to buy bread. I can only conclude that my local Netto supermarket are trying to encourage their customers to buy toilet rolls.

Andy Quin
Huddersfield

CONSIDERING the final legacy of the Queen Mum was a massive tax evasion, she can now really look the East End in the face. She was more of an East Ender than any of us knew.

John Townsend
Nottingham

I HAD to feel sorry for Paul McCartney's children when I read that Heather Mills is a strict vegetarian like their late mother Linda. The poor things have only been enjoying bacon sandwiches for four years when Paul re-marries and they are suddenly off the menu again. No wonder they stormed out of the wedding.

Guy Willoughby
Jarrow

IF anyone reading this heard the fart I just did, could they please drop me a line and let me know how far away they are.

A Wilkes
West Midlands

ABOUT 20 years ago, rumours abounded in London about an auction of a pair of Selina Scott's used knickers. Do any readers know if these rumours were true? If so, do they know the whereabouts of the knickers and whether their owner would be prepared to sell them.

Steve Gerr
Devon

A MATE of mine told me his girlfriend's cousin was a roadie for Stevie Nicks in the 80s, and that he had the special job of 'cocaine man'. His duties included having to powder the songstress's starfish with the aforementioned substance before she went on stage every night. Do I win a T-shirt?

Cam Hunter
e-mail

SPORT TALK

THE WORLD CUP may have gone, but England is still smarting from the Ronaldhino free kick that put us out of the tournament. Was it a goalkeeping blunder by David Seaman, or a spectacular fluke shot by the zombie-faced Brazilian? We've been innundated with letters giving your point of view.

...I used to love watching David Seaman on Match of the Day. The next time I see his face on telly, I'll put a bloody brick through the screen...and send him the bill!

R. Winston, London

...Watching Seaman let that goal in made me sick to my stomach. I think he should be put on the sexual offenders register.

Jan Stewer, Wimbledon

...If Seaman had spent a little less time having his hair cut like a girl, and a little more time moving backwards towards the far post, maybe it would have been England's name on the World Cup instead of Brazil's.

Dan Whidden, Derby

...Seaman earns a fortune playing for Arsenal. If he had a shred of decency in his body, he would spend every last penny on research into time travel, then go back in time to just before the kick was taken and stand a little nearer to the back post.

William Brewer, Devon

...Seaman has apologised for the second Brazilian goal. But it takes two to tango. What about the man who actually kicked the ball into the net? He showed no regret whatso-ever. In fact, he looked rather pleased with himself.

H. Hawk Leicester

...I think Seaman should be hanged on Match of the Day. And Gary Lineker could pull the lever. This would not only prevent him messing up again, but would act as a deterrent to other goalkeepers thinking about letting in a similar goal.

Peter Gurney, Hull

...Gordon Banks would have saved that shot, and he's only got one eye. That makes Banks twice the keeper that the two-eyed Seaman will ever be.

Thomas Cobbley, Dublin

...I don't blame Seaman for the blunder that let in Brazil's second goal. I blame his hairdresser. If he'd gelled his ponytail into a spike above his head, he could have used it to tip the ball over the crossbar.

Ann Dall, Wales

...Let's all stop attacking David Seaman. It's only a game after all. The most important things were that all the matches were played in good spirit and everyone taking part enjoyed themselves. And that the fucking krauts lost in the final.

Peter Davy, Edinburgh

GEORGE BEST IS A CINEMA PEST

UP THE ARK CORNER

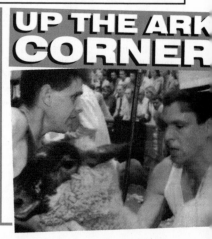

Lord Help Me

with Abdul Latif, Lord of Harpole

Dear Your Grace,

I was a fan of the seventies children's show Fingerbobs. I have recently been trying to construct my own Fingermouse, but have faced a few problems. I have cracked the tricky nose bit, but as far as the ears are concerned I have hit a brick wall. Lord help me.

Adam Collins, Farnborough

Lord Harpole says...

Don't worry, Adam, the Lord of Harpole will provide the answer. Being brought up in Bangladesh, I'm afraid I never saw the Fingerbobs show. So I called the BBC on your behalf and asked to speak to the presenter, Mr. Yoffi, but unfortunately he wasn't answering his extension. If he cares to call in at my restaurant, the Rupali, Bigg Market, Newcastle upon Tyne, I will provide him with a delicious free curry, including drinks up to the value of £3 in return for the information you seek.

SORTED

Dear Your Highness,

Can you tell me which one is Ant and which one is Dec off TV children's favourites Ant and Dec? I think that Ant is the slap head and Dec is the 14 year-old.

Richard Harrison, Gwynedd

Lord Harpole says...

Don't worry, Richard, help is at hand. I, Lord Abdul Latif of Harpole have written a poem to help you remember which is which.

When Dec and Ant are on TV,
It's hard to tell which one they be,
So speak these words from out your neck,
Young Ant to tell from his friend Dec,

The head that has a balding pate,
Belongs to Ant and not his mate,
The one with hair on Dec is called,
His mate's the other one that's bald.

SORTED

©Abdul Latif, Lord of Harpole. No part of this poem may be reproduced in any manner or by any means without written permission from the Rupali Restaurant, Bigg Market, Newcastle upon Tyne.

UP THE ARSE CORNER

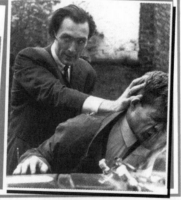

YOU ARE DR. MIRIAM STOPPARD THE REF

Test *your* knowledge of footballers' problems. What would *you* do in this situation if *you* were Dr. Miriam Stoppard the Ref?

During a match, the ball is knocked into touch by a member of the attacking side. As the throw-in is taken, an opposing defender approaches you on the edge of the 18 yard box and confides that he is having trouble maintaining an erection. He is 21 years old, his partner is 23. She is very understanding, but it is causing tension in their relationship and he fears she may start to look elsewhere for sexual fulfilment. *What do you do?*

a. *Suggest he asks his GP for a course of vasodilatory drugs to increase blood flow in his penis.*

b. *Tell him to relax, and experiment with non penetrative forms of sex.*

c. *Stop the game and award an indirect free kick against the defending side.*

The correct answer is b. The commonest cause of erectile disfunction amongst footballers is stress. Worrying about the problem will only make it worse. If he can relax with other forms of sex play, his mind will be taken off the problem and nine times out of ten, the condition will vanish of its own accord.

Next week - The Janet fucking Street fucking Porter Story

Rievaulx Abbey plc

MONK

£21~30k (pro rata) depending on age and experience.

Hours~ 168 pw

We are an established monastery looking to appoint a highly motivated and experienced monk to run and expand our team of brethren. The successful applicant will demonstrate:

* *Strong chanting skills*
* *Proven track record in wandering around cloisters*
* *Ability to keep bees under pressure*

If this is you and you're looking to join one of Britain's most dynamic and challenging closed communities, e-mail *dominic47@cofe.com* or write enclosing your cv and details of your current package to: *Brother Dominic, Personnel and Recruitment Unit, Rievaulx Abbey, North Yorkshire.*

Closing date for applications 30th June 2002.

Quote Ref V1

Rievaulx Abbey ~ Buzzin' RTA

FANCY A PINT?

NO THANKS. I'M IN THE CAR

Mount Grace Priory

Monk - £30K + sandals

MGP *is seeking a dynamic and experienced Monk to work as part of a team drawing and illuminating large capital letters to tight deadlines.*

The successful applicant will be a self starter with excellent sitting quiet skills and a proven ability to say nothing for years on end. A sound knowledge of gazing heavenward with the fingertips together is essential.

For further information and a job application pack, log onto www.mountgracepriory.com/monks or contact Brother Maynard, Human Resources Manager, Mount Grace Priory, Ripon.

mount grace priory

Monk £35k + frugal fare +relocation package

The Brothers of Canterbury Ltd

are seeking to recruit a highly motivated and ambitious monk with a strong and proven track record of not touching his own genitals to head a team of novices. The appointee will be required to plan and implement long term cross platform prayer strategies.

If you have:

* *At least 5 years experience of loving the Lord at senior level*
* *A positive approach to working as part of a team droning in Latin*
* *The drive and vision to work in a dynamic non-communicating Trappist environment*
* *A pious attitute towards life*

Then **WE** want to hear from **YOU!**

Send a cv along with the name address of two referees to: The Brothers of Canterbury Ltd, Canterbury Priory, Canterbury.

St. Peter's Monastery

Saint Peter's Monastery

MONK (residential) 50k pa + bonus

St. Peter's is a creative, dynamic and successful monastery founded in 1232. Following restructuring we are looking to recruit a confident and enthusiastic go-getting monk who would fit in with our highly motivated professional performance management framework team.

Building upon our existing business base, maintaining and strengthening our partnership agenda and maximising our mead production are the three key strategic priorities for this exciting and demanding role.

The successful applicant will have a clear commitment to growing herbs, getting up at three in the morning and bell ringing, combined with sound experience of living off porridge. A small bald patch on the top your head would also be an advantage.

St. Peter's Monastery ~ "achieving progress through quiet reflection"

PRONTOMONK
Monk Temping Agency

At PRONTO Monk Temping Agency, we can help with all your staff problems. Whether you need one monk for half a day or a full order for a year, we can provide the monks to cover any eventuality. All our personnel have full calligraphic, chanting and bee keeping skills and are available at short notice.

Whatever your order requirement, PRONTOMONK Temping Agency can provide it~

* •**Benedictines**
* •**Dominicans** •**Carmelites**
* •**Gregorians** •**Franciscans**
* •**Carthusians**•**Trappists**
* •**Cistercians**

Call 0802 222 33 or visit our website at www.prontomonk.com

"You'll thank Heaven for PRONTOMONK!"

FEATHER FORECAST

TODAY: The south west of England will start out with patchy eider down, but quickly become primary flight in the early afternoon. Northern parts will see a band of ostrich and maribou which will spread its way across the country reaching the midlands and south by the evening.

OUTLOOK: Duck down and sparrow flight will dominate the weekend, but there will be some unsettled patches of goose quill by late Sunday.

THREE DAY OUTLOOK

Saturday: Plumes over Wales, the South and the South East

Sunday: Outbreaks of eider down and penguin from the West

Monday: Chiefly sparrow with changes of plumage dying out overnight

---

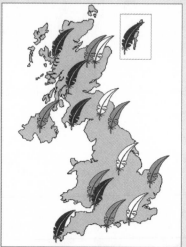

Britain's stars were paying tribute last night after Bernie Clifton's comedy ostrich was killed in a freak accident. Bernie was too upset to comment after the brightly coloured 6 foot bird fell 30 feet onto paving stones at the Clifton's home in Surrey.

The gangly bird had climbed onto the roof to adjust the TV aerial after the picture had become fuzzy during a televised football match. It is thought that the ostrich, a veteran of several Royal Variety performances, lost its footing, or was knocked off balance by a gust of wind.

Bitz

WE'RE DISCUSSING WHETHER MAN'S EXISTENCE PRECEEDS HIS ESSENCE AND IF THE NATURE OF BEING IS ULTIMATELY NOTHINGNESS. DO YOU WANT TO JOIN US?

NO. THAT'S TOO DEEP FOR ME.

CAUTION 200ft DROP

SCIENTISTS DISCOVER WORST THING

Some lab-bunnies yesterday

ASK ANYONE what the worst thing in the world is, and they'll tell you war, disease or famine. But not according to scientists from the University of Budapest. They've discovered that the worst thing in the world is actually a paper cut on your bell-end.

The five man team led by Professor Namoff Reszla researched the problem for over a decade before publishing their conclusions in the prestigious 'Nature' magazine.

clippers

"We subjected a succession of volunteer students to a wide range of horrible things, such as snapping their front teeth off with nail clippers and pulling back

■ *by Our Medical Correspondant*
Dr Roland Pianno

their big toes and sawing through the tendon bit underneath with a Stanley knife," said Professor Reszla. "We got laboratory rabbits to watch all the terrible things. Then we gauged how much they winced using a small wince-measuring probe inserted in the back of their necks."

schooners

In the experiment that got the most dramatic results, Professor Reszla drew a sheet of A4 typing paper sharply across a student's glans, leaving a 2cm paper cut.

"The rabbits' response was fantastic," he said. "The reading went off the scale. Rabbits which

had shown a wince reaction of 30% when we cut someone's tongue up the middle with tinsnips were suddenly showing 95% or more. One rabbit winced so hard it broke its back. There was no doubt we had discovered the worst thing in the world."

junks

But the study, which was commissioned by Bird's Angel Delight, has angered animal rights activists across the world. "We shouild not be exposing rabbits to this sort of barbarity. It's barbaric barbarism." fumed Ada Littlejohn of Nottingham.

"Why can't they get some of these murderers and paedophiles, put them into clamps and force them to watch someone getting a paper cut on his herman gelmet?"

PALACE SHELL-SHOCKED

ROYAL watchers were last night scratching their heads after Clarence House sources revealed that the Queen mum has laid an egg.

discovery

Palace staff made the discovery after her butler heard grunting sounds from her rooms late on Tuesday night. Fearing that she had fallen or was choking on a fishbone, staff entered the room and discovered her sitting on the bright blue speckled rugby ball-sized egg.

nickleodeon

She was very protective at first and refused leave the egg, breaking the arm of a footman who attempted to pick it up. However, after a few minutes she appeared to lose interest in it, and royal GP Gladstone Gamble was able to remove it to a nearby incubator.

BELOW: An egg similar to the one laid by the Queen Mum and (inset) a Queen Mum similar to the one that laid an egg

ANOTHER ROYAL EXCLUSIVE

■ *by HAZELNUT MONKBOTTLE*

Queen mum expert Dr David Starkey said: "No monarch has ever laid an egg before, but the constitutional implications are quite clear. If whatever hatches out is male, it will take precedence over the Queen in the line of succession. We are faced with the very real possibility of ending this Golden Jubilee year with some bizarre human/chicken monster on the throne."

sky sports 1

But there were no such worries from members of the public who have already begun to gather outside the palace gates waiting for news. "I love the royals and anything to do with them", said 82 year-old Ethel Moron, who had travelled over 300 miles from Darlington with her friend Ada Fuckingstupid. "I don't care what weird beaked hybrid comes out the egg, I'm sure it will do a marvellous job."

"God bless it," she added.

Cliff Face Drop Driver OK

A WOMAN whose car plunged nearly 6ft off Cliff Richard's face has escaped serious injury.

Her Ford Orion veered out of control in the veteran pop star's hair and smashed through his glasses before plummeting off his chin.

The woman, who hasn't been named, spent the night on a ledge halfway down Richard's trousers, after the car flipped and landed on its roof. She was spotted when she flashed her headlights at passers by, who alerted the emergency services.

Firemen freed the 27-year-old woman on Wednesday night and yesterday she was "comfortable" in hospital.

HRH Her Royal Highness Queen Elizabeth The Queen Mother
Her Marvellous Life in Pictures

Even now, weeks after her funeral, it's hard to believe the Queen Mother really has gone. Over the 101 years of her long and marvellous life she became as much a part of the British landscape as London buses, bobbies on bicycles two by two, Westminster Abbey, the tower of Big Ben or the rosy red cheeks of the little children.

But now is not a time to allow our overwhelming feelings of sadness and despair to sweep over us. Instead of weeping inconsolably and commiting suicide in order to be with her again, we should try to smile through our tears and celebrate her marvellous life. A life which shone like a marvellous beacon of marvellousness amidst a world full of whatever the opposite of marvellousness is.

1900 From the day she was born, the infant Queen Mother showed signs of being more royal than the other babies in the hospital. She quickly mastered the art of having everything done for her, and by the age of 11 months she was able to wave at people out of her pram and choke on food. These were skills she was to call on every day of her life for the next hundred marvellous years.

1912 In April, the 12 year old queen Mother set sail for America aboard the ill-fated RMS Titanic along with 2340 other souls. The ship hit an icecube in the Atlantic and began to sink. With great presence of mind, she commandeered 3 lifeboats, one for herself, one for her ladies in waiting, and one for her luggage. Selflessly, she steered her boat amongst the hundreds of drowning passengers, lifting their spirits by waving and politely enquiring how long they had been in the water.

1917 With the dark cloud of war hanging over Europe, The people of Britain are encouraged to make do and mend. In June, the King took announced that food rationing was being considered and that everyone must tighten their belts. Showing her mischievous sense of humour, the Queen Mother immediately ordered 5000 slightly smaller belts from the haute couture houses of Paris. The belts, made of everything from leather to panda skin, and encrusted with diamonds and rubies, duly arrived, along with a bill for over 1 million guineas to the British taxpayer. The Queen Mother's delightful joke had cost a mere shilling from every man, woman and child in Britain.

1928 As patron of St. Mary's Hospital, London, the Queen Mother was invited to take tea in the laboratories of Alexander Fleming, at the time a young professor struggling to invent antibiotics. During the visit, she was offered a swan sandwich on which a small amount of crust had inadvertently been left. Horrified at the crust, she left the sandwich on the bench, where Fleming discovered it three weeks later with all penicillin fungus growing out of it. He later named the strain of mould in honour of the woman whose refined taste had made it possible, Penicillium queenmumensis.

1931 During a State Safari in Rhodesia, The Queen Mother and her husband George VI between them bagged more than 200 Zulus in a single day's shooting. In today's climate, shooting black men for sport may be frowned upon by the politically correct lobby. But in those days it was a perfectly innocent pastime. Indeed, as there are many more black men nowadays than there were in the thirties, it could be argued that the Queen Mum was actually an early conservationist.

1933 Europe in the early thirties was a place of rising social tensions. With war once again brewing on the horizon, the world could seem a frightening place to live. But throughout it all the Queen Mother never once lost her marvellously impish sense of humour. She was often known to sneak out of Buckingham Palace in the early hours and make her way to Jewish districts of London where she mischievously put half bricks through windows and daubed cheeky swastikas on brickwork.

1940 Queues formed in high streets as people lined up for their meagre weekly rations of powdered egg, bacon and sugar. Displaying solidarity with her people, the Queen Mum queued up too, ration book in hand. After standing outside the butchers for nearly eight minutes, she recalled parliament and told them she feared the country would become demoralised if they thought the royal family didn't have enough meat. A bill was forced through, and the Windsors spent the rest of the war on a stone of sausages each every day!

1945 The Queen Mother's unpleasant experiences of having to meet a few working class people during the war had taken their toll, and doctors advised that for her own health she should take it exceptionally easy for a while. Retiring to a darkened room in Balmoral Castle, she placed her forearm across her brow and swooned onto a chaise longue, where she remained completely motionless for 21 years. In 1966 she emerged, declaring herself "greatly refreshed" by her rest. Amazed onlookers could only shake their heads in admiration as she got immediately back to work, sitting in a gold coach waving at people!

1951 During the post war period of reconstruction, the Royal Family decided that they should bring their image more up to date, as it was feared that they could seem out of touch with the ordinary people of Britain. In a monumental lapse of judgement, the King sent nude photos of the Queen Mother to the Readers' Wives section of Fiesta magazine. The pictures, tame by today's standards, showed the Queen Mother posing on the formica top in the kitchen of Buckingham Palace. Half a million copies of the magazine had rolled off the presses before Palace officials got wind of the King's actions. A constitutional crisis was narrowly averted when the entire issue was taken out into the middle of the North Sea and dumped in 10,000 ft of water.

1966 Everyone remembers where they were when England won the World Cup in June of 1966. Especially the Queen Mum! With the score at 3-2, this marvellous lady couldn't contain her excitement any more, dashed from the royal box and ran onto the pitch. BBC commentator Kenneth Wolthamstow spotted her and uttered the words "the Queen Mum is on the pitch, she thinks it's all over." The commentary was later re-recorded on the orders of stuffy palace officials.

1978 The Queen Mother's acts of kindness were legendary, but in 1978 they nearly saved a man's life. During a visit from royal doctor Sir Gladstone Gamble one of her butlers collapsed after swallowing his own tongue. Seeing the poor man choking on the floor, she gave the doctor permission to go and assist him as soon as he had finished shaving her bunions. Unfortunately, due to a particularly tough bunion, it was 25 minutes before the butler could receive medical help and by then he had already been dead for quarter of an hour. But the Queen Mother's attempt to save him didn't go unnoticed, and she awarded herself the Victoria Cross in recognition of her extraordinary act of self-sacrifice.

1985 She was famously loyal to her servants, several of them staying with her for many decades. One of them, affectionately known as 'Backdoor Bobby', joined her household as a boy of 13 and stayed with her for more than 50 years. After knowing him for half a century the Queen Mother came to look upon him almost as a human being, and so it broke her heart when she had to dismiss him after he took her afternoon tea with an insufficiently polished teaspoon on the tray.

2002 At the end of a marvellously long life, filled with marvellousness, Britain's favourite grandmother still hadn't lost her sense of fun. On the day she died, relatives wept tears, not of grief and sorrow, but of hysterical laughter. Called to Clarence House to say goodbye, they were treated to a sidesplitting impression of 'Staines Massive' comedian Ali G, complete with Tommy Gear hat, comedy hand gestures and sexually explicit language.

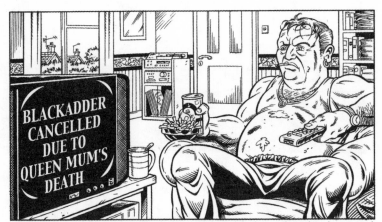

2002 And so, on March 31st our beloved Queen Mother was taken from us before her time. The British people were stunned into going about their daily business as if nothing had happened. But the loss of the most marvellous woman ever to stalk the face of the earth touched people's hearts a thousand times more deeply than the deaths of their own grandmothers ever could. A million times more tragic than ten jumbo jets full of blind orphan toddlers flying into the side of a mountain, the moment of her passing changed the world forever until normal programmes resumed 25 minutes later.

TO RECEIVE SEXY MESSAGES FROM BORED GINGERBREAD WOMEN, TEXT 'PASTRYCHAT' TO 81125.
MESSAGES COST £25 EACH.

SPOILT BASTARD

SUICIDAL SYD

HE'S ALWAYS TRYING TO POP HIS CORK!

I'M SO GRIEF-STRICKEN BY THE RECENT DEATH OF HRH PRINCESS MARGARET (AND VERY PROBABLY THE QUEEN MUM TOO BY THE TIME THIS GETS IN THE SHOPS) I THINK I'LL KILL MYSELF.

...ANYONE FANCY A GAME OF RUSSIAN ROULETTE?

ACE!

BUT...

RIEN N'AVEZ PLUS, COMRADES. FAITES VOS JEUX.

BAH!

20 BETROOTS ON NUMBER 6.

THE VIBRATING BUM-FACED GOATS

HIGH IN THE CHEVIOT MOUNTAINS LIVED OLD JED SIMMONS, OWNER OF A TRULY REMARKABLE HERD OF GOATS. FOR THESE WERE VIBRATING ROBOT GOATS, EACH OF WHICH HAD AN ARSE FOR A FACE.

SPRING WAS HERE, AND JED SIMMONS' TWO GRANDCHILDREN WERE HELPING HIM OUT DURING THE GOAT-OILING SEASON

HELLO? WHO'S THIS CITY GENT COMING UP THE MOUNTAIN?

HE LOOKS AWFULLY OFFICIAL, GRANDPA

I AM MR PEARSON FROM THE MINISTRY OF AGRICULTURE, AND I HAVE HERE AN ORDER TO DESTROY YOUR ENTIRE HERD OF BUM-FACED LIVESTOCK

KILL MY GOATS? BUT WHY?

THESE ARSE-FEATURED GOATS ARE INFECTED WITH PILES!

I SHALL HAVE TO SHOOT THEM WITH A BOLT-GUN, THEN BURN THEM ALL ON A BIG FIRE

BUT THESE ROBOTIC GOATS ARE ALL I HAVE

I CAN'T HELP THAT

AS SOON AS I'VE EATEN MY PACKED LUNCH, THE SLAUGHTER WILL BEGIN

SUDDENLY ONE OF THE BUTTOCK-FACED BEASTS LUNGED AT THE MINISTRY OFFICIAL

HA HA! LOOKS LIKE MR PEARSON'S BEEN GIVEN THE BUM'S RUSH!

MY SANDWICH! I DROPPED IT ON THE GROUND, AND NOW IT'S ALL COVERED IN GRIT AND DIRT!

YOU'LL GET NO SYMPATHY FROM US!

YOU MURDERER OF ELECTRIC RUMINANTS!

WHATEVER MR PEARSON MIGHT BE, WE CAN'T JUST STAND BY AND WATCH WHILE HIS SANDWICH IS RUINED

THAT'S NOT WHAT VIBRATING GOAT KEEPING IS ALL ABOUT

SWIFTLY, JED JAMMED THE SANDWICH INTO THE BUMCLEFT OF ONE OF HIS MECHANICAL HOOFED MAMMALS

STAND BACK, EVERYONE

I'LL GET THE MOTOR FIRED UP

SOON THE TUSH-FACED HERBIVORE WAS VIBRATING VIOLENTLY

IT - IT'S WORKING!

THE GRIT AND SOIL IS LITERALLY BEING SHAKEN OFF THE SANDWICH!

MY SANDWICH IS AS GOOD AS NEW. I DON'T KNOW HOW TO THANK YOU

YOU'VE SHOWN ME THAT THERE'S MORE TO LIFE THAN THE PETTY RULES AND REGULATIONS OF THE MINISTRY

AND FROM THAT DAY ON, MR PEARSON LIVED IN A CAVE ON THE MOUNTAINSIDE, WHERE HE LED THE SIMPLE LIFE OF AN OSCILLATING BOLLOCK-FACED CHICKEN FARMER

CHAMPAGNE CHARLIE!

Corks Pop as Merry Widower hits Medical Negligence Jackpot!

Over the moon - Charlie receives his winnings from hospital administrator Norbert Dentrissangle and the bungling anaesthetist who performed his wife's tragic toenail op.

DERBYSHIRE plumber Charlie Wheelbarrow was HALF A MILLION POUNDS richer last night - thanks to a botched operation which killed his wife.

By our Medical Correspondent
Gripper Stebson

Judges ordered the bonanza payout after bungling docs gave Mary Wheelbarrow, 67, more than **TEN TIMES** the recommended dose of anaesthetic during a routine op.

Wednesday

A beaming Charlie said: " Mary went in on the Wednesday morning to have an ingrowing toenail removed. Apparently, the anaesthetist misread a dial on a new machine or something, and she never regained consciousness."

Thursday

He continued: "I was absolutely gobsmacked when the judge awarded me the money. It's beyond my wildest dreams. This is the best day of my life."

A delighted Charlie received his winnings from Norbert Dentrissangle, chief administrator of the Derbyshire St Mungo's Hospital Trust at a special ceremony outside the hospital where his wife perished.

Friday

Friends at Charlie's local pub, the Red Lion were also joining in the celebrations. Landlord Eddie Bremner said: "We're all absolutely chuffed for him. This couldn't have happened to a nicer bloke. The champagne's already on ice for the next time he comes in."

Robin

But Charlie is determined that his new found fortune is not going to change his life. "I may be rich, but I'll still drink in the same old pub with the same old friends. I'm still the same old Charlie underneath," he laughed.

Kato

But he does have plans for some of the money. "I'll have a nice long holiday, a new car, and move to Florida," he told us.

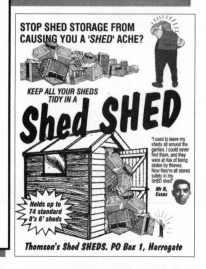

WORLD CUP WILLIE

YOUNG CHARLIE BRANT WAS SO FOOTBALL MAD HE TATTOOED THE ENGLAND FLAG ON HIS BELL-END...
...WITH A PIN AND SOME INK...

AAAGGHHH! NNNGGHH! AAAAGGGHH!

NNNAAAGHH! NNAGGH! AAAAGGGH!

AAAGGHHH! NNNAAGHH! NNAAGGGHHH! MAM! IT'S GONE SEPTIC! AAGGHHH!

104

A Theological Question of Sport

with Christian Hop, Skip & Jumper
Jonathan Edwards

Heaven can pate

Dear Jonathan,

I was wondering recently about triple Olympic Gold medalist Duncan Goodhew. It is well known that he lost all his body hair when he was six years old as a result of falling from a tree. When he dies and goes to Heaven, will he have a full head of hair?

Joan Dunbarr, Ilkley

Jonathan answers... You assume that Duncan is going to Heaven and not the other place, but that is up to God alone to decide. However, after three Olympic golds for Britain and a Commonwealth record, I think it's a fair bet that he will be going up, rather than down! However, you must understand that the Heaven that we speak about is not a physical place that we can see or touch. It is a spiritual plane of existence to which our immortal souls transfer after the death of our physical bodies. As such, concepts of appearance, and indeed being, are irrelevant. But in answer to your question, yes, he will have hair. And pubes.

Hand of God

Dear Jonathan,

I am a Christian, but I have found my faith tested lately. If God is perfect and loves us all, how can he allow such terrible things to happen in the world, such as Maradona handling the ball into the net, or Mike Tyson biting Evander Holyfield's ear off?

Jake Turvey, London

Jonathan answers... Firstly, don't worry about your faith being tested, because coming through these tests will make it stronger. As you say, God is perfect and all powerful, and He created the world we live in. Our faith in Him is strengthened in the good things that we see, such as Botham making mincemeat of the Aussies in 1976, or England sticking 5 past the Krauts last year. However, because Adam ate from the tree of knowledge, all of us are born in sin and we are given choice. And as such, Tyson has the free will to bite his opponent's ear, Maradona chooses to handle the ball, and Tim Henman elects to fall to pieces and fail to reach the finals every Wimbledon.

Let us play

Dear Jonathan,

The Old Testament tells us that there is only one God, and that anyone who follows other Gods or false prophets will suffer His wrath. As a triple-jumping Christian, how do you explain the fact that in the 1980 Olympic games, that same God sat back and allowed India, a predominantly Hindu country, to take the men's hockey title from the Christian nation New Zealand?

Frank Oasis, Barnstaple

Jonathan answers... You cannot look at these things in isolation. Yes, the Indian men may have taken the gold, but at the same games their female counterparts were beaten by the largely atheist Soviet Union in a match to decide the bronze medalists. In the games before, the Indian men's team finished 7th. It is all very confusing. From our limited human perspective, we shouldn't try to understand what is happening. We just have to have faith that is is all part of His greater plan for Olympic hockey.

Do **YOU** have a Theological sporting query? Write to:
Jonathan Edwards, A Theological Question of Sport, Viz Comic, Po Box 1PT, Newcastle upon Tyne, NE99 1PT.

ELEPHANTS NEVER FORGET.....YEAH!

Mrs Mop looks quite a mug, when Davey won't receive her plug!

DAVEY Socket

The Pesky Power Point

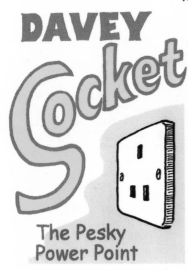

YIKES! HERE COMES MRS MOP... AND SHE'S GOING TO PLUG IN HER VACUUM CLEANER!

THAT'S ODD! I CAN'T SEEM TO GET THE PLUG INTO THE SOCKET!

NOT GOING IN

OH WELL. NEVER MIND

GUESS WHAT READERS? MRS MOP'S VACUUM CLEANER IS FITTED WITH A EUROPEAN TYPE TWO PIN PLUG!

NO WONDER IT WOULDN'T PLUG IN!!

CHORTLE! ARF!

More electrical laughs with Davey next week!

Letterbocks

It's the page that rings your doorbell every time you sit down for a shit.

B-mail letters@viz.co.uk

Letterbocks, Viz Comic, PO Box 1PT, Newcastle-upon-Tyne, NE99 1PT.

THE politically correct lobby would have us believe that the Black and White minstrel show was racist. What nonsense. There could have been any number of black faces underneath that make up as membership was open to anyone, regardless of their colour. The same cannot be said for seventies pop band Earth, Wind and Fire. Were there any white faces in their line-up? I think not.

*Lt. Col. W Bunter (retd)
Aldershot*

THEY say that size isn't important. If that's true, why can't I get these shoes on?

*Matthew Elliott
e-mail*

I'VE JUST got back from Tesco's and I swear I saw Bob Carolgees looking at the 'Star Drops' on the household products aisle, but it might not have been him.

*Paul Green
e-mail*

GEORGE Best ruined his liver with the drink. But after thirty years of banging six Miss Worlds a day before breakfast, his cock must be in an even sorrier state.

*Paul Scott
London*

IT'S wonderful that after all the pleasure he has given to football fans, ex Northern Ireland international George Best should be given a new lease of life. After wrecking his own liver through drink he had to give up alcohol. Now, thanks to the wonders of medical science he can jump off the wagon and hit the bar with a vengeance.

*M Whittle
Nottingham*

DID you just hear that?

*P Roberts
e-mail*

PS. There it is again.

★Sorry, we didn't hear anything. Did any of our readers? Please write and tell us if you just heard anything. Mark your envelope 'I think I just heard something' and send it to the usual Letterbocks address.

IF ALL of Al Quaida are hiding in a cave, why don't the Americans simply sit by the entrance with a blunderbuss and starve them out? It always worked for Hank in the Beano when the 3 bears had been stealing from his store.

*Tim Woods
e-mail*

I AM currently chairperson of Wakefield Diarrhoea Association. If anyone would like to join, please send me £10, and maybe then we can find out what causes this terrible affliction which blights mosts of us at some stage of our lives.

*Fat Al White
Wakefield Diarrhoea
Association
Wrenthorpe*

IT'S stupid to think that forcing giant pandas to watch pornography will make them want to reproduce. Surely it will just make Mr Panda want to get a blow job, shove his cock up Mrs Panda's arse and then masturbate all over her friend's face. That'll never get them pregnant.

*D Fecate
Royston*

I WAS dumping rubbish at my local tip the other day, and was saddened by all the seagulls there. Surely they belong at the seaside. So the next time I clean out the garage, I'm going to dump all my rubbish on the beach to encourage these wonderful birds back to their natural habitat.

*Robin Gilbert
South Wales*

AS expected, the moaning minnies have come out of the woodwork to complain that Sir Mick Jagger has done nothing to deserve his knighthood. Well I disagree. I recently met Marianne Faithful in the flesh, and never mind a knighthood, I'd want a Dukedom and a life peerage to eat a mars bar out of her twat.

*J. Brown
London*

BOTH the Beatles and The Who tragically lost a member in the last year and one in the 80s. Contrast this with the so-called dangerous Rolling Stones who haven't had a death since 1969. Come on, lads.

*Graeme Castleroad
Cheshire*

THE OLD folk around my way tell me 'No news is good news'. Bollocks! Camelot have just broke the news to me that I've won £14 million on the Lotto. So you can stick your £5 prize money. I wouldn't wipe my arse on any note under a twenty.

*Dave Batten
Plymouth*

PS. Just joking about the fiver.

ISN'T IT marvelous how Falklands hero Simon Weston hasn't aged over the last 20 years. People in Los Angeles would pay a fortune for the secret of eternal youth that Simon is so lucky to possess.

*O Lionnel
Essex*

CONGRATULATIONS to all our sporting heroes who competed in the recent commonwealth games. Once again, England's athletes showed they were second to none when competing against the Isle of man, Tonga and Christmas Island. Perhaps we should guarantee ourselves gold medals all the time by only competing against these nations.

*T Shaw
e-mail*

LAST year I was at an auction in Wisbech while the BBC were filming an episode of Bargain Hunt. However, when it came on the telly last month I was disappointed to see that they didn't show the box of porn that sparked a bidding frenzy and went for a handsome £250. Even Dickinson put in a couple of cheeky bids for the 'box of delights'.

Mr Allgood
e-mail

DULUX say 'you find the colour, we'll match it.' Well I found the colour, on one of their fucking colour charts, and they couldn't even match that, so what chance they've got with the handle off an inflatable boat I don't know.

Dan Sullivan
West Bromwich

PS. My lounge does not look 'Aztec Gold'. It's fucking orange.

WE READ a lot in the newspapers about strategies to prevent another September 11th happening, but upon checking my calendar today, I noticed that yet another one is planned for later this year. Will they never learn!

Moose
e-mail

ON A recent Johnathan Ross show, David Bowie said he doesn't change his baby daughter's nappy. What a hypocrite. He wasn't afraid of shit when he was a bummer, why now?

N Foukes
Cardiff

Widow left in dire straits **LETTER OF THE DAY**

Dear Miriam... MY HUSBAND has died and I don't know which way to turn.

I am 33 and have 3 children aged seven, five and three. I had been happily married for 8 years when my husband died of cancer this summer. He had told me that he had life insurance and I would be taken care of in the event of his death. It turns out that he had missed a payment and that the policy lapsed last year.

What little savings we had went on funeral expenses and I have missed the last 3 mortgage payments. The building society have now written asking for the payments and are threatening reposession of the house. In addition to this, the local authority are taking me to court over non payment of council tax. I have been living on credit cards since his death, but now even thay are demanding some money. I have no income apart from my family allowance and that doesn't even cover our weekly food bill. The debts are spiralling out of control and I can't see any way out. I am at my wits end, Miriam. Please help.

✱ Losing someone close to you is always a traumatic experience that only time will heal. On a practical level, all your money worries can be solved with one phone call to Dr. Miraiam Stoppard Finance. Tell me your details and I'll give you an INSTANT DECISION in principle.

You can make a fresh start with a Dr. Miriam Stoppard Consolidation loan. Pay off all existing loans, credit cards, HP, overdrafts etc and replace them with a single manageable monthly payment - with cash left to spend on whatever you like. CCJs, Mortgage arrears - no problem! Typical credit example £10,000 x 60 months = £214.58 p/mth. Total £12,874.80 APR 10.9%.

Loans subject to status and secured on property. Your home is at risk from Dr. Miriam Stoppard if you do not keep up payments on a mortgage or other loans secured upon it.

✱✱✱

Material girl

Dear Miriam... I AM in love with a wonderful girl, but she has very expensive tastes.

I am 19 and still live with my mum. My girlfriend is 22 and likes to go out every night for fancy meals. But she is old fashioned and believes that the man should always pay. I am a cleaner in a fast food restaurant and earn very little money.

I have suggested that we stay in some nights, but she refuses and says we must go out. Now she has seen a diamond ring she likes in a jewellers, but I told her it was too expensive. She said that if I really loved her, I would buy it. I don't want to lose her, but it costs £500 and it would take me a year to save up for it. What can I do?

✱ Why settle for a £500 ring in 12 months time when you can buy your girlfriend a £3000 ring tomorrow and have £2000 left to take her on holiday.

Your poor credit rating and the fact that you live with your mum does not exclude you from an unsecured loan from Dr Miraim Stoppard Finance. Both homeowners and tenants can apply, subject to status.

A £5000 loan from Dr Miriam Stoppard Finance will cost you just £41.96 a month over the next 300 months at a variable APR of 9.4%. That's just £1.35 a day. Call now for for an immediate in principle decision.

Your mother's home may be at risk from Dr Miriam Stoppard if you do not keep up payments on a mortgage or other loans secured upon it.

Top of the

We're gonna live forever, Gonna live forever, Live forever, Forever. So sang Oasis in their hit song Live Forever. It's unlikely that the words of that song will come, as Spandau Ballet sang, 'True' but with advances in medical technology and Dolly the sheep, pop stars are living longer than ever before. It's a sobering thought that the likes of H out of Steps and Pop Idol Will could still be alive in 100 years time.

But how long exactly do the stars think they've got? And what steps are they taking to prolong their lives? We asked them and then got Pop Gerontologist, Doctor Fox to assess how many, as David Bowie sang, 'Golden Years' they can expect before finally ending up in a, as Bernard Cribbins sang 'Hole in the ground'.

Pop Peter Pan Young One Bachelor Boy **Cliff Richard** still shows no sign of dying. So what's his secret formula for living forever? Surprisingly, the ageing rocker bases his lifestyle on that of the tortoise, some of whom live to be over 250 years old! "I've got a big wrinkly neck, and I eat lots of lettuce," he told us. "Round about October, I curl up and my manager puts me in a box of hay in the garage, where I remain fast asleep for half the year. In the Spring he takes me out and wipes my eyes with damp cotton wool," he added. "I've also painted 'Sir Cliff' on my back with Humbrol."

Dr. Fox says: "*On the face of it, Cliff's plan is a good one. Without the stress of constant touring, and with his vitamin-rich lettuce diet, he could live well in excess of 180 years. However, there is a risk that he could be eaten by rats or wake up early and wander into next door's garden, fall asleep in a pile of leaves and get shovelled onto the bonfire by mistake.*"

Four-foot-six Who frontman **Roger Daltrey** famously sang that he hoped he died before he got old, but as he approaches pensionable age he's glad his dream only came true for fellow band members Keith Moon and John Entwistle. "I once heard that your heart only beats a certain number of times in a lifetime," he told us. "So I try to keep my pulse rate as low as possible. For example, I always listen to my old rock LPs at 16 rpm, and I go everywhere in a sedan chair carried by slaves. I'm so relaxed my heart only beats 3 times a minute, so I reckon I've got a good few years

left in me yet."

Dr. Fox says: "*Roger's laid back approach is a good recipe for longevity. But there are other things he could do to postpone his inevitable death. For example, tests on mice have shown that looking at fish reduces stress and can double lifespan. Roger owns tens of thousands of fish, so if he could manage to watch them all he could improve his chances. However, thanks to his high octane lifestyle in the 60's, he's already used up the vast majority of his heartbeats. I predict he's only got a few weeks to live.*"

In her 1979 hit, disco diva **Gloria Gaynor** boasted that she would survive, and so far she shows no sign of letting her listeners down by dying. "I think I'll survive well past 120," she told us. "I reckon the secret of long life is to keep yourself busy. Although I no longer record or perform, I do voluntary work at a local quarry 4 days a week, shovelling wet grit into sacks."

Dr. Fox says: "*Whilst exercise is undoubtedly good for older people, it should ideally be gentle. I'm worried that Gloria Gaynor may be doing herself more harm than good shifting 15 tons of damp grit 4 times a week. However, if she cuts down to a couple of days a week, and remembers to lift the sacks with her back straight and knees bent, I see no reason why she shouldn't still be with us in 50 years' time.*"

Bee Gees Maurice, Robin and **Barry** are well known for their ludicrous high-pitched singing, piano key teeth and hissy fits. They look no older now than they did in their heyday 40 years ago, but in the words of their song, how much longer can they keep 'Stayin' Alive' before they're all dead? "We hope to make it well past 100," squeaked Maurice. "We're on a special diet drawn up for us by a Hollywood nutritionist. Basically, we each drink a gallon of purified mineral water each day, and we're only allowed to eat nuts and fizz-bombs. Lots of other stars follow the same plan, including Bob Hope, McCauley Culkin and Gary Coleman out of Diff'rent Strokes."

Dr. Fox says: "*I fear for the Bee Gees. They should be wary of fashionable dieticians promising long life. Years of experience have shown that you can't beat a traditional balanced diet, such as chips, beans and fish fingers, supplemented with regular injections of monkey hormones, for keeping the Grim Reaper at bay.*"

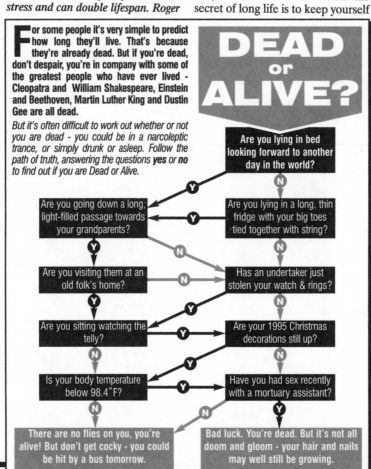

For some people it's very simple to predict how long they'll live. That's because they're already dead. But if you're dead, don't despair, you're in company with some of the greatest people who have ever lived - Cleopatra and William Shakespeare, Einstein and Beethoven, Martin Luther King and Dustin Gee are all dead.

*But it's often difficult to work out whether or not you are dead - you could be in a narcoleptic trance, or simply drunk or asleep. Follow the path of truth, answering the questions **yes** or **no** to find out if you are Dead or Alive.*

DEAD or ALIVE?

Are you lying in bed looking forward to another day in the world?

Are you going down a long, light-filled passage towards your grandparents?

Are you lying in a long, thin fridge with your big toes tied together with string?

Are you visiting them at an old folk's home?

Has an undertaker just stolen your watch & rings?

Are you sitting watching the telly?

Are your 1995 Christmas decorations still up?

Is your body temperature below 98.4°F?

Have you had sex recently with a mortuary assistant?

There are no flies on you, you're alive! But don't get cocky - you could be hit by a bus tomorrow.

Bad luck. You're dead. But it's not all doom and gloom - your hair and nails may well still be growing.

OAPs!

Fame! I'm gonna Live Forever!
Or did they?

Back in the 80s, the kids from Fame told the world that they were going to live forever. And twenty years on, the question on everyone's lips is how is their bid for immortality faring. We look at see how they are progressing and award each one a 'live forever' rating out of ten.

Lee Curreri
Born 4th January 1961
Lee, who played mop-top music prodigy Bruno, is doing quite well in his bid to live forever, having

sucessfully completed 41 consecutive years without dying. He quit the stage 10 years ago and now works in a cheese freezing warehouse in New York, where he believes the cold, calcium enriched air will improve his chances of immortality.
Live forever rating: **8/10**

Erica Gimpel
Born June 25th 1964
Actress Erica Gimpel has sucessfully completed 38 years of immortality, though is sadly now confined to

a wheelchair after being shot in the spine in an episode of ER. This is doubly tragic, as in the Fame TV series Erica played feisty student Coco Hernandez who lived to dance on car bonnets. Happily, she can still walk and dance in real life.
Live forever rating: **7/10**

Jesse Borrego
Born August 1st 1962
Texas born Jesse has the Japanese symbol for long life tattooed on his arse. After his

character Jesse Valasquez was axed from the show, he learned how to fly - high! - by joining the United States Air Force. He left after 4 years and picked up his sucessful acting career, appearing in the TV movie 'Hell Swarm' and episode 19 of the first series of 'Hunger'.
Live forever rating: **8/10**

Gene Anthony Ray
Born May 24th 1963
39 year-old Gene, who played dance ace Leroy Johnson has quit acting and

moved to Milan, where he runs a business photographing tourists holding a snake. He hopes the Mediterranean diet of sun dried tomatoes, olive oil and pepperami will help him achieve his aim of living forever. And he's doing fairly well so far, with a score of 39 years not out.
Live forever rating: **7/10**

Valerie Landsburg
Born August 12th 1958
California-raised Valerie, who played bubbly but unattractive dancer Doris

Schwartz is leading the race to immortality amongst the fame veterans. After network bosses axed the series in 1987, she quit acting and moved to Nantucket where she sank her savings into a squid ink farm. After that failed, she moved to Boston wher she now farms cuttlefish for budgies.
Live forever rating: **9¹/₂/10**

Albert Hague
Born October 13th 1920
Veteran actor Hague played long-suffering Benjamin Shorofsky, bearded Professor of

Music at the High School for Performing Arts. Initially doing well in the imortality stakes, he suffered a setback in November last year when he was bitten in the scrotum by a gila monster after a prank he was playing at San Francisco Zoo backfired. He was making a good recovery when he fell out of the hospital window and died.
Live forever rating: **0/10**

How Long Will YOU Live?

It's a sad fact that, unless you are *Dr Who* or *Christopher Lambert* off *Highlander*, one day you are going to die. However, it's also certain that you will probably live longer than your grandparents did, especially if they died young. 30% more people now live up to 20% or more longer than 95% of their ancestors - and it's a figure that's increasing by up to 15% per year.

In 1970, average life expectancy was 35. Nowadays, most of us can look forward to sitting in a pool of urine blowing bubbles out of our noses in care homes till well past the age of a hundred.

Your family history, what you eat and drink, and the things you do each day all affect how long you will live. So when exactly will YOU die?

Find out exactly how long you've got left before your heart stops beating, starving your brain of oxygen and your consciousness flickers out forever into the vast, black, timeless void of eternal nothingness that is death by taking our fun lifestyle quiz.

1. You make yourself a packed lunch to take into work. What do you put in it?
a) A lettuce sandwich on wholemeal bread, an apple and a bio yoghurt.
b) A ham sandwich on white bread, a sausage roll and a carton of orange juice.
c) A 2lb tub of Utterly Butterly and a spoon.

2. How do you cope with stress at work?
a) Cut yourself some slack. Listen to Andean Pan pipe music, fiddle about with an executive toy and perhaps prune a Banzai tree on your desk.
b) Leave the office for an hour and hit a couple of baskets of golf balls at the local driving range.
c) Bottle it all up until you turn the colour of Alex Ferguson and black out.

3. When you stick the butter knife into a toaster to retrieve burnt toast, how often do you unplug it first?
a) Sometimes.
b) Rarely.
c) Never.

4. You go to a department store to buy some trousers, but notice that the gents' department is on the second floor and the lift is broken. What do you do?
a) Take the stairs.
b) Take the escalator.
c) Take a taxi home and order an enormous elasticated pair from a mail-order advert in the Sunday Mirror.

5. How much money do you owe to Bermondsey Dave?
a) Nothing.
b) 0 to £5.
c) Over £5.

6. You decide to have a nice quiet night in watching TV with the family. How much do you have to drink?
a) Nothing serious, just a few cans.
b) A bottle of wine left over from Christmas, half a bottle of cooking sherry and some gin.
c) All the drink in the house followed by a pint of gassed milk, the two-stroke oil from the garden strimmer and a tin of Brasso filtered through a slice of bread.

7. What sort of cigarettes do you smoke?
a) Healthy Marlboro Lights from Holland and Barrett.
b) Medium tar cigarette such as Benson and Hedges.
c) Giant rollies made from tea bags and newspaper.

8. How often do you go backpacking in Australia?
a) Never.
b) Rarely.
c) Often.

9. How often do you wear a seatbelt in the car?
a) Always. It's clunk! click! every trip.
b) Just on long journeys, but don't bother for short trips.
c) Never, because you met a bloke in the pub whose mate was in a crash and he was thrown clear of his car and the fireman told him that if he had been wearing a belt he would have been killed.

10. How often do you go to swimming parties at Michael Barrymore's house?
a) Never.
b) Sometimes, but I never take my trunks.
c) Often.

11. Which of the following would best describe your arteries?
a) Like the inside of a gleaming pipe off the Castrol GTX advert.
b) Like the Bakerloo line - a bit grubby but functional.
c) As tight and furry as Sooty's arsehole.

12. When you get up in the morning, how long does your uncontrollable coughing fit last?
a) 3 seconds to 5 minutes.
b). 5-10 minutes.
c) Until you go back to bed.

How long have YOU got?

Mainly As: *Congratulations! The Queen may as well begin writing that telegram now. Thanks to your healthy lifestyle you are almost certain to reach the ton, and if you avoid household accidents and hereditary illnesses, you could even double that.*

Mainly Bs: *Not bad. You are guaranteed at least seventy years on this earth, but you could make eighty or ninety with a few minor adjustments to your lifestyle - don't park right outside the pub door every day, park 20 yards down the road to give yourself a bracing walk.*

Mainly Cs: *Oh, dear. With your lifestyle as it is, you'll be lucky to make it to the end of this article. Drastic action is needed now. After you've finished your tea tonight, don't sit in front of the telly, go out and run further than you have ever run in your life before.*

The ARTFUL Podger

TUBBY T.V. ARTS PONCE MARK LAWSON HATES HIGH BROW LITERATURE. HE PREFERS TO REVIEW PORNY MAGAZINES!

BAH! THE PRODUCER HAS GIVEN ME ANOTHER BIG THICK BOOK (WRAPPED IN BROWN PAPER) TO REVIEW FOR HOMEWORK. IT'LL BE DEAD BORING, WITH NO PICTURES IN IT. WHAT A BORE!

AND I WAS PLANNING TO LOOK AT PORNY MAGAZINES TONIGHT

I KNOW! I'LL DUMP THIS WORDY CODSWALLOP IN THE BIN...

DROP!

THEN NIP INTO THIS NEWSAGENTS TO ACQUIRE SOME NAKED GIRLIE MAGAZINES!

PHOARR!! THIS LOT SHOULD DO. I ALMOST NEED A SPECIAL WEE-WEE JUST LOOKING AT THEM

MARK! IS THET YOU?

WHAT ON EARTH ARE YOU DOING WITH THAT VILE PORNOGRAPHY!?

CRIPES! GERMAINE GREER!! OH, I WAS JUST ERM...

I WAS JUST ASKING THE SHOP KEEPER TO REMOVE THIS FILTH FROM DISPLAY... BECAUSE IT, ERM... OFFENDED ME! YES. THAT'S RIGHT! IT OFFENDED ME.

HUR-RUMPH! THAT PUT PAID TO MY PERVY PURCHASES! NOW I'M NEVER GOING TO GET MY PAWS ON ANY PORN. UNLESS...

JUST AS I THOUGHT! THE LOCAL PARK IS A REGULAR DUMPING GROUND FOR OBSOLETE WANK MAGS. LOOK, A SEXUALLY FRUSTRATED GENT IS DISPOSING OF HIS SHAMEFUL STASH IN THOSE BUSHES EVEN AS I SPEAK!

CHUCK!

NO BALL GAMES NO DOG SHIT NO PORN TIPPING BY ORDER

I'LL SNEAK ROUND THE BACK OF THOSE BUSHES AND RETRIEVE IT!

SECONDS LATER...

RUMMAGE! GROPE!!

COME ON... I KNOW IT'S IN HERE SOMEWHERE!

FUMBLE!

AH! GOT IT...

HANG ON A MINUTE! THIS ISN'T PORN. IT'S POETRY!!

YES, IT'S MY LATEST BOOK-LENGTH POEM. I DECIDED TO THROW IT AWAY BECAUSE IT DOESN'T RHYME

YIKES! TOM PAULIN

FANCY MEETING YOU HERE! I WAS JUST... ERM... ADMIRING YOUR WORK!

YOU LIKE IT? MMM! PERHAPS I WAS A BIT HASTY THROWING IT IN THE BUSHES. HERE, LET ME READ IT TO YOU, SLOWLY. IT WILL ONLY TAKE A FEW HOURS...

OH, FUCK!

SOME BITS DON'T RHYME, BUT JUST IGNORE THEM, OKAY?

THE NEXT DAY AT BBC 2...

PAULIN'S PRATTLING POETRY RECITAL TOOK ALL NIGHT. I DIDN'T GET SO MUCH AS A GLIMPSE OF A DIRTY BOOK

AND NOW I'LL BE IN TROUBLE FOR NOT DOING MY HOMEWORK!

WELL LAWSON. WHAT DID YOU MAKE OF THAT BOOK I GAVE YOU? HAVE YOU FINISHED REVIEWING IT YET?

ERM... NO SIR. I LOST IT, SIR

THAT'S A PITY. I THOUGHT IT WOULD HAVE BEEN RIGHT UP YOUR STREET

ALRIGHT THEN. PARSONS, TELL US WHAT YOU MADE OF DAVID O'SULLIVAN'S 'HISTORY OF EXPLICIT PORNOGRAPHY IN THE 20TH CENTURY' WITH OVER 300 FULL COLOUR PHOTOGRAPHS

?

AHEM AHEM...

I ABSOLUTELY LOVED IT. A FARRAGO OF FILTH? MAYBE. A PLETHORA OF PORN? PERHAPS. BUT FOR ME THIS IS A WORK OF PURE PORNOGRAPHIC GENIUS

WHAT O'SULLIVAN DOES IS VERY CLEVER. IN A SENSE HE'S CREATING A THREE-WAY DIALOGUE BETWEEN THE SEXUAL IMAGERY, THE VOYEURISTIC VIEWER, IF YOU LIKE, AND HIS COCK. MY COCK SPOKE TO ME. IT SAID "PULL ME, PARSONS, HARD AND FAST." AND I DID. IN FACT, I ALMOST WANKED MYSELF BLIND

YES, I AGREE. I'M NOT NORMALLY A BIG FAN OF EXPLOITATIVE PORNOGRAPHY, BUT SOME OF THE IMAGES IN THIS BOOK - ESPECIALLY THE GIRL-ON-GIRL STUFF, WAS ENOUGH TO MAKE ME START QUESTIONING MY OWN SEXUALITY

BAH!!

KYLIE-EIDOSCOPE

Get set for non-stop Kylie-on-Kylie-on-Kylie action with your fantastic **FREE**

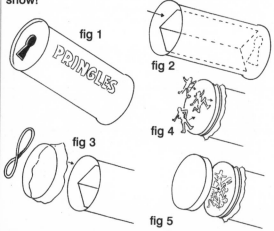

"It's especially for YOU!"

Just imagine peeping through the keyhole of a hotel door and seeing Kylie Minogue having lesbian sex... *with herself!* YOU should be so lucky.

Well now that dream can come true, thanks to this FANTASTIC FREE GIFT. The Viz *Kylie-eidoscope* allows you private access to your own Kylie lesbian orgy any time you like. It's simple to construct and even simpler to use. Just look through the *Kylie-eidoscope* keyhole, turn the end and watch as a myriad of bare Kylies writhe and contort in a non-stop, lust-fuelled technicolour lesbian orgy where *no two positions will ever be repeated!* You'll be enjoying the most erotic show imaginable, and passers by will think you are just looking for the last Pringle in the tube whilst rummaging for change in your pocket.

INSTRUCTIONS

1 Cut a keyhole shaped hole in the bottom of an empty Pringles tube using the template provided (fig 1)

2 Take a Pringles tube-sized piece of tin foil and bend it at a 45°angle. Insert it into the tube as shown (fig 2)

3 Cover the open end of the tube with a piece of clear polythene and secure with an elastic band (fig 3)

4 Carefully cut out the little Kylies and sex toys around the dotted lines and drop them on top of the polythene (fig 4)

5 Replace the translucent tube lid (fig 5)

6 Turn the translucent lid, sit back and enjoy the show!

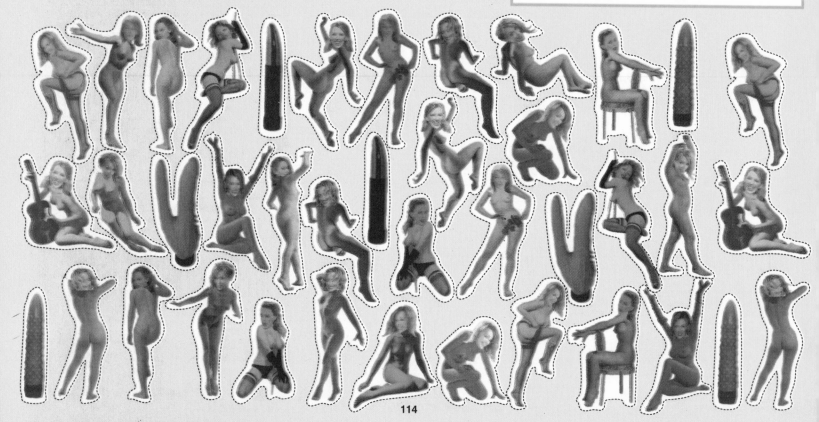

114

TINRIBS

AS A TREAT, WE WILL BE GOING ON A SCHOOL TRIP TO THE SAFARI PARK TODAY

YOU WILL DRIVE THE COACH, MR SNODWORTHY

AND SHORTLY

COR! ISN'T THIS EXCITING, TINRIBS?

SHORTLEAT SAFARI PARK
SCHOOL TRIP

HI. I'M BARBIE. I LOVE YOU VERY MUCH.

NOW THEN. TO DIMINISH ANY PLEASURE YOU GAIN FROM THIS OUTING, I'M GIVING YOU THESE DULL WORKSHEETS TO COMPLETE DURING THE DAY.

HEH, HEH!

HEAD MASTER

BOO!

HAND IN YOUR WORKSHEETS TO MR SNODWORTHY AT THE END OF THE TRIP, WHO WILL HAVE TO STAY UP ALL NIGHT MARKING THEM

EH?

HEAD MASTER

THUS A TEDIOUS TIME IS HAD BY ALL EXCEPT FOR ME. HOORAY!

BAH! I HATE DOING MARKING

BUT IF ALL THE KIDS WERE KILLED BY WILD ANIMALS, THERE'D BE NO WORKSHEETS TO MARK. HMMM....

>AHEM< OH DEAR, WE'VE RUN OUT OF PETROL

THE CHILDREN WILL HAVE TO GET OUT AND PUSH — I HOPE THEY DON'T GET EATEN BY LIONS (CHEH HEH)

I KNOW HOW TO KEEP THOSE LIONS OFF US, HEAD MASTER

HEAD MASTER

...WITH THE AID OF MY FANTASTIC ROBOT PAL!

USING ONE OF TINRIBS' TIN CAN SUPPORTS, WE SLIT OPEN MR SNODWORTHY'S BELLY...

YARRRGH...

ZZZIP

THEN WE PULL OUT THE JUICIEST BITS OF GUTS AND OFFAL

THERE. THOSE TASTY TITBITS WILL OCCUPY THE LIONS WHILE WE PUSH THE COACH

GROAN THE PAIN...

SCHOOL TRIP

SLAVER CHEW

SHORTLY I'LL MAKE THIS RHINO CHARGE AT THE KIDS

THUNDER

SNORT

IT'LL TRAMPLE THEM TO DEATH — THEN IT'S BYE-BYE TO MARKING WORKSHEETS

HYAH! GEDDUP THERE!

HI. I'M BARBIE.

WOW!

THAT CHARGING RHINO HAS SKIDDED ON TINRIBS

CHONK!

GAH!

I'VE BEEN SPEARED THROUGH THE HEAD!

GRR — THAT PESKY ROBOT KEEPS SPOILING MY MURDEROUS PLANS

BUT I'LL FIX HIM

I'M TRAINING THIS GORILLA TO ATTACK THAT MECHANICAL TWIT

HI. I'M BARBIE. I LOVE YOU VERY MUCH.

THWACK

JAB!

I SIMPLY NEED TO GOAD IT CRUELLY WHILST PLAYING A RECORDING OF TINRIBS'S VOICE

HEH HEH! NOW IT'LL GO APESHIT MENTAL WHEN IT HEARS THAT ROBOT'S ELECTRONIC VOICEBOX

SEEK 'IM OUT, BOY!

OOG!

HUNH?

THE GORILLA IS HEADING THE WRONG WAY

WOW! IT'S ATTACKED PROFESSOR STEPHEN HAWKING ON THAT OTHER COACH

CAMBRIDGE UNIVERSITY TRIP

LET-GO-YOU-BIG-APE!

WE ARE CAMBRIDGE UNIVERSITY BRAINBOXES, AND PROFESSOR HAWKING WAS GOING TO MARK THE EXTRA-DIFFICULT WORKSHEETS WE'VE COMPLETED

BUT NOW HE'S BEEN KNACKED BY THAT BIG MONKEY, YOU'LL HAVE TO MARK THEM

SO IT'LL BE SOME TIME BEFORE MR SNODWORTHY GETS THROUGH ALL THOSE WORKSHEETS, TINRIBS...

ICE

...YOU MARK MY WORDS!

HI. I'M BARBIE. I LOVE YOU VERY MUCH

TICK TICK CROSS TICK

CHARLIE & CHUBBY... CCTV TELLY VOYEURS

FULCHESTER CCTV CONTROL ROOM... NOW THEN, CHAPS, KEEP A KEEN EYE OUT ON THE CITY CENTRE TODAY. IT'S BUSY AND THERE'S PICK-POCKETS AND MUGGERS ABOUT. REMEMBER THE DANGER FROM TERRORISM. BE ALERT!

YES SOR. WILL DO, SOR.

YURGH. HUNH.

RIGHT THEN, CHUBBY. LET'S GET STARTED, EH?

HMM. HNNH! HNNH!

ON THE STREET...

GIZ THAT BAG YOU COW!

EEEEK!!

SNAP!

WILL YE LOOK AT THAT, NOW.

GIVE US YER FUCKIN' CAR, OR I'LL SLIT YER FUCKIN' THROAT!

EEEEEK!!

CCTV IN OPERAT

NOW THEN, NOW THEN. I'LL ZOOM IN.

WILL YE LOOK AT THE FOKKIN' TITTIES ON HOR.

HUURGH! HUURGH!

I BET YE'D LIKE TO GET YER FOKKIN' DORTY LITTLE HANDS ON THEM, YE FILTHY BASTORD.

HUURGH! HUURGH!

DIE, INFIDELS!

AAAAIIIEEEEE!!

X1

LOOK. YE CAN SEE ALL O' HER FOKKIN' LITTLE KNICKERS.

HUURGH!

I BET YE'D LIKE TO GET YER LITTLE FAT COCK INSIDE THEM KNICKERS, YE DORTY LITTLE MAN.

HUURGH! HUURGH! HUURGH!

LOOK, THIS ONE'S GOT NO BRA'S ON. DAT'S DISGOOSTIN'. MIND, YOU'D RATHER SEE A FAT ONE, WOULDN'T YA?

HUURGH!

I BET YE'D LIKE TO USE YER BIG DORTY HANDS TE PULL DOWN HER KNICKERS, AN' KISS HOR ALL ON DE TITTIES.

HUURGH! HUURGH! HUURGH!

BOOM!

FULCHESTER'S HOSPITALS ARE OVERFLOWING IN THE AFTERMATH OF THIS AFTERNOON'S MAJOR TERRORIST ATTACK. THERE HAVE BEEN MANY CASUALTIES, AND THE DEATH TOLL IS RISING.

POLICE ARE CURRENTLY EXAMINING CCTV FOOTAGE TAKEN IN THE VICINITY OF THE INCIDENT...

DID YE SEE THE BARMAID'S TITS? YOU LOVED 'EM DIDN'T YE?

HUURGH!

MEANWHILE... LOOK AT THE JUGS ON THAT! I BET YOU'D LAV TA RAB 'ER BIG BOOBIES... PUT YOUR LITTLE SAUSAGE RIGHT UP HER, EH, YOU'D LAV THAT, WOON'TCHA? EH?

YOU CAN SEE 'ER NIPOOZ.

HUURGH!

LAV TU SACK ON THEM WOON'TCHA? EH? YOU DIRTY FAT BARSTARD.

HUURGH! HUURGH! HUURGH!

HELPFUL HERBERT ...BUT HIS GOOD DEEDS ALWAYS GET HIM INTO SCRAPES!!

118

PLAYTIME FONTAYNE

IT'S BAD NEWS, I'M AFRAID. HEAD OFFICE HAVE INSTRUCTED ME TO MAKE CUTBACKS. I'M SORRY BUT IT LOOKS LIKE I'M GOING TO HAVE TO MAKE ONE OF YOU REDUNDANT.

BEFORE I PROCEED, I'D LIKE YOU ALL TO UNDERSTAND THAT THIS IS THE MOST DIFFICULT PART OF MY JOB. I DON'T TAKE SUCH DECISIONS LIGHTLY.

IP- DIP- DOO, DOGGY DOES A POO, CAT DOES A WEE-WEE... OUT GOES **YOU!**

119

It's the page that once coughed a docker's omelette into its hand on the Bakerloo Line.... ...and wiped it on a lady's coat.

Letterbocks

letters@viz.co.uk

Letterbocks, Viz Comic, PO Box 1PT, Newcastle-upon-Tyne, NE99 1PT.

MY OLD grandmother used to be the tea lady who looked after Chris Tarrant on Who wants to be a Millionaire? She told me in secret that the relatives of the main contestants got into some right fucking scraps to sit in a certain seat on the programme. Have your readers noticed that all the winners' relatives sit in the first seat of the second row. It's a fucking fix said my gran. When she complained to old Tarrant about the mess it caused, he called her an old twat.

Vic Reeves
Rotherham

(And yes, my name is Vic Reeves)

I WOULD like to inform tennis racquet manufacturers Slazenger that I just just spent £21.95 on a Wilson racquet because their own product at £19.95 had a picture of Tim Henman on it. If Slazenger want to continue losing business, then I suggest they continue getting Mr Huffy to endorse their products. On the same note, if Wilson decided to double the cost of their racquets, I'm sure most people would happily pay.

B. Henry
Hexham

I HAVE to complain at the way the English language is being hijacked by all and sundry. In my youth, gay meant happy. Now it's solely used to describe the activity of a buggerist. Let's say it how it is.

Colonel AKP Hepcott-White (Rtd)
Surrey

"THERE'S nothing worse than constipation on your big day" the advert for Senecot says. Surely the shits would be far worse.

Dave Oliver
Hartlepool

I'VE written a pop song all about Kylie Minogue's arse and I wonder if any pop stars would like to record it. It's called Kylie's Arse, and it's very catchy. I'll not do any verses, but the chorus goes-

Kylie's arse, Kylie's arse,
Kylie's arse, Kylie's arse,
Kylie's arse, Kylie's arse,
I'm in love with Kylie's arse,
(He's in love with Kylie's arse)

If it was a hit, I'd be happy to split the profits 50/50 with the pop star.

Chuma
e-mail

Are you a pop star who would like to record Chuma's Kylie's Arse? Perhaps you're Sting or David Bowie looking for new Christmas single. Or perhaps you're Boneo out of U2 looking for a new anthem to head your latest tour. If so, write to us at the letterbocks address and we'll put you in touch with Chuma. Mark your envelope 'I'm a pop star'.

CAN I thank the lady in front of me in the queue last Saturday for amusing me when her bank card was declined at the supermarket checkout. Can I suggest that she avoids future embarrassing incidents and delaying more affluent customers by paying her bills on time and learning the meaning of the term APR.

DP Morgan
Cardiff

THERE is something wrong with my new girlfriend. Each time I try and stick my cock in her mouth, she turns her head to put it in her ear. Do you think it's a fetish?

R Skelton
Plymouth

I'VE heard that Professor Stephen Hawking is working on a theory that would predict the location in the universe of everything. If he has any luck with it, perhaps he could contact me through your magazine and tell me where I've left my car keys.

Jools Chappell
e-mail

HAS Keith Richards had extreme plastic surgery as many pop stars do, and if yes, how does he smell? I claim £5 for spotting the prosthesis.

P. Marsh
Walsall

SOME time ago I was told an interesting rumour about actress Joanna Lumley. It seems she has a plastic rectum. This is because in her early days of fame, she would get her boyfriend to sprinkle cocaine on his cock and do her up the arse. Unfortunately, doing this in excess caused her arse to collapse, hence the need for the plastic one. I hope to meet her one day and ask her to confirm or deny this, or perhaps she could contact your magazine and do the same.

Brian Boyd
e-mail

Are you Joanna Lumley? If so, write and tell us if you've got a plastic arse.

I AM disgusted at the example the police set the public. I was recently fined for having an out of date tax disc on my car. However, whilst watching The Bill on UK Gold, I noticed that every one of the police cars' tax was out of date by at least 3 years. Once again, it's one rule for one, another rule for another.

Mr Badger
Throckley

I WAS recently ear bashed by my flat mate for leaving the tap running as it wastes water. In the next breath he explained that because of global warming, everywhere will eventually be flooded. If this is the case, surely the best thing to do is to leave the tap on so all of this water goes down the drains.

Tom Norfolk
Norwich

THEY SAY that there is no such thing as a free lunch, but I once found half a kebab on the pavement, and it cost me nothing.

Patrick Wood
e-mail

THEY SAY that carbon monoxide is the silent killer in the home. Not in my house it's not. It was my husband Fred.

Rose West
Durham

I'M NOT happy with the way our beautiful language is being taken from us. In my youth, foxy meant fox-like. Now it has connotations of sexual attraction. I can't describe a small reddish-brown dog as being foxy anymore without being taken for some sort of beastialist.

Colonel AKP Hepcott-White (Rtd)
Surrey

I THINK the bin men in my area have got a cheek going on strike for being underpaid. They only work one day a week, the lazy fuckers.

Patrick Millner
e-mail

HOW come no matter how many people are unemployed, the number of job centres and people working in them never changes? We have the same number now as when we had 3.5 million people out of work. With just 900,000 on the dole, two thirds of job centre staff are sitting on their arses with nothing to do.

Mark Humphries
e-mail

HAS anyone noticed that James Bond's codename, 007, is always pronounced wrongly? The first two characters are clearly zeros, but they are invariably pronounced as the letter 'O'. 'Double nought seven' or 'double zero seven' would both be acceptable. You would have thought that with all the millions spent on making the films they would have got a simple thing like that right.

J. Welch
e-mail

THE other day, I dropped a tin of Alphabetti Spaghetti in Tomato Sauce onto the floor whilst opening it. When I bent down to clean them up, I noticed they spelled out the spooky message 'SMALL PECKER - 2.15 KEMPTON PARK - A MONKEY TO WIN. I checked the

---

DO YOU REGRET THAT TATTOO NOW?

YES!

YES!

YES! SKINS

Table Football Results

Division 1

Blue	6	10	Red
Red	10	8	Blue
Red	4	10	Blue
Blue	10	3	Red

Champion's League

Rosso	10	6	Blau
Azzurro	7	10	Rouge

UEFA Cup (2nd leg)

Azul	10	9	Rojo

(20-17 agg)

TOP TIPS

A BEER mat cut diagonally in half and fastened together with lengths of string makes an ideal bra for Tara Palmer-Tompkinson.

Rob Jackson, Tinshill

IN THE same way that a lazy eye can be cured by covering the other eye with frosted glass, a lazy ear can be cured by pushing a cork into the good one.

D. C. Dry, Boston Spa

WHEN mailing faeces to Her Majesty the Queen (or other famous personalities, such as Gareth Gates), avoid getting poo on your tongue by using self-sealing envelopes.

Tim Kovacs, Otterwa, Canada

SHOPPERS. When you have finished and are leaving the supermarket, kindly offer your shopping list to people who are going in, as they may have forgotten to make one.

Kennon Baird, California

GARETH Gates. Avoid embarrassing bouts of stuttering by simply singing your replies to questions.

Matt Douse, Beverley

GENTLEMEN. Save money on expensive dating agencies. Simply stand across the road from your local lonely hearts club and when you see someone you like come out, follow them home at a discreet distance. After they have entered their home, leave a dignified amount of time before knocking on their door and asking them out for a drink.

Stewart Cowley, London

LETTERBOCKS fans. Save two quid every deci-month by picking up a free copy of Metro every day. Most of the letters in Viz get reprinted in there eventually.

Rob Leese Jones, e-mail

I'M A GUITAR

YOU'RE A LYRE!

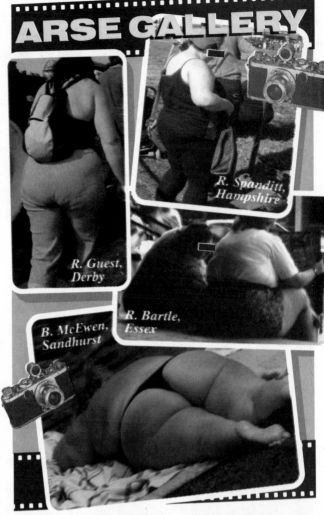

ARSE GALLERY

R. Spanditt, Hampshire

R. Guest, Derby

R. Bartle, Essex

B. McEwen, Sandhurst

---

paper and sure enough, a horse of that name was running. I put £500 on it (a monkey) at 25-1 and lo and behold it won! Have any other readers won shitloads of money as a result of spilt food?

Greg Brooks e-mail

MELVYN Bragg accepted his peerage so that he could begin to abolish the House of Lords from within. Well after three years of sitting in his Ermine robes grinning like a Cheshire cat, could he let us know how far he has got?

B. Tippit Wales

IF I had a penny for every time I'd read Viz and found it amusing, I'd have just under 2 pence.

Duncan e-mail

IMAGINE if you shat out of your cock instead of your arse, how thin your turds would be.

Dr. McFee Yorkshire

HOW big a hypocrital cunt is Paul McCartney? Sacking his roadies for sneaking a bacon sandwich. Yet on the single Ebony and Ivory, he openly boasts that his piano is made of the rarest of woods and elephants' trunks! Why didn't he have a barbecue with the left over

trees, frying the rest of the poor fucking elephants?

William Budd e-mail

WHEN I was a boy, galvanise meant to coat iron with a thin layer of zinc to prevent rust. Now, apparently, it means to rouse a group of people forcibly by shock or excitement. How much longer are we going to allow our language to be stolen from us?

Colonel AKP Hepcott-White (Rtd) Surrey

HOW come grumble vid star Ben Dover can manage to mess around with loads of birds just by dishing a few crappy compliments about? I told Doreen (my mate Dave's nan) that her homemade fairycakes were delicious. I thought I was well in, but she went berserk when I woke her up at 3am by slapping my cock on her chin.

W. Hardman e-mail

Lord Have Mercy

With **Abdul Latif,** Lord of Harpole

Dear Lord Harpole,

I have defrauded a charity. Last week my friend said he was going to visit Cragside House, a National Trust property in Northumberland. I have been a member of the National Trust for 10 years, and I lent him my membership card so he could get in without paying. It clearly says on the back that the card is non-transferable. It seemed so insignificant at the time, but now I feel so guilty as I realise the gravity of what I have done. Lord have mercy.

T. Contiboard, Newcastle

Dear Mr. Contiboard,
Don't feel too bad. Whilst what you did was technically wrong, you have supported the charity for a long time. What's more, I'm sure your friend went into the gift shop or cafe for refreshments. He may even have considered joining the Trust himself. Pop along to my restaurant, The Rupali, Bigg Market, Newcastle-upon-Tyne, have 3 Aloo Murgihis and you shall be forgiven.

Dear Lord Harpole,

I am a butcher, and the other morning I arrived early for work to take a delivery of oven ready chickens. I have to confess that whilst I was alone in the storeroom I had impure thoughts about them. I am ashamed to say that at lunchtime, I went back into the storeroom and acted upon those thoughts. I feel so guilty. Lord have mercy.

Frank Plywood, Quality Butchers, The High Street, Fulchester

Dear Mr Plywood,

I notice from your address that you are the butcher who supplies poultry and meat products to certain of my rival restaurants. Here at the Rupali Restaurant, I always make sure that I buy only from Butchers whose relationship with their meat remains on a professional basis. Come to the restaurant and eat 3 Vindaloo Special Sooka Jhinghas and all shall be forgiven.

Dear Lord Harpole,

I have killed a man. I committed murder and got clean away. During the war, I was burgling a house in the East End of London. I knocked some saucepans over in the kitchen and the owner, who was asleep upstairs came running down armed with a knife. The was a struggle and somehow I stabbed him through the heart. I panicked and ran off. An hour later, there was an air raid and his house took a direct hit. There was nothing left. That was fifty years ago, and a day hasn't gone by when I haven't thought about the terrible crime I committed. Lord have mercy.

J. Fibreboard, Hackney

Dear Mr. Fibreboard,

The taking of a human life is indeed the worst of all crimes. But I feel that after fifty years of remorse and mental torture you have punished yourself enough. But just to make doubly sure, you must consume 3 of my world famous Curry Hells. And if that sounds expensive, remember any Curry Hell consumed in full at the Rupali Restaurant is absolutely FREE!

GOLDFISH BOY

AFTER LOSING HIS PARENTS IN A BIZARRE FAIRGROUND ACCIDENT, YOUNG JOHNNY JOHNSON WAS TAKEN IN AND RAISED BY KINDLY GOLDFISH ON THE HOOK-A-DUCK STALL. AFTER SEVERAL YEARS, HE HAD BEEN WON BY FATHER BROWN THE LOCAL VICAR, WITH WHOM HE NOW LIVED.

CHRISTMAS EVE...

PLEASE ACCEPT MY CONDOLENCES ON YOUR HUSBAND'S DEMISE, MRS. ERNSHAW

THANK YOU, VICAR. I AM COMFORTED BY THE THOUGHT THAT MY DEAR ALBERT WILL NOW BE SITTING AT THE LORD'S RIGHT HAND. SNIFF!

ALAS, I SUSPECT THAT MAY NOT BE THE CASE. HE ONCE VOUCHSAFED TO ME THAT AS A SIX-YEAR-OLD HE STOLE AN APPLE FROM A NEIGHBOUR'S TREE...

... AS A RESULT, I FEAR THAT THE DEVIL WILL BE SEWING HIS EYES OPEN WITH RUSTY WIRE AS WE SPEAK, AND WILL SHORTLY BE CASTING HIS FLAYED, NAKED BODY INTO A LAKE OF FIRE FOR THE REST OF ETERNITY

OH DEAR

I'LL MISS HIM SO MUCH, VICAR

YES. IT'S ALWAYS A SHAME WHEN A LOVED ONE PASSES ON AT THIS TIME OF YEAR...

...IT REALLY SPOILS CHRISTMAS

I'LL FEEL QUITE ALONE TONIGHT, SITTING IN MY EMPTY HOUSE. ALBERT AND I USED TO SIT TOGETHER AND WATCH THE EUROTRASH CHRISTMAS EVE SPECIAL, YOU KNOW

EUROTRASH!?! WHY, THAT'S MY FAVOURITE PROGRAMME

ERM.... FORGIVE ME IF I SEEM A LITTLE FORWARD — BUT WOULD YOU LIKE TO COME AND SPEND CHRISTMAS WITH ME AT THE VICARAGE, MRS. ERNSHAW?

WHY, I'D LOVE TO, VICAR...

...AND CALL ME ELSPETH

THAT EVENING...

GOD, I'M SO EXCITED, GOLDFISH BOY. THE WIDOW ERNSHAW IS MOVING IN FOR CRIMBO. SHE'LL BE HERE ANY MINUTE

HOW DO I LOOK?

DING!
DONG!

AH! THAT'LL BE HER, NOW!

(Advt.)

Old Testament † The Mark of a Man of the Cloth

ELSPETH! WELCOME TO THE VICARAGE. MERRY XMAS!

THANK YOU, VICAR. PERCY AND I ARE SO LOOKING FORWARD TO OUR STAY

PERCY!?! WHO THE F....

...WHO'S PERCY?

HE'S MY PET PELICAN. ALBERT BROUGHT HIM BACK FOR ME FROM CYPRUS IN 1945

WELL, MAKE YOURSELF COMFORTABLE, ELSPETH. I'LL GO AND MAKE A POT OF TEA

AH, TEA! THE CUP THAT REFRESHETH, BUT DOTH NOT INEBRIATE

INDEED!

PUT A LITTLE TOT OF BRANDY IN MINE, WOULD YOU, VICAR?

HEH! HEH! SHE'LL BE PUTTY IN MY HANDS. FOR WHAT I AM ABOUT TO RECEIVE MAY THE LORD MAKE ME TRULY...

GLUB! GLUB! GLUB!

SQUAWK! SQUAWK!

CLUNK! CLUNK!

BAD PERCY! BAD PELICAN! STOP IT!

WHAT ON EARTH...?

NAUGHTY PERCY! DROP IT!

JESUS H. CHRIST! GOLDFISH BOY!

OH, THANK HEAVENS! HE'S ALRIGHT!

YES, VICAR. I DO APOLOGISE. PERCY HAS ALWAYS BEEN A SOD FOR FISH. HE CAN'T GET ENOUGH OF THEM

ANYWAY, LOOK AT THE TIME! EUROTRASH IS ABOUT TO START

GOODNESS ME, YES. I'LL GO AND FETCH THE TEA

SO···· MEERY CHREEESTMAS, MA EEENGLEEESH CHERMS. OUR FIRST CALL IS LAPLAND FOR THE ANNUAL NAKED LADYBOY SANTA CLAUS CHESS TOURNAMENT····

30 MINUTES LATER···

ET, SALUT, MAINTENANT!

WHAT AN INFORMATIVE PROGRAMME, VICAR

YES, THE FEATURE ABOUT THE NUDE CAMPANOLOGISTS OF HOLLAND BROUGHT TO MIND THE COLLECTION OF ECCLESIASTICAL ETCHINGS I ACQUIRED ON A COACH-TRIP TO AMSTERDAM····

PERHAPS YOU'D CARE TO COME UPSTAIRS FOR A PRIVATE VIEW OF MY C··· I MEAN THEM··· ···THE ETCHINGS

OH! YES, VICAR GIGGLE!

I···I FEEL QUITE LIGHT-HEADED, VICAR. GIGGLE!

MINT!

I'LL JUST PUT PERCY OUTSIDE SO AS HE DOESN'T EAT GOLDFISH BOY AGAIN, ELSPETH

OUTSIDE!?! WHY, THE PELICAN IS A TROPICAL BIRD, VICAR. PERCY WOULDN'T SURVIVE FIVE MINUTES ON A NIGHT LIKE THIS

BUT I CAN'T PUT GOLDFISH BOY OUT. THE WATER IN HIS BOWL WOULD FREEZE SOLID

WELL, WHY NOT LET HIM GO IN THE RIVER OR SOMETHING? I MEAN HE LOOKS TO HAVE OUTGROWN HIS BOWL ANYWAY

BUT··· BUT···

JUST MAKE UP YOUR MIND, QUICKLY, VICAR, BEFORE MY URGE TO SEE YOUR····

···YOUR ETCHINGS SUBSIDES

SO····

I'M SORRY ABOUT THIS, GOLDFISH BOY, ONLY MRS. ERNSHAW IS A VULNERABLE WIDOW····

···AND SHE'S HAD TOO MUCH TO DRINK

TO THE RIVER

THE LORD IN HIS WISDOM DOESN'T SEND THESE OPPORTUNITIES MY WAY VERY OFTEN

FAREWELL, OLD FRIEND, AND GOOD LUCK!

HEH! HEH!

BACK TO THE VICARAGE

5 MINUTES LATER···

I'M TERRIBLY SORRY, ELSPETH. I DON'T KNOW WHAT'S WRONG. THAT'S NEVER HAPPENED TO MY ETCHINGS BEFORE

DON'T WORRY ABOUT IT, VICAR. YOU CAN TRY TO SHOW THEM TO ME LATER ON

PERHAPS YOU'RE JUST UPSET ABOUT LETTING YOUR GOLDFISH BOY GO

YES, PERHAPS YOU'RE RIGHT

WELL, DON'T WORRY. I'M SURE HE'LL BE FINE. HE'LL HAVE A WONDERFUL TIME SWIMMING FREE

HE'LL MEET LOTS OF NEW FRIENDS, AND I'M SURE HE'LL HAVE A MUCH HAPPIER, LONGER LIFE IN THE RIVER THAN HE WOULD HAVE IN THAT BOWL

YES! YES OF COURSE! YOU'RE RIGHT

NEXT DAY···
THE ANGLERS' ARMS

TIME, GENTLEMEN, PLEASE!

CAUGHT-DECEMBER 2002

ROBBIE FUCKING WILLIAMS

THE MAN WHO CAN DO NO WRONG

SIGH, I'M BORED OF BEING REPORTED AS GREAT ALL THE TIME. I WISH I COULD BE NAUGHTY, LIKE THE SO SOLID CREW!

I KNOW!! I'LL SLIP A FIREARM INTO MY GIRLFRIENDS BAG!!

≥TEE HEE!!

FLASH! CLICK!

WOW! THIS'LL MAKE A FRONT PAGE SCOOP!!

THANKS ROBBIE! WHAT A SHINING EXAMPLE TO SET!

EH?!

BAH! I GO OUT WITH SO MANY BIRDS I FORGOT- MY CURRENT ONE IS A POLICEWOMAN DOING A GUN AMNESTY!

I'LL HAVE TO BE ALOT WORSE THAN THAT... I KNOW! I'LL DATE RAPE THIS YOUNG GIRL!!

TRA-LA-LA!

SKIP! SKIP! SKIP!

GRIND!! GRIND!!

COCKTAIL OF PRESCRIPTION DRUGS

GOSH - ALL THAT SKIPPING HAS MADE ME EVERSO TIRED... I THINK I'LL HAVE A DRINK...

TIP!!

GLUG GLUG GLUG!

HO HO HO!

HOW DO YOU FEEL NOW?

ERM- I... I FEEL...

...I FEEL CURED!!

HUNH? I HAD CANCER AND AIDS AND IT'S ALL CLEARED UP NICELY. I FEEL RIGHT AS RAIN AND ITS THANKS TO YOU AND YOUR WONDERFUL CONCOCTION!!

I LOVE YOU!

FLASH!

YOU'RE THE BEST, ROBBIE!!

LATER... I KNOW! I'LL TERRORISE THE OLD LADY THAT LIVES IN THIS BUNGALOW

...I'LL START BY LOBBING A BRICK THROUGH HER WINDOW!

SO... HUNNGH!!

LOB- SMASH!

OUCH! OOF!! ACHTUNG!!

VE SURRENDER! PLEASE- DO NICHT GO LOBBING ANYMORE BRICKS THROUGH OUR WINDOWS!

CAN YOU BELIEVE IT? I'VE ONLY GONE AND INFILTRATED SADDAM HUSSIEN, BIN LADEN + ADOLF HITLER'S SECRET HIDING PLACE!

COR ROBBIE! YOU'RE A HERO!!

FLASH!

CONGRATULATIONS, ROBBIE! THEY WERE ABOUT TO SET OFF A BOMB TO BLOW UP THE WHOLE WIDE WORLD, AND YOU STOPPED THEM!! THERES A REWARD FOR THIS...

...A WEEKEND AT BLACKPOOL!

COO!

YOU KNOW, THIS ISN'T SO BAD AFTER ALL. I THINK I'LL RELAX AND DO A BIT OF SUNBATHING...

FLASH!

THE NEXT DAY...

BAH!!

PIE

BLOBBY WILLIAMS

CUNT ROBBIE LETS FANS DOWN BY PUTTING ON A BIT OF WEIGHT- THE FAT BASTARD

GILBERT RATCHET

Panel 1: AW BOO! OUR TELLY HAS BROKEN DOWN JUST BEFORE CHRISTMAS
I'LL MISS ALL THE FANTASTIC YULETIDE PROGRAMMES

Panel 2: I KNOW — I'LL GO AND WATCH THE TELLY IN THE OLD FOLKS HOME DAY ROOM
EXTINCTION'S ALP NURSING HOME
THEY NEVER SWITCH IT OFF IN THERE

Panel 3: BUT — OH CRIKEY!
I CAN'T SEE THE SCREEN BECAUSE OF THAT BIG PILE OF DEAD ELDERLYS IN THE WAY

Panel 4: I'M AFRAID THIS COLD WEATHER IS KILLING OFF MY ELDERLYS LIKE FLIES, GILBERT
BUT I'M LOATHE TO TURN THE HEATING ON BECAUSE IT'S RATHER EXPENSIVE

Panel 5: NOT TO WORRY, MISTER
I'LL INVENT A MORE ECONOMICAL CENTRAL HEATING SYSTEM FOR YOUR OLD FOLKS HOME

Panel 6: SEE — THE **WHIP-O-MATIC** FORCES FATSO RADIO HEART FM DJ **JONO COLEMAN** TO CARRY A WARDROBE UP AND DOWN SOME STAIRS
WHACK WHACK
THE HEAT GENERATED IN HIS ARMPITS IS THEN PUMPED AROUND THE BUILDING THROUGH A SYSTEM OF COPPER PIPES

Panel 7: THAT'S SMASHING, GILBERT
WHACK WHACK
LOVELY WARMTH
PLEASE ACCEPT THIS PORTABLE TELLY AS A REWARD

Panel 8: OOPS! I'VE ACCIDENTALLY SET THE WHIP-O-MATIC TO FULL POWER
WHACK WHACK WHACK WHACK WHACK
CLONK!
JONO IS CHARGING UP AND DOWN LIKE A MAD THING

Panel 9: WHACK WHACK WHACK WHACK WHACK
WOW! THE ARMPIT-HEAT PRESSURE IS REACHING BURSTING POINT...
HISS
QUAKE
...RUN FOR IT!

Panel 10: BOOM!
EXTINCTION'S ALP NURSING HOME

Panel 11: YOU IDIOT, GILBERT — YOU'VE BLOWN UP MY LUCRATIVE NURSING HOME
I'LL TAKE THAT TELLY BACK, THANK YOU

Panel 12: SHORTLY
HELLO
LOOKS LIKE MR ROBINSON IS OFF TO POST HIS CHRISTMAS CARDS

Panel 13: THEY'RE NOT **JUST** CHRISTMAS CARDS, GILBERT...
EACH ONE CONTAINS OUR ANNUAL "ROBINSON FAMILY NEWSLETTER" WHICH REPORTS IN DETAIL EVERYTHING THAT'S HAPPENED IN THE ROBINSON HOUSEHOLD OVER THE PAST YEAR

Panel 14: HERE — READ ALL ABOUT JULIAN'S A-LEVEL RESULTS, AND LITTLE JOCASTA WINNING A ROSETTE AT HER PONY CLUB...
HELLO ALL!! WELL, WHAT A YEAR ITS BEEN FOR THE ROBINSON FAMILY!!! blah blah PROMOTION TO SENIOR MANAGER blah blah HOLIDAY IN PRAGUE blah blah LOFT CONVERSION blah blah HOME-MADE JAM blah blah
NOT TO MENTION THE LATEST UPDATE ON OUR LOVELY RENOVATED FARMHOUSE IN PROVENCE

Panel 15: PERHAPS YOU COULD INVENT A **POST-O-MATIC** TO HELP ME DELIVER THESE TO ALL MY FRIENDS AND RELATIONS
I'VE A BETTER IDEA, MR ROBINSON

Panel 16: MY **TELL-SOMEONE-WHO-CARES-O-MATIC** WILL AUTOMATICALLY STUFF YOUR POXY "FAMILY NEWSLETTERS" RIGHT UP YOUR FUCKING ARSEHOLE
STUFF! CRAM!
OH MY!

Panel 17: WE ARE MR ROBINSON'S FRIENDS AND RELATIONS, GILBERT, AND WE'D LIKE TO OFFER YOU A TOKEN OF OUR THANKS
HERE'S A LUXURY GIANT-SIZED DIGITAL WIDESCREEN TELLY

Panel 18: CHRISTMAS DAY..
...AND NOW ON CHANNEL 5, IT'S DENIS NORDEN'S FESTIVE HISTORY OF THIRD REICH BLOOPERS
TELLY CHRISTMAS, READERS!

Have Your Say!

The recent fiasco of the Paul Burrell trial and the Queen's last minute intervention has focused the public's attention on the Monarchy, and in particular their relationship to the judiciary. Should the Queen be above the law, or should she be treated as any other citizen? We went on the streets to find out what **YOU** think...

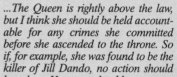

Regal illegal - HM the Queen on her way to work yesterday. But look! No seat belt - and the powerless police (circled) can only stand and watch.

...I think the Queen should have been called into the witness box to give her evidence just like anyone else, regardless of the constitutional implications. However, they should have made a special gold witness box with ermine trim, a red carpet and all diamonds stuck in the front.

William Malthus,
wine taster, London

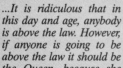

...It is ridiculous that in this day and age, anybody is above the law. However, if anyone is going to be above the law it should be the Queen, because she does a marvellous job and always has a smile for everybody. And she can't answer back.

Audrey Beech,
grandmother, Liverpool

Of course the queen should not be allowed to get away with any crime, except of course for the murder of suspected paedophiles. I for one would applaud her majesty for taking a firm hand with regard to these perverts.

George Kelly,
ferry captain, Derbyshire

...The Queen is above the law, and quite right too. I run an all-night garage, and if her Majesty chose to burst in at 3am with a sawn-off shotgun, trying to wrench the till of the counter and screaming at me to fill her bag with cigarettes, I would be deeply honoured.

Ernie Ludlow,
retailer, Bishop Stortford

...Of course the Queen must be immune from prosecution. Were she to be convicted of a crime and sent to prison, just think of the consequences. The thought of the likes of Rose West getting her common little hands on Her Majesty's vagina in the showers simply doesn't bear thinking about.

Edna Carstairs,
doll's hospital anesthetist, Hull

...I can't see what all the fuss is about. It's not as if she's a menace to the public. The only crimes Her Majesty commits are respectable ones, like shooting pheasants out of season, ignoring traffic lights in her gold coach and systematic tax evasion.

Trafford Lovething,
disc jockey, Manchester

...No one has a greater love and respect for Her majesty the Queen than me. She does a marvellous job, often in thankless circumstances whilst the carpers stand and criticise. However, the law is the law and everyone must obey it. I think she should be hanged and I for one would happily pull the bloody lever.

Alan Riot,
laughing gas fitter, Lancaster

...Once again, it's one law for the rich and one law for the rest of us. There's the Queen with £7 billion to her name, who will never spend a day behind bars in her life. On the other hand, just because my brother is unemployed, hasn't got a penny to his name and has murdered six women, he gets thirty years in Pentonville. It beggars belief.

Barry Heraclitus,
burglar's mate, London

...It would be absolutely pointless sending her to prison for any crime she committed. The prisons are like Buckingham Palace these days. You couldn't make it up. We're going to hell in a hand cart.

Richard Littlejohn,
rocket scientist, Wapping

...I was burgled two months ago. Everything was taken and excreta was smeared on the walls. The detective who came round to investigate told me that if Her majesty was responsible, the authorities would not be able to touch her. It turns my stomach whenever I see her on the telly with that smug grin on her face.

Mrs Dobson,
housewife, Nottingham

...The Queen should be allowed to commit any crime she likes. Prince Charles, however should only be allowed to commit crimes up to armed robbery and rape, whilst Princes William and Harry could do burglary and car theft. Minor Royals, like the Duke and Duchess of Kent could could steal items of small value from corner shops.

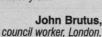

John Brutus,
council worker, London.

...The first principle of the British legislature is that the reigning Monarch is above the law. Therefore, were the Queen to make herself subject to the law like eveyone else, she would in fact be be *breaking it* and could expect to feel its full weight. However, luckily for her, being above it she would then get away scot free.

Joynson Taylor-Garret,
solicitor, London

...The Queen is rightly above the law, but I think she should be held accountable for any crimes she committed before she ascended to the throne. So if, for example, she was found to be the killer of Jill Dando, no action should be taken. However, should DNA tests show she had aided John Christie in his murder spree in the late forties, she should be brought to book.

Reg St. John Stevas,
dustman, Leeds

...The whole area is a minefield. What if the young Princess Elizabeth had stabbed her father in the chest? The precise moment at which he died, she would be guilty of his murder. And yet at the same moment she would have become Queen and therefore immune from prosecution. Does this mean that Prince Charles can now murder his own mother with impunity? If so, what kind of example is that to set to his children.

Frank Palance,
policeman, Goole

You only Clive Twice

Pretend OAP actor finally comes of age

EXCLUSIVE!

VETERAN ACTOR Clive Dunn was last night celebrating after finally reaching the age he has always pretended to be.

Dunn, 80, spent most of the seventies playing doddery octogenarian Corporal Jones in TV's Dad's Army, despite actually being only about 30 or something.

"In those days, if I wasn't on set I had to dress up like I was even younger than I actually was, wearing big collars and leather jackets just to prove I wasn't as old as I made out," he told reporters.

bother

"But now I am actually as old as I was only pretending to be then, I don't have to bother any more. It's great."

Dunn intends to spend his retirement in Portugal, being like what he only used to pretend to be, but for real.

jack

"It's a bit strange," he added. "Next year I'll have to dress up younger than I will be in order to look as old as I used to have to dress up older than I was to look, when I was younger." -*Reuters*

Dunn, yesterday, finally as old as he always pretended to be and (inset) as he was when he was pretending to be as old as he is now

SCHOOL SPANNER

SHIVERING IN CLASS IS AGAINST SCHOOL RULES! STOP THAT AT ONCE OR YOU'LL GO BLIND!

WE CAN'T HELP IT, SIR. THE RADIATOR IS BROKEN AND WE'RE COLD.

ISN'T THERE ANYTHING YOU CAN DO, MR. CARETAKER?

I'M AFRAID NOT, TEACHER. THAT RADIATOR IS OF PRE-BRITISH STANDARD MANUFACTURE. I HAVE NO TOOLS SUITABLE FOR ITS SPECIFICATIONS.

HANG ON, SIR! YOU'RE FORGETTING I'M THE SCHOOL SPANNER!

ER, I FAIL TO SEE THE RELEVANCE OF THAT, JENKINS.

I CAN GRIP THE TROUBLESOME BOLT WITH MY TEETH! MY MOUTH IS ADJUSTABLE FOR ALL PLUMBING WORK AND RELATED MAINTAINANCE.

I DON'T THINK THAT WILL BE A GOOD IDEA, JENKINS.

Nnghh

CRRK

JEESUS!

HOORAY! THE RADIATOR IS WARMING UP NICELY

TRUE TO YOUR WORD, JENKINS, YOUR ADJUSTABLE JAW WAS JUST RIGHT FOR SUCH A NON-UNIVERSAL FITTING.

NNH...MY PLEATHURE.

LATER...

TCH. MY CAR WON'T START! IF I'M NOT HOME AT THE USUAL TIME, MRS. TEACHER WILL ASSUME I'M HAVING AN AFFAIR AND DIVORCE PROCEEDINGS MAY COMMENCE!

PERHAPS I CAN BE OF ASSISTANCE, SIR?

TANG! TANG! TANG! TANG!

PLEASE REMEMBER I'M A SPANNER, NOT A HAMMER, SIR.

NNNNGH!... GUST A GOOSE GONNECTION...

CRUNCH!

TWIST!

...GAT'S GOT IT, GIR!

EXCELLENT WORK, JENKINS! YOU'VE SAVED MY MARRIAGE. HOWEVER CAN I REPAY YOU?

UM... I THINK I MIGHT NEED A DENTIST FAIRLY SHARPLY, SIR. ANY CHANCE OF A LIFT?

NO. FUCK OFF.

VROOOM!

POOR SPANNER. USED AND ABUSED BY HIS CLASSMATES AND TEACHER AND NOW HE HAS TO WALK HOME TO BOOT!

READER'S VOICE ↑

HO-HO! DON'T FEEL TOO SORRY FOR ME, READERS!

...I'VE GOT A LIFT HOME ON THE SCHOOL BIKE!

VIZ 115 ©LEW STRINGER 2002

Starts THIS WEEK... The Eddie George Story — Part 1 – The Early Years

London, 11th September 1938...

Congratulations, Mrs George. It's a boy!

I'll call him Sir Edward.

Goo! Goo!

At school, Eddie wasn't interested in music...

You've missed your guitar solo again, George! Pay attention, boy, or you'll never grow up to be in a band!

Sorry, Sir!

Ha! Ha!

But Eddie had other dreams...

I don't *want* to be in a band. Pop music is *boring*!...

I want to be *Deputy Chief Cashier* of the *Bank of England*

30 years later, that dream came true...

Bring me the quarterly audit returns for the gross domestic product of the minimum lending rate please, Miss Pondicherry.

Yes, Mr George

And turn up the exchange rate mechanism up a quarter of one percent, will you?

DEPT. OF CASHIER EDDIE GEORGE

Hey! The Bank of England *ROCKS*! This job is *DA BOMB*!

Don't miss part 2 - Eddie becomes Assistant Director of the bank's Gilt Edge Division!

CHRISTMAS IN OTHER LANDS

South America

There is one Christmas tradition that all mums would be happy to forego - *that's washing up the plates after dinner!* But for the inhabitants of the Amazonian rain forest, dirty dishes are not on the Yuletide agenda. That's because the local tribespeople have their own plates surgically inserted into their lower lips during infancy for religious or possibly decorative reasons. So after dinner, it's a simple matter of sitting back with the rest of the family and enjoying the Christmas film.

Japan

Children in Japan receive far smaller presents than their lucky English counterparts. That's because only the tiniest parcels can fit under the traditional bonsai Christmas tree. But woe betide any child who is not sufficiently grateful for their diminutive gift. Failure to write a Thank You note to the Japanese Santa Claus - who is believed to be a 2 inch tall bleeping electronic elf - is an unpardonable sin which must be paid for by committing ritual suicide on Boxing Day.

Tibet

For the Buddhist monks who inhabit the Himalayan mountains of Tibet, Christmas carol singing is a rather subdued affair. Their strict monastic vow of silence means they are forbidden from uttering a single sound. But if you think noiseless carol singing is tricky, their after dinner game of charades is made doubly difficult!

United States

The American state of Texas executes hundreds of criminals every day, and Christmas Day is no exception. However, the guards try to make it a special day for the condemned men, trimming 'Old Sparky' with tinsel and fairy lights, and even pulling a cracker with the prisoners before pulling the lever.

Next month ~ January in Other Lands

FLASH HARRY IN THE 21st CENTURY

FLASH HARRY, TRAVERSING THE GALAXY, SEEKING OUT NEW CIVILIZATIONS AND EXPOSING HIS GENITALS TO THEM, HAS LANDED ON THE PLANET KRYPTOBELLIS III...

IT'S ONE SMALL STEP FOR MAN...ONE GIANT EYEFUL FOR SOME KRYPTOBELLIS III BIRD

AH! HERE'S ONE NOW... WATCH ME GIVE HER THE FRIGHT OF HER LIFE!..

...AN' IT'LL REALLY TURN ME ON

'ERE, LOVE... WAHAY! HMM!?

FLIP!

EH!.. AREN'T YOU SHOCKED? SHOCKED? WHY? YOU'RE OBVIOUSLY A STRANGER TO KRYPTOBELLIS III... BUT... 'ERE...

...IS THIS MAN BOTHERING YOU, MISS?

Bungle in the Jungle

DOCTORS at a North hospital were left red-faced last night after a woman complained of bowel pains following surgery. For X-rays showed that the careless quacks had left a FIVE FOOT NURSE inside the woman during her operation!

Gladys Jungle underwent surgery for womens things at St. Malcom's Hospital, York in November 2000. "I came home after four days, and everything was just fine," she told us.

"Then in the December I started to get thumping pains in my side. The doctor said it was my biological clock ticking, and just to take some aspirins."

quality street

The aspirins worked for a while but by Christmas it was worse than ever, and on Boxing Day, Gladys, 62, was rushed back to hospital by her husband.

"This time they told me I'd eaten too much Quality Streets, and it was probably indigestion. In the new year, I went to see my GP, but he told me to stop wasting his time."

roses

Gladys continued to suffer in silence through the New Year, until in December last year, the pain became unbearable.

"I wanted to get it sorted once and for all," she said. "I'd had a little win on the Bingo so I decided to go private."

celebrations

At the private hospital in Fulford, a proctological examination was carried out under anaesthetic.

"Everything looked normal," said Dr. Ashtar Iqbal, the consultant in charge. "I was just about to withdraw the probe when I thought I saw someone waving frantically from behind the patient's liver."

Jungle - hospital bungle led to nurse in bowels

Gladys was taken to X-ray where stunned colleagues confirmed the diagnosis.

"Surgeons leave things inside patients all the time, but they're usually pretty small things, like scalpels, watches or mobile phones. I've never heard of a whole nurse being left in before," Dr Iqbal said.

The misplaced nurse was removed in an operation lasting four hours, and Gladys was allowed home a week later.

miniature heroes

Ironically, it was later discovered that an anaesthetist had been left inside Mrs. Jungle during the operation to remove the nurse.

"It's a disgrace. His muffled shouting and carrying on keeps me awake all night," she said yesterday. "I've got no money to go private, and I'm on a three year waiting list to have him out."

giant haystacks

The Hospital's Chief Administrator was unavailable for comment. "He's being removed from 53-year-old heart bypass patient at the moment," a spokesman said.

MY HEARTBEAT HELL!

"Seek thrills OR DIE!"

-Docs' stark warning to speed demon Damon

EX-FORMULA ONE champion Damon Hill today revealed his biggest fear since quitting the sport: *"Without thrills I'm a dead man."*

In 1997 Hill was at the top of the F1 tree. Every day brought him his fix of excitement behind the wheel of a 200mph racing car. But ironically, it's only since his retirement from the world's most dangerous sport that Hill has really begun to fear for his life.

In his new book, 'Thrillseeker - The Damon Hill Story' (*Cheese on Toast Books, £19.99*), he tells how a high-octane F1 career has left him a helpless adrenalin junkie. And without the excitement his body craves, he fears his pulse rate may drop to zero and he will die.

I remember driving my last Grand Prix for Jordan in 1999, a pretty exciting race. Afterwards, I went back to my home in Dublin and sat down in the front room with my wife Georgie to do a crossword puzzle.

"I'd done about half the clues when everything went black. The next thing I remember, I was waking up in the intensive care unit of my local hospital.

pulse

"Apparently, the lack of excitement in just sitting at home had caused my pulse rate to plummet to the point where my heart stopped. The doctors had managed to get it started again, but they told me I was lucky to be alive. Next time I might not be so lucky. That's when I realised that without a constant rush of adrenalin, I was a dead man".

After his brush with death, Hill faced a choice. If he wanted to stay alive he had to drastically change his lifestyle.

"Even something as simple as drinking a cup of tea could be so mundane as to plunge me into a coma. Every time I fancy a cup now, my wife makes twenty and laces one of them with deadly poison. The thrill of knowing that I have a 1 in 20 chance of dying each time I have a cuppa is just enough to keep my heart from stopping.

"For most people, a trip to the garden centre is a relaxing way to spend a Sunday afternoon, but for me it could literally be a death sentence. When we go these days, Georgie takes the kids in the car, whilst I fire myself out of an enormous cannon and meet her there. It may sound extreme, but it's the only way I can shop for bedding plants and stay alive.

fruits

"My condition has made it very difficult for the whole family to share the fruits of my success. For instance, we have a swimming pool in the garden which the kids used to love to play in. But now they won't go anywhere near it. I've had to put ravenous crocodiles in it because simply splashing about on a lilo could prove fatally humdrum for an adrenalin

> ## "Every time I fancy a cuppa, my wife makes twenty and laces one of them with deadly poison"

junkie like me. The only way I can enjoy a relaxing swim is to be chased up and down with the imminent threat of being torn limb from limb by giant reptiles."

The hours of darkness offer no respite for thrill-dependent Hill. An uneventful forty winks could proove lethal, and so the former F1 champion has to go to extreme lengths to maintain a pulse until the morning.

"Like everyone I need sleep, but unlike everyone else, mine has to be action-packed. So these days I sleep in an enormous centrifuge. The G-forces recreate the sensations of driving round an F1 race track and that keeps my heart going. My wife Georgie is very understanding. She finds it difficult to get to sleep whilst being subjected to such huge centrifugal forces, but she knows that if I had anything less than 6G for the full 8 hours, I might not wake up at all."

sulphured apricots

In his book, Hill doesn't pretend that life is easy, and he openly admits that things have changed.

"I don't pretend that life is easy, and I openly admit that things have changed. Even collecting the post in the morning has turned into a dice with death. When I tread on the top step, a mechanism is triggered which releases a 10-ton stone ball from the attic which chases me down the stairs. I usually grab the post off the mat with a fraction of a second to spare before diving into the kitchen for my breakfast."

But despite his affliction, Hill is determined that he is going to live as normal a life as possible.

"It would be so easy for me to just throw in the towel and spend all day lying in my centrifuge. But that's not my style. I think it's important that I do all the things with my family that any normal person would do, although obviously I can't risk letting the excitement levels drop. For instance, I make a point of doing the weekly shop at Asda, but I have my own special shopping trolley. It's got an atom bomb underneath and it's wired up to explode if my speed drops below 20 mph. It may sound risky, but if it keeps my pulse rate high enough to get me to the checkout alive, then that's fine by me."

Damon Hill will be signing copies of his book whilst strapped to the wing of a pilotless 1922 Tiger Moth plummeting towards a tank of man-eating tiger sharks at Borders Books, Charing Cross Road on 15th September from 10.30am.

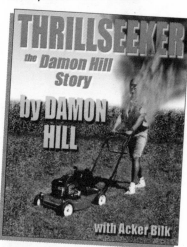

THRILLSEEKER the Damon Hill Story **by DAMON HILL**

with Acker Bilk

Extracts from 'Thrillseeker - the Damon Hill Story' © Damon Hill & Acker Bilk

Next Week: The Hit Men and Hill - *"The Ninja Assassins who attack me while I'm on the toilet... and I pick up the tab!"*

BILLY NO MATES

BILLY HAS THROWN AWAY HIS PORNOGRAPHY IN AN ACT OF TEEN ANGST MADNESS...

MMNOORAH! WHAT HAVE I DONE? WE'VE GOT A SCHOOL TRIP TO A CHURCH TODAY AND I NEED A **WANK**!!

...ANYTHING WILL DO - A SWIMWEAR CATALOGUE, A CATWALK FASHION MAGAZINE ARTICLE - ...**ANYTHING!**

BUGGER! ALL I CAN FIND ARE THESE PHOTOS FROM MY GRANS 95th BIRTHDAY...

oh god...

KEEP OUT

BILLYS ROOM

NO NOBODY EVER

THWAK! THWAK! THWAK! THWAK! SPLOOGE!

...oh GOD...

TOTAL UTTER GUILT

...AND THIS CLASS, IS THE CONFESSION BOX, WHERE GUILTY PEOPLE CAN BE FORGIVEN FOR THEIR SINS FOR GIVING THE PRIEST A BIT OF DINNER TABLE CONVERSATION...

AND OOH **LOOK**- CLOISTERS!!

HELLO MY SON

ERM... HI... I, ERM... WELL, ER, HAD AN, ERM...WELL, YOU SEE, I DIDN'T HAVE ANY MAGAZINES TO ERM... YOU KNOW...

YES..?

...WHAT'S THIS..?

ERM.. WELL, I... OOH... COR! LOOK AT **THEM**!!

I'M SORRY?

PHWOOAR!

KIDS ILLUSTRATED **BIBLE** THE GARDEN OF EDEN

THWAP! THWAP! THWAP!

THWAP! THWAP! THWAP! THWAP!

ERM, HELLO..?

...WHATS GOING ON?

AND HERE IS THE CONFESSION BOX AGAIN...

THWAP! THWAP! THWAP! THWAP!

HA HA HAAAA!

SWING!

HO HO HOOOOO!!

NEEUGHH!! MAKE IT STOP! I WISH IT WOULD ALL JUST **END**!!

MM -NUGHN!!

SHORTLY... THIS SHOULD MAKE SURE IT NEVER HAPPENS AGAIN...

:CROAK!:

HELLO BILLY.

EH?!

WHAT?

WELCOME TO **HELL**

MMNOORAH!

I'M AFRAID YOU WILL BE CAUGHT TRAGICALLY WANKING WITH YOUR PANTS ROUND YOUR ANKLES BY LAUGHING GIRLS...

...FOR THE **REST** OF ETERNITY!

NOOOOOOO!!

THWAP! THWAP! THWAP! THWAP!

YES. AND

Letterbocks

It's the letters page that's been undressed by kings, and seen some things that a letters page ain't supposed to see.

Letterbocks, Viz Comic, PO Box 1PT, Newcastle-upon-Tyne, NE99 1PT.

E-mail letters@viz.co.uk

I'M NOT a racist or a homophobe. But the thought of being held down and buggered by some big black bloke puts me right off going to any of these so-called Caribbean countries for my holidays.
*J. Johnson
Durham*

RIBENA Toothkind, my arse. I recently lost a crown trying to get the plastic straw off the carton.
*Jon
Weston*

THEY SAY that those who live by the sword will die by the sword. What nonsense. I'm a blacksmith specializing in period weaponry, and I've just been diagnosed with terminal cancer of the throat.
*M. Plywood
Yorkshire*

WHEN MY grandad died, everyone said that that his little dog Paddy, a faithful companion for 14 years, would die of a broken heart. But they were all wrong, as we had him put down the day after the funeral.
*T. Walker
London*

WHOEVER says what goes up, must come down has clearly never stuck a milk bottle up their arse.
*P. Purvis
London*

I SEE many people have approached the newspapers to attest that Michael Barrymore is actually a strong swimmer despite his claims to the contrary during the hearing into the death of Stewart Lubbock. However, the papers themselves have been less than truthful all along, constantly referring to Barrymore as a 'TV funnyman' and 'entertainer'.
*Martin Daulby
e-mail*

IT HAS recently occurred to me that the reason vaguely spooky Vision On artist Tony Hart could never return the pictures we sent into the gallery, was that they were covered in spunk. Of course, I may be wrong, but in the current climate there is no room for complacency.
*N. Lowson
Wood Green*

HAS ANYONE ever noticed that you never see a ginger couple. If these Tamworths don't fancy each other, how can they expect us normal people to shag them?
*Snowbeast
e-mail*

I WAS disgusted to see my next door neighbour's girlfriend posing naked in this month's Men Only. I know for a fact that they are not married and there she was displaying herself in the Readers' Wives section. Have these people no shame, lying to magazines in order to make money.
*H. Corrs
Nottingham*

AS AN American citizen, I am both shocked and outraged that Germany's Justice Minister, Herter Daeubler-Gmelin, has compared US President George W Bush to Adolf Hitler. Any fool can tell you Hitler had a moustache.
*T. King
New Hampshire, USA*

I HAVE fallen off a ladder in the last three years and injured myself. Does anyone know of an organisation which deals with personal injury compensation? It would be good to know that there was a team of experienced solicitors dedicated to my case (and to know that they have helped thousands of people like me). Perhaps they could work on a no win/no fee basis?
*D.J.A.
Cleveleys*

WHY IS it that on the advert for bingo, all the women playing are young, half-decent looking girls, rather than the motley crew of old bags that really turn up?
*T. Hooper
Wales*

THE WAY he prances about, anyone would think that Elton John was a puff.
*J. Izzi
e-mail*

PLEASE publish more pictures and stories of lovely animals like Sultan the skateboarding horse. We need them to gladden our hearts in these distressing times.
*Jean Smith
Cambridge*

I SAW Lloyd Grossman in the Playhouse in Newcastle the other day. Inexplicably, no violence ensued, even though I said "Look! There's that cunt Lloyd Grossman" very loudly as he walked past.
*Rob Smith
e-mail*

MY GIRLFRIEND has just dumped me. She wrote saying she "had to really leave because a no-good-fucking-smartarse-scumbag-wanker wasn't someone to spend a life with". Do you think I should mention that she has split an infinitive AND ended a sentence with a preposition when I write begging her to stay with me? Or should I correct her later?
*Darren Anderson
Thornton-Cleveleys*

ON THE 11th September last year, I moved into a flat with my girlfriend and, knowing full well I would be expected to remember the anniversary of us moving in together, I was racking my brains to think of a way to remember the date. Imagine my relief when I finally got the TV wired up in our new living room and saw the tragic events unfolding in New York, on a day that none of us will ever forget for many years to come.
*Dave Willis
e-mail*

I'M ALL for change and progress, but was in two minds about whether we should adopt the Euro until I heard that each country was allowed to produce their own. Now I'm all for it, as it will allow us to join a united Europe whilst retaining our own Queen's head on the currency. It also means that we can easily identify the notes and coins produced in other EU countries and refuse to accept them in our shops.
*J. Butler
Derby*

MARTIN Brundle sang the praises of the 16 strong Ferrari pit crew during the Italian Grand Prix last week after they changed Michael Schumacher's tyres in 8.4 seconds. That's nothing. I stopped at some lights for 5 seconds in the centre of Liverpool last week, and some kids had my

GO P FOR A CUP OF TEA? I ASK YOU... WELL I'M NOT PAYING THAT!

THIS BOY SURE PLAYS A MEAN GUITAR

hub caps, wing mirrors, radio and my briefcase out the boot. And there was only 3 of the bastards.

Bill Moss
e-mail

COULD YOU please say something nice about Milwall Football Club? The national press seem to have it in for us, and so it would be nice to read something positive for a change.

Neil Andrews
The New Den

* Not off hand, Neil, but we'll open it up to the Viz readers. Can you think of something nice to say about Milwall Football Club? Write to us at the usual address, marking your envelope 'I've Thought of Something Nice to Say About Milwall FC'. There's half a brick, a broken bottle and a Stanley knife for the writer of the nicest letter.

HATS OFF to Sir Alex Ferguson who treated the false accusations of sexual harassment against him with the contempt they deserved. He showed that if you are innocent of a crime, then you have absolutely nothing whatsoever to worry about.

Barry George
Belmarsh Prison

WHILST recently employed as a temporary toilet cleaner at the extremely swanky Law Society Rooms in London, I took the opportunity to write 'Wanky Shit' in permanent marker on the back of one of the cubicle doors, accompanied by a crude picture of a penis ejaculating over a large pair of breasts. I'm not proud of what I did, but I wonder if any other readers have defaced the palaces of the mighty with this sort of puerile, adolescent graffiti.

James Richardson
e-mail

I HAVE a mate who swears he gave Tara Palmer-Tomkinson one behind the back of a gazebo at one of the Duchess of Kent's housewarming parties in the pissing rain. He is so adamant that it happened that I'm sure he wouldn't mind me sharing this information with the readers. The fact that he lets my neighbour's dog lick Marmite off his nob may lead some people to question the credibility of his claim, but I know him personally and believe him to be telling the truth.

S. Kemp
e-mail

I THINK it's marvellous that we see so many women bus drivers these days. It's about time that women were given the opportunity to show that they can perform perfectly well in what were previously thought of as male only jobs. Good on 'em and more power to their elbow, I say. Mind you, I'm glad they only let them out in the little 25 seat cityhoppers. I wouldn't fancy being near one behind the wheel of a double decker when she's trying to back it into the depot.

J. Lightfoot
Newcastle

I WAS surprised to learn the other day that comedian Richard Blackwood is the half-brother of supermodel Naomi Campbell. It must be quite unusual to have two such multitalentless people in the same family.

A. Sommers
Carlisle

I WONDER what a dog's shits would be like if all it ate were four big bags of Cheesy Nachos popcorn per day. If any readers have a dog and would like to find out, could they please let me know what happens. I have got a dog myself, but it's not the kind of experiment I want to embark upon.

M. Hepple
Luton

I RECENTLY saw flabby faced politician and famous spitter Roy Hattersley cleaning up after his dog. Has anyone else seen a famous person shovelling pet crap?

J.P.
Burnley

TOP TIPS

WIVES. If your husband is pestering you for a hand job and you can't be bothered, simply sit on your hand for ten minutes until it goes dead, and it will feel like someone else is doing it.

F. Muir, London

MARS BAR fans. Buy a Snickers bar and pick out the peanuts. Hey presto, a Mars bar and a handful of peanuts, all for the price of a Snickers.

Tim Woods, e-mail

MIDGETS. Draw less attention to your disability by dressing up in children's clothes and passing yourself off as a toddler.

Madeleine McDonald,
Edinburgh

SWISS people. Claim neutrality during the next world war so as you can hoard Nazi loot and pilfer Jewish gold.

Barney Waygood, Edinburgh

HOUSEWIVES. Look in the dictionary to find the difference between the words 'need' and 'want', then carefully choose the right one to use when talking about buying new dresses.

Eggman, e-mail

BANGKOK holiday makers. Avoid confusion and potential embarrassment by never banging a woman with a hairier arse than yourself.

Mark Bruce, e-mail

FOOL potential car thieves into thinking there is a large dog in your parked vehicle by leaving the windows slightly open.

George Thrakes,
Chester-Le-Street

OLD people. Attach a sweeping brush to the front of your mobility trolley. Now, instead of being a menace on the pavements, you can provide a valuable service to your community.

Ben Reeves, Hove

PROSTITUTES. If selling your body for sex makes you feel cheap, then simply raise your prices.

Tony Fisher, Ipswich

HUSBANDS. get your wife to swallow your spunk by simply wanking into the milk before making her a cup of tea.

Michael Smyth, e-mail

JINX thieves by fitting mirrored glass to your house and car. When a thief breaks a window, Hey Presto! - seven years bad luck.

John Hymns, Macclesfield

GIVE your office that fabric shop feel by pushing all the desks together and fixing rulers along one edge with blu-tac.

Superjohn, e-mail

MAKE your postman's day by opening the door as he comes up the path and saying "If there are any bills you can take them back. Ha! Ha! Ha!"

Stu Perry (Postman), Isle of Man

E-mail toptips@viz.co.uk

* We've had a bulging mailbag on the subject of whether or not Joanna Lumley has got a plastic arse, though significantly enough, none from Ms Lumley herself. Perhaps she simply feels it beneath her to write and deny such rumours, or perhaps there is a more sinister reason for her silence. Here are a few of the letters we received.

...A FRIEND of mine who was a make-up artist and trainee cameraman at various places told me that, apparently, she had so much anal sex that her poor backside gave up the ghost, and she had to have extensive reconstruction under the pretence that she was away at a health resort, type of thing. It sounds unlikely to me as, unless something the size of a marrow was employed, regular bumsex would not wreck the arse quite so drastically.

K. Whyjelly
Lincolnshire

...I HEARD this story about 5 years ago at a dinner party in Hampstead. What the previous writer says is apparently the case, that Joanna has a valve, rather than a sphincter. This results in her needing special equipment before she can drop a log. I also heard that her husband did not know of this until after they were married, which I suppose means they didn't have bumsex before marriage. Of course, it might all just be rumour, but the man who told me seemed to speak with great authority.

I. Wilson
e-mail

...I DON'T know whether it's true or not, but why don't the BBC commission Donal McKintyre to go undercover in their ladies' bogs to expose the truth. Let's face it, it's got to be more exciting than his last series.

T. Kelly
Hull

...APPARENTLY, I've heard (*The rest of this letter has been omitted on legal advice.*)

J. Giles
Hampstead

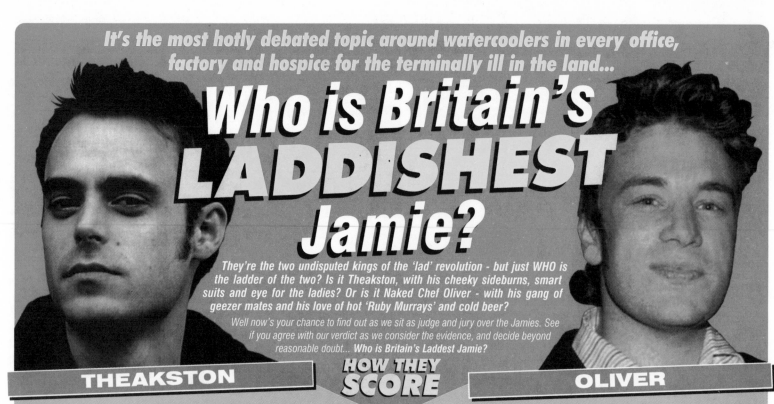

It's the most hotly debated topic around watercoolers in every office, factory and hospice for the terminally ill in the land...

Who is Britain's LADDISHEST Jamie?

They're the two undisputed kings of the 'lad' revolution - but just WHO is the ladder of the two? Is it Theakston, with his cheeky sideburns, smart suits and eye for the ladies? Or is it Naked Chef Oliver - with his gang of geezer mates and his love of hot 'Ruby Murrays' and cold beer?

Well now's your chance to find out as we sit as judge and jury over the Jamies. See if you agree with our verdict as we consider the evidence, and decide beyond reasonable doubt... Who is Britain's Laddest Jamie?

THEAKSTON | HOW THEY SCORE | OLIVER

The Birds — 7 / 7

Love 'em and leave 'em Theakston has been romantically linked to a bevy of beautiful beaver. Hardly a day goes by when he doesn't appear in the paper at a glitzy premiere with some classy piece on his arm. English rose Joely Richardson, yodelling wrist-slasher Mariah Carey and her out of All Saints are just three of the lairy Priory presenter's past girlfriends. However, with none of his conquests successfully impregnated, a question mark must still hang over this laddie's taddies.

Bossy wife Jules has doormat Jamie firmly under her thumb. Bounced into an early marriage after splitting his first and only kipper, the cockney pot-jiggler has never had the chance to sow his wild oats, unlike the fanny ferrets who he pays to be his mates in the adverts. Instead of being linked with a string of glamorous girlfriends, Jamie's been stuck in the kitchen, frying up a string of sausages for his pregnant potboiler missus.

Transport — 9 / 3

Theakston's chosen vehicle leaves Oliver in its wake... quite literally! That's because the Top of the Pops six-footer gets from A to B in a sleek formula one powerboat. Travelling at speeds up to and in excess of 200 mph, getting top marks in this round is plain sailing for laddish Theakston, especially since he's probably got several open-topped sports cars as well. And a helicopter.

If you saw Oliver strolling round Tesco's scoffing olives out of his shiny black open-face motorcycle helmet, you'd be forgiven for thinking that he rode a powerful sports motorbike, such as a Ducati 996 or a Suzuki Hayabusa. But you'd be wrong. The monkey-faced loudmouth loses lad points thanks to his choice of a pastel blue woman's scooter, which could be burnt off at the lights by Stephen Hawking.

Cocknality — 5 / 8

It's hard to imagine public school-educated Home Counties boy Theakston stuck halfway up a chimney whilst his dad sticks pins in his feet. And with his upper class accent he'd find difficulty discussing jellied eels and the Krays with a pearly King. Down at the Old Bull and Bush.

Cockney lads don't come born any more through and througher than chirpy fuckgob Oliver. With his string of cheeky catchphrases, including "pukka", "sorted", "lovely jubbly" and "you plonker, Rodney", he's as Londonish as the roast beef and Yorkshire pudding that he cooks.

Rock and Roll — 6 / 8

The closest former auctioneer Theakston gets to a rock'n'roll lifestyle is presenting Top of the Pops once a week. But basking in the reflected second-hand laddishness of real rockers such as Liam Gallagher, Robbie Williams and H who was out of Steps is a poor imitation of the real thing, and Jamie makes a poor showing in this round.

If cooking is the new rock'n'roll, then rock'n'roll is the new cooking. And rock'n'roll cook Jamie's no exception to the rule. Every night Oliver twists off his apron and swaps his chicken drumsticks for some wooden ones, keeping the rhythm in his very own group! Whether he's beating drums or eggs, he's number one in the chef AND pop charts all year round.

Lack of Domestication — 9 / 5

Real lad Theakston's probably got no time for poncing around with a feather duster and a tin of shake 'n' vac. You putatively couldn't eat your dinner off his plates, let alone the floor. His hoover may be clogged with pizza boxes, birds' knickers and spent johnnies, and the pan of his shitter could well look like the starting line at Brand's Hatch. Such top untidiness earns blokeish Jamie a tidy score and he cleans up in this round.

You could eat your dinner off the floor of this Jamie's house, and it'd be an 8-course dinner he'd cooked himself like some sort of girl. As Oliver's army of viewers know, he keeps his fashionable penthouse mews loft conversion so spick and span it sometimes looks more like some expensive television studio set than a real lad's home. A flat performance in this round.

Drinking — 7 / 8

A bar-room kicking for Theakston in this round. Although he doesn't mind a drink, it's always fine wines for connoisseur Jamie. More at home in a posh gentleman's club than a spit & sawdust pub, quilted silk dressing gowned Theakston's always happiest ensconced in a leather armchair, sniffing snootily at a balloon of vintage port costing upwards of £10 a bottle.

Oliver is rarely seen without a bottle of his favourite designer lager in his hand. He even appeared in one Safeway advert with a stinking hangover after spending the previous night down the "rub-a-dub" with his "chinas". As a naked chef, he may know a thing or two about fine wines, but good old British Budweiser is this lad's tipple of choice.

Going with Pros — 10 / 5

Last Christmas, a pissed-up Theakston put his money where HER mouth was when he treated himself to a forty quid romp with a whore. He may have been too drunk to stand up, but his gut stick was certainly Live and Kicking. And not only did he pose for saucy suck-off snaps in the fashionable London bondage brothel, but he then proudly boasted of his red-blooded exploits to a Sunday newspaper. Uberlad Theakston tops this round with maximum points.

At eight months pregnant, Jules's jewels may well be out of bounds to husband Jamie. But we know from the Tesco advert that he is not averse to going behind his wife's back, nipping to his mum's for a curry whilst pretending to buy lightbulbs. So it would be no surprise to see his trademark scooter parked up outside a backstreet brothel whilst he gets his helmet polished inside. However, there is no evidence to suggest he uses prostitutes, so it's only half marks in this round.

Tongue Girth — 0 / 10

Oh dear! With his pathetic, normal sized tongue, Theakston loses marks in the final round.

Top marks for this Jamie who, looking like he's trying to spit out a pound of liver whenever he speaks, has Theakston well and truly licked.

THE VERDICT — 53 / 54

Mockney toff Theakston gets the bitter taste of defeat after a pitiful showing leaves him bottom of the lad pops.

When it comes to being Jamie the lad, Oliver's got all the old ingredients of a luvverly jubberly recipe for success.

Sorted!

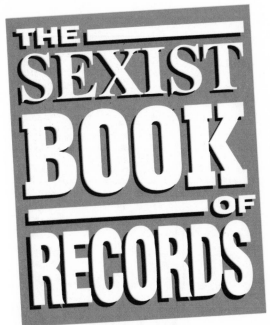

THE SEXIST BOOK OF RECORDS

The World of Women

Motorway driving

Least successful journey

On April 16th 1994, Mrs Enid Maelstrom of Nottingham (GB) set out in her car to visit her sister Martha in nearby Clifton, a journey of 6 miles. Intending to join the M1 at junction 26, she sat at the end of the sliproad looking anxiously over her shoulder for an opportunity to join the carriageway for 7hours 32minutes 14seconds. During her mammoth wait, Mrs Maelstrom stalled the car 196 times and burst into tears 14 times. Nottinghamshire Police CCTV footage later showed that at least 654 other road users had flashed their headlamps and slowed down to assist her manoeuvre, all to no avail. Her ordeal only came to an end when she reversed up the sliproad, causing a coach to swerve down a banking, killing eighteen.

The Human World

Longest middle lane journey

The furthest distance a woman has ever driven exclusively in the middle lane of a motorway is 449miles *723km* in the case of trainee teacher Lucy Stone (GB) on a journey from Exeter to Glasgow on August 6th 1999. Joining the M5 at junction 31, she took up her position in the middle lane and, driving at a steady 40mph, remained there blissfully oblivious to traffic conditions, until she left at junction 15 of the M8 over 13 hours later. The wheels of her Ford Fiesta only strayed onto the tarmac of the slow lane on four occasions; once at the start of her trip, once at the end, and twice when she swerved on and off the road in order to refuel at Sandbach services. Had Miss Stone ventured to look out of her side windows at any point in her odyssey, she would have seen an estimated 10,000 vehicles pass her in the outside lane, 3,000 on the inside lane, and a 15 foot wide Bessemer Converter with police motorcycle outriders which was forced onto the hard shoulder to get past her near Penrith.

Hair

Most negligibly different haircut

Gladys Taupin from Nottingham (GB) holds the record for the most negligibly different haircut. Every Wednesday afternoon from October 1978 until her death in September 1999, Gladys visited Michael's Ladies Hairdressers in Clifton, Nottingham with her friend Dolly. After paying for a shampoo and set, and sitting under a drier with plastic shells over her ears, she would leave the shop with her helmet of tight, white curls exactly the same as when she entered. Her husband, Harold, was required to say that each of the indistinguishable hair-dos was lovely. He later estimated that he had complimented her on her hair on 682 occasions, despite being unable to discern a single hair's difference.

Largest cost/effect discrepancy

On June 14th, 2002, after reading Women's Hair magazine, Tracey Hatfield from Hertfordshire (GB) decided to 'do something' with her hair. Entering Zizzors Hair Design, Windsor, she handed a picture clipped from the magazine to the chief stylist Zohzie. She was shampooed, wet-combed and styled for 7 hours at a cost of £862.97. Two of her friends commented favourably on her new style, whilst her husband Terry didn't notice.

The World of Teenagers

Miscellaneous

Ponytail tension

In November 2001 it was reported that a ponytail belonging to Donna-Marie Bell of Ashington, Northumberland (GB) was exerting a force of 2.5 kilonewtons on her scalp. The ponytail, which was 8.5cm *3.5ins* long, was achieved by folding over a single standard scrunchie 18 times. Whilst the scrunchie was in place, Miss Bell's ears and nose migrated around 5cm up her face, giving her an appearance which has been likened to someone sneaking up behind Zsa Zsa Gabor and letting off a klaxon. It has been estimated that having such a ponytail would be same as hanging a long wheelbase landrover from your hair.

Least erotic masturbatory material

Whilst staying at his grandmother's house in Carlisle (GB), 14-year-old Scott Beale found himself alone, and decided to look for erotica to assist him in a putative masturbation session. A search of the house elicited nothing remotely pornographic, and Scott eventually found himself in the lavatory with an open copy of the Radio Times, abusing himself over a two inch black and white photograph of Radio 4 Midweek presenter Libby Purves. Notwithstanding his predicament, Beale managed to ejaculate over the image after just 45 seconds, a mere 30 seconds longer than usual.

Purves • last ditch choice for Beale

THE SEXIST TIMES

PHWOOOOAR! World scaffold leering record comes home!

A Dagenham bricklayer yesterday brought the World record for leering at women from a scaffold back to Britain.

Terry Bartram, 38, jeered offensively at 3787 women from his building site scaffold overlooking Cheltenham High Street.

suggestions

This included shouting sexual suggestions to 2302, thrusting his hips forwards whilst pulling his fists back at 1079, requesting 458 to get their tits out, wolfwhilstling at 326, calling 172 a dirty cow and offering 26 the opportunity go up there and suck his big cock.

Father of two Terry was jubilant. "I just went for it', he told us. "I lost count of how many birds I'd verbally abused after ten minutes. Luckily someone was keeping tally."

The record attempt started when Terry clocked on at 8.27 am, and finished when Bartram clocked off at 9.15 pm after putting in four hours of overtime.

overtime

The record averages out to one jeer every twelve seconds throughout the entire shift. However, Terry peaked at 4.25pm when a local sixth form college turned out and he barked like a dog at 508 women in a single 6 minute period. During the course of the day he laid a grand total of two bricks.

Bartram - jubilant

15th Nov 2002

THE CRITICS

Panel 1: Natasha! Crispin! So glad you could come in to have a chat about our new project.

No problem, Liz... Only too pleased to do our bit for Public Service Broadcasting.

Panel 2: After all, where would the nation's cultural life be without the BBC?

Who else could stand up against the endless stream of mindless pap served up by ITV?

Ah, now you've hit the nail on the head...

Panel 3: At the very heart of everything we're planning to do here lies the simple, uncompromising core belief...

Panel 4: ...We must make a programme that gets bigger ratings than Pop Idol.

Panel 5: The series we're planning will be the most talked about show ever... and it will make an invaluable contribution to human cultural progress....

Panel 6: Genius Search 2002... The quest to find the 21st Century's first artistic genius.

Panel 7: Previously unknown contestants will be invited to apply from all areas of the arts... Then they'll be voted off, week by week, by a viewers' phone poll.

Panel 8: Obviously, a serious programme like this needs heavyweight presenters with impeccable intellectual credentials... Unfortunately, Ant and Dec weren't available so we thought we'd ask you two.

Panel 9: Also, we're relying on your expert inside knowledge of the arts to help us find the right contestants.

Panel 10: Leave it to us, Liz... With our rigorous powers of objective critical judgement, we'll tirelessly scour the entire country for undiscovered talent...

Panel 11: A week later...

Here you go, Liz... Your first three embryonic geniuses...

This young composer, Lucien Mockney-Pseud, from London, is bravely struggling against the incestuous Musical Establishment to gain recognition for his minimalist sequences of sampled fire alarms...

Awight, Uncle Crispin. 'Ow ya doin'?

Clomidia Rashe, also from London, is a conceptual video artist... Her ten-hour slow-mo video pieces of the inside of her own anus during defecation probe to the very fundament of New British Art...

Natasha, darling! Haven't seen you since that opening at dear Hugo's last week.

Sebastian Scrawlle-Badleigh is an up-and-coming London novelist. His unbelievably brave decision to write his debut novel without using any vowels is set to turn literature upside down...

Hi guys! Pops said to tell you that Arts Council cheque's in the post, yah? Thanks for getting me on the show.

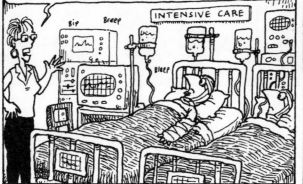
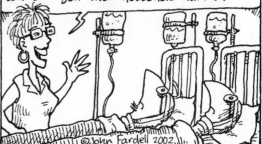

BILLY PUNTER

THE PROSTITUTE-HUNGRY CONFERENCE DELEGATE of GREYFRIARS HOTEL

Have YOUR say...

Ready, Steady, Yawn - Schumacher romping to another predictable victory yesterday.

The Ferrari redwash of this year's Formula One championship has left millions of viewers yawning. And now Grand Prix chiefs are locked in emergency talks in a desperate bid to inject excitement back into F1 before disillusioned fans turn off altogether. We went onto the street to ask what *YOU* would do to bring the thrills back to the world's most glamorous sport.

"...If any team establishes a lead of more than 20 points in the constructors' championship, they should be forced to put women drivers in their cars to allow the other teams to catch up. And if they get 30 points in front they should have Damon Hill."

J Fraser, traffic warden, Crewe

"...F1 bosses should take a leaf out of Starsky & Hutch's book, and require drivers to crash through big piles of cardboard boxes when entering the pit lane. On their way back onto the track they should have to smash through a couple of fruit barrows and force a woman with a pram to leap out of their way."

Dan Rogers, taxi driver, Dundee

"...These days, the pit stops have become dull and predictable. They would be much more exciting if the refuellers weren't allowed within 10 feet of the car and had to use children's supersoakers instead of the heavy safety nozzles they use now. The combination of jets of petrol and white hot engines would certainly liven things up a bit."

P Sweeny, policeman, Letchworth

"...On the starting grid, the dolly birds holding up the number boards should be forced to go topless. No only would this add millions to the viewing figures, it would also save race organisers money on bras."

R Crawley, window cleaner, Bolton

"...F1 bosses should take a leaf out of Keannu Reeves's book. Cars should be fitted with a bomb which is wired up to explode if the car goes below 300mph."

Dan Rogers, taxi driver, Dundee

"...Something has to be done to slow Michael Schumacher down. Just before the race he should be made to eat one square of Ex-Lax chocolate for every point he is ahead in the championship."

J Wilson, housewife, Shropshire

"...They should force Schumacher to drive each race wearing Little out of Little & Large's glasses. I reckon that would slow him down by up to 2 seconds a lap, and give him a really bad headache."

Ray Morris, vicar, Truro

"...If I was Bernie Ecclestone, I'd go home, rub my face in my wife's tits, and then bang her on an enormous pile of crisp £50 notes."

Bob Pavarotti, builder, Sussex

"...If Schumacher is leading by more than 10 seconds when he comes in for a pit stop, Professor Sid Watkins should slit the tendons behind his knees."

Jesus Garcia, student, Hull

"...Half the drivers should go round the track clockwise and half anti-clockwise. This would bring back the good old days when fans enjoyed spectacular fatal crashes and thrilling fireballs in practically every race."

E Beedle, prostitute, Oxford

"...F1 bosses should take a leaf out of Michael Caine's book. On the final lap of each race, the cars should have to drive up a ramp into the back of a specially converted coach. The coach could then swerve off an alpine pass, ending up teetering over a precipice, keeping grand prix fans on the edge of their seats until the next race."

Dan Rogers, taxi driver, Dundee

"...I miss Murray Walker's excitable commentaries. They should replace dreary James Allen with Ian Paisley, and get him to down half a pound of amphetamines before the off."

Umberto Eco, grocer, Rotherham

Miriam
SOLVES YOUR PROBLEMS

Dear Miriam... This morning I went to open a tin of beans for my husband's breakfast. The trouble is, I couldn't find the tin opener anywhere. I am 29 and he is 32. We've had this problem before, but the tin opener has usually turned up after a minute or two. But this time it is different. I've been searching for ten minutes now, and I've reached the point where I'm searching in the places that I've already looked in. My husband has to go to work in twenty minutes. What can I do?

✳ *This is a common problem. Many people your age lose the tin opener from time to time. Just relax, and I'm sure you will find it eventually. In the mean time, it is important to feel positive. Try to focus on the things in your kitchen that you can find, such as serving spoons, teacups or the washing machine. You may also like to send for my leaflet 'Lost Tin Openers' or call my premium rate helpline.*

LETTER OF THE DAY

- -

Dear Miriam... I got in my car the other day and noticed that the fuel gauge was almost on empty. I spoke to my boyfriend about it that night and he said that I was probably running out of petrol.

I am 21 and he is 22 and we have been going out for 6 months. He has suggested that we go to the garage and put a tenner's worth of petrol in, but I'm not sure. My boyfriend thinks I'm just being silly, but it's nearly £2.80 a gallon and I don't want to be rushed into something I may regret. Please help me.

✳ *You are right to be cautious. Weigh up the pros and cons. Putting a tenner's worth of petrol in will cost you £10. On the other hand, if you don't, your car will eventually judder to a halt. But it is your car, and you must do what you feel is right for you. I'm sending you my leaflet 'Does My Car Need Petrol?' which will give you all the advice you need to make your decision.*

- -

Dear Miriam... I've just moved a vase from my dining room, and put it on the corner table in the front room. The trouble is, I don't know whether it goes with those curtains.
I am 48 and my husband is 50. I've asked him what he thought, but he just shrugged and carried on watching the telly. I could put it back where it

was, but then I'd have to move that lamp that my husband's sister Dolly bought us last Christmas, and that goes with the carpet in the dining room. I am at my wits end.

✳ *I've read your letter several times and I simply cannot see the problem. The vase goes lovely with them curtains. Which means that Dolly's lamp can stay where it is. If you are worried in the future, you can call for reassurance on my helpline 'Does that Vase go with them Curtains?'*

Dr. Miriam Stoppard
Premium rate problem lines you can trust

Mnah! Mnah! Does this soup need more salt?
0000 994 387

Which shoes with these trousers? Black or brown?
0000 994 388

Oh, look. What kind of bird is that on the bird table?
0000 994 399

Can you give me a hand with the other end of this wardrobe?
0000 994 390

Calls cost enough to keep Dr. Stoppard in very fancy earrings

---

Justice
WITH
Jacobs
THE FAT SOLICITOR

Bandit at 3 o'clock

Q It's 3 in the morning and I have just woken to find I am being burgled by a man in a balaclava. He has stabbed my husband in the stomach and now he is coming screaming at me with a 12 inch knife. I am 32 and my husband was 33. We have been burgled several

times before, but this is the first time that we have been attacked. I am within reach of a very heavy lamp with a square alabaster base, and wonder if I am within my rights to hit the intruder over the head with it.
Mrs. B, Essex

A *The fat solicitor regrets that he is unable to answer any legal queries, as he is eating a really, really big pie.*

JUST DIAL J FOR JUSTICE
The Fat Solicitor dishes out legal advice on major topics...

NEIGHBOUR TROUBLE?
Gary summarises the 1966 Boundaries Act whilst eating a whole packet of Hob-nobs
0000 994 388

FAULTY GOODS?
Your statutory rights explained whilst Jacobs stuffs two Battenbergs in his big fat face
0000 994 389

Calls cost 50 sausage rolls/min and terminate in the nearest Greggs.

Christobies
Auctioneers and Valuers Ltd
Knightsbridge

Are privileged to announce
a sale of

Chasabilia and Daviana

on **Saturday 10th August 2002**
at the **Salerooms, Knightsbridge, London**
Viewing on **Wednesday, Thursday, Friday, 7th, 8th, 9th**

Sundry lots to include:

Several public house upright Pianofortes, assorted scraggy Beards, a bald Drummer (*sold as seen*), Dr. Marten 'Airwair' shoes by Griggs and Co. (*12 pairs*), a large collection of elasticated Braces, bass Guitars, sundry loopy Snooker equipment (*24 lots*), various collarless shirts, gorblimey trousers (*several pairs*), flat Caps (*2 lots*), 1 silver Disc circa 1978, etc etc.

In all 628 lots, the whole comprising the property of Messrs. *Charles Hodges* and *David Peacock Esq*, late of Margate, England.

Angharad & Reece
Auctioneers
206~208 New Zealand Street, Bloomsbury, London

For Sale By Auction
Monday 12th August 2002
(viewing 9th~11th)

A circa 1930 wood veneer oak buffet Sideboard with thick rectangular moulded top above a central section with drawer and compartments carved with stylised panels and scrolling, the side cupboards quarter veneered, framed by acanthus carved columns with square plinth base raised on large bun feet, and containing 1 crate of Courage mild.
Est. £10~15

A Yoghurt
for the
Rest of My Days

We asked Celebrities, if they could only eat one kind of yoghurt for the rest of their life... which would it be?

No. 103
Robert Powell

Strawberry for me. Yum! Yum!

COLONEL BLIMP
THE SHORT-SIGHTED GIMP

BLUSTERING BOMBADEERS, READERS! I'M OUT FOR SOME HOT SUB DOM ACTION!

WHAT'S THIS? SOMETHING ABOUT SWINGERS, EH?

CHORTLE! MY LUCKS IN HERE!

OHO! I'VE SPOTTED A DOMINATRIX COUPLE! I FANCY A BIT OF THAT!

EXCUSE ME SIR, YOU DON'T MIND IF I TAKE OVER WITH YOUR GOOD LADY WIFE FOR A WHILE DO YOU? I'LL LET YOU WATCH OF COURSE.

SCREAM!

ARF ARF! SCREAM LOUDER YOU NAUGHTY BITCH! NOW SMACK MY ARSE WITH THE BACK OF A HAIRBRUSH AND URINATE INTO MY MOUTH! BARK BARK!!

BOOT!!

...AND STAY OUT!

YAHROO!

OOH, THAT PAINFULL BOOT UP THE RING WAS MARVELLOUS! ACCEPT THIS TENNER, I SHALL BE RECOMMENDING THIS PLACE TO ALL MY FRIENDS!

GALLOPING GUNNERS!

M+S

WHAT HAVE WE HERE? 'S+M'!

BY JOVE! LOOK AT ALL THE DELIGHTFUL WHORES ON DISPLAY! JUST LIKE AMSTERDAM!

I'M GOING TO GET STUCK INTO THAT ONE, MAKE NO MISTAKE!

INSIDE... HELLO MADAM, I WOULD LIKE YOUR BIGGEST BUTT PLUG HAMMERED RIGHT UP MY JACKSIE, AND I'D ALSO LIKE TO BE GAGGED AND STRANGLED UNTIL I NEARLY PASS OUT.

...THAT'D BE SUPER!

OOH, YEAH! YOU FILTHY SLUT! TAKE THIS YOU BITCH, YOU LOVE IT!!

WHACK! WHACK! WHACK!

WHACK!

WHACK!

JUMPING GENERALS!

I DON'T KNOW MY OWN STRENGTH!

ERM, EXCUSE ME SIR...

GASP! IT'S HER PIMP! I BET HE'S GOING TO CUT ME UP GOOD FOR MESSING HIS BEST HO'S FACE!

...I CAN HARDLY WAIT!

ACTUALLY, I WANTED TO THANK YOU. YOUR WINDOW DISPLAY HAS HAD THE PUNTERS FLOCKING BACK TO THE SHOP!

PLEASE ACCEPT A £10 MARKS & SPENCER VOUCHER!

IT'S ALL VERY WELL GIVING ME THIS VOUCHER, BUT WHERE AM I GOING TO FIND A MARKS & SPENCERS? THE WHOLLY INCONSIDERATE WHOREMONGER!

CAPERING COLONELS! LOOKS LIKE I SPOKE TOO SOON!

S+M CLUB

BRUISED MEMBERS ONLY

I'LL SEE IF THEY SELL ANY NICE SHOES!

HELLO! HELLO!? I WOULD LIKE TO BE FITTED FOR A PAIR OF BROGUES! HELLO?

BLUBBERING BABBOONS! THIS PLACE IS DISGRACEFUL!

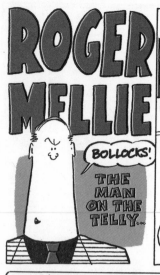

JESUS! OKAY, ROGER, WAIT THERE! I'LL COME STRAIGHT OVER WITH THE FTV LAWYER...

SMASHIN', TOM...

...OH, AND CAN YOU GET ONE OF YOUR KIDS TO PISS INTO A BOTTLE AND SNEAK THAT IN...

...ONLY THEY'LL WANT A SAMPLE BEFORE THEY'LL LET ME GO.

A WEEK LATER AT FULCHESTER COURT...

THE CROWN VERSUS ROGER MELLIE...FINAL CALL FOR ROGER MELLIE, COURT Nº 3

COURT Nº 3

WHERE THE HELL IS HE? HIS TRIAL WAS DUE TO START HALF AN HOUR AGO!

SORRY I'M LATE, TOM. I STOPPED OFF AT THE THREE HORSESHOES FOR A SWIFT COUPLE...

...ENDED UP HAVING ABOUT EIGHT OR NINE. Y'KNOW HOW IT IS...

...AND THEN I COULDN'T FIND ANYWHERE TO PARK NEAR THE COURT

COURT Nº 3

WELL, YOU'RE FOR IT THIS TIME, ROGER, YOU'LL LOSE YOUR LICENCE FOR SURE!

DON'T WORRY, TOM, I'M A PRO... GOT A LITTLE SPEECH READY...

THERE WON'T BE A DRY EYE IN THE HOUSE

5 MINS LATER...

PRISONER AT THE BAR... YOU HAVE BEEN FOUND GUILTY OF BEING DRUNK IN CHARGE OF A MOTOR VEHICLE. DO YOU HAVE ANYTHING TO SAY BEFORE I PASS SENTENCE

YES, YOUR HONOUR

... I WOULD LIKE TO REQUEST THAT YOU DO NOT TAKE AWAY MY LICENCE. I ASK THIS NOT FOR MYSELF...

...BUT FOR THE MANY CHARITIES WHO I DO SO MUCH WORK FOR. IT IS THESE WHO WOULD SUFFER IF I COULD NOT DRIVE TO THEIR FUNCTIONS...

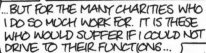

...CHARITIES SUCH AS "THE JUDGES' BENEVOLENT FUND", "JUDGE CONCERN", "THE ROYAL SOCIETY FOR THE PREVENTION OF CRUELTY TO JUDGES" AND MANY MORE...

...IT IS THESE WHO WOULD SUFFER THE PUNISHMENT, YOUR HONOUR.

SHORTLY...

MR. MELLIE, MR. MELLIE... A £20 FINE AND NO LOSS OF LICENCE...

...ARE YOU PLEASED WITH THE SENTENCE?

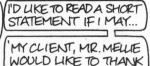

I'D LIKE TO READ A SHORT STATEMENT IF I MAY...

MY CLIENT, MR. MELLIE WOULD LIKE TO THANK THE PUBLIC FOR THEIR SUPPORT DURING THIS DIFFICULT TIME...

BBC

HE IS NATURALLY RELIEVED THAT IT IS ALL OVER AND HE CAN PUT THE EPISODE BEHIND HIM AND LOOK TO THE FUTURE...

MY CLIENT HAS NO MORE TO ADD AT THIS MOMENT...

...THANK YOU.

SO, MR. MELLIE... ARE YOU GOING HOME TO YOUR FAMILY NOW?

NO, I'M JUST HAVING A QUICK FAG BREAK...

...I'M BACK ON IN TEN MINUTES WITH MY BROTHER ON SOME TV QUIZ FRAUD CONSPIRACY...

CARLTON T.V. VERSUS ROGER MELLIE ...COURT Nº 6

...THEN I'VE GOT A SHOPLIFTING AT ELEVEN AND A POSSESSION OF AN ILLEGALLY MODIFIED FIREARM AT HALF PAST...

HI, TOM. WHAT TIME'S KICK OFF?

...AND I'M UP FOR DROWNING SOME BLOKE IN A SWIMMING POOL THIS AFTERNOON.

147

Letterbocks

★★Star Letter★★

Every time I visit the hairdressers, the gorgeous blonde girl who cuts my hair thoughtfully gives me a tissue when she has finished. Obviously, she knows I'm going straight home to have a wank over her. The last time I went, however, she wasn't there and a bloke with a moustache cut my hair instead. Imagine my disgust when he also gave me a tissue. I don't think I'll be going back there again.

Mick Sterbs, Coventry

Letterbocks
Viz Comic
P.O.Box 1PT
Newcastle NE99 1PT

E-mail
letters@viz.co.uk

This Harry Potter film is all well and good, but I can't help thinking it's all a bit far fetched. I mean, how many schools do you know where there's a ginger kid with two mates?

Tim Woods
e-mail

The press has been complaining that Michael Jackson was cruel to put a towel over his baby's head before dangling it off a fourth floor balcony. I think he deserves a round of applause. If the tot had been able to see how far he could fall, he would have been terrified. Jacko showed responsibility and fatherly kindness by covering his head before pulling his cheeky stunt.

Ron Hubbard
Cardiff

Has anyone lost a flat, orange cat and some flies in the car park of Llantrisant Tescos? I found them yesterday and wonder if there is a reward.

Kris
Pontyclun

Isn't talking behind someone's back actually talking in front of them?

Ed Short
e-mail

I've just taken my grandson to the London Dungeons to where we greatly enjoyed the Jack the Ripper Experience. Perhaps when he's my age, he will take his own grandchildren to see the Peter Sutcliffe Experience.

J. Farmer
London

First 1977, now 2002. Has anyone else noticed that every time the Queen has a jubilee, the firemen go on strike? I for one will be investing in a fire extinguisher and an asbestos blanket well in time for 2012.

Jim O'Reilly
e-mail

Your story about Albert Tatlock's 7 years of bad luck (issue 120) says that in 1983, he put a £5 each way bet on the Grand National, and his horse came in 4th. But each way bets in the National pay out for 4th place; therefore this was *good* luck. Might I suggest that you pay someone to check for such oversights before publication? I realise that this would probably mean a rise in the cover price to something like £3 or £4 per issue, but I for one would be absolutely delighted to pay the price.

Gladys Stovies
e-mail

If so many people are falling ill through chefs not washing their hands after using the toilet, then how come I never get ill after rimming our lass?

Mick
Sheffield

I am the landord of a pub in Bodmin, and it's like the Island of Dr Moreau in here. Never mind, they still pay the outrageous prices I charge for my pissy beer. Cunts.

Coxy
Bodmin

If spare ribs are spare, how come my local chinese restaurant charages a fortune for them?

Ching Woo
Chingford

My old mum always used to swear by something she called 'washing up liquid'. It was a gooey, funny smelling concoction apparently for cleaning kitchenware, and even now I know some people who still use it. With this in mind, might I suggest that staff in in-store 'restaurants' at Tesco, Sainsbury, Safeway and Asda give it a try on thier sodding cutlery.

Doug Richardson
Wolverhampton

I am training to be a teacher and use my placements as an excuse to play footie in the playground and be the best. I was wondering, do any other Viz readers take a similarly light-hearted approach to what is essentially a vital profession? For example firemen who mess about on the pole.

Johnson Wilmot
Netherby

If Barry Chuckle off The Chuckle Brothers (the short, bandy-legged one) is reading this, the Morris Ital you sold me in 1983 had a fucked clutch. Now you've got a bit of money in your pocket from your hilarious shows, I think it's only fair you give me the 30 quid it cost to get fixed.

Oz 'Psycho' Barritz
e-mail

How good it is to see McDonalds taking the message of the Anti-Globalisation Lobby to heart. On a recent vist to their Champs-Elysees branch in Paris, I found the staff inattentive, the food massively overpriced and the toilets overflowing with raw effluent. If only other multi-nationals would follow this example of respecting local tradition and custom.

Miller
France

I am only just getting over the sad demise of the TV producer Desmond Wilcox. I always hoped that he would outlive his wife Esther Rantzen by many years.

Hedgepig
e-mail

DROWSY WASPS RUINED THE CIRCUS

148

Regarding the issue of whether Gibraltar should join Spain or remain part of Britain, if I lived there I would opt to join with Spain. Just think how much better the weather would be.

**Philip Welton
Stoke on Trent**

You'd think that after 23 years, some of these so called 'Children in Need' might have grown up like the rest of us.

**Moose
Valley Park**

Has anyone else noticed the troubling facial resemblance between kiddies TV presenter Cat Deeley and the 1970s style inflatable "Sexy Doreen" doll, the one with 3 willing holes and real hair?

**Ant & Dec aged 9
e-mail**

I think the firefighters should work for free because it is very exciting to run into burning buildings and much warmer for them than all us folk who have to stand around in the cold watching.

**S Duncan
Westminster**

I'm on holiday in Spain and I've just been watching some bullfighting on the telly. What a load of rubbish. I'd like to see those matadors face a real predator (like a tiger), not a herbivore. Now that would be a show.

**Anthony E Miller
Madrid**

My middle name is Kenelm, which is Anglo Saxon for 'Bold Helmet'. Can any of your readers beat that?

**Matthew Hunter
e-mail**

Only the other day I came home from work and found a mixture of men's and women's clothing scattered about my lounge. Imagine my surprise when I discovered my boyfriend upstairs, naked in our bed

having sex with my best friend. I hit the roof. However, he soon cleared it all up by explaining that 'It was only a bit of fun, and it meant nothing'. How foolish I felt for making such a fuss.

**Alicia Trump
North Berkshire**

Can anyone tell me how to spell Basil Brush's laugh? The end bit is easy; it's the cackle before that is proving a little tricky.

Is it "erha-yah-ha-hah-hayh-ya, BOOM! BOOM!'" or what? I am willing to swap the spelling of a bum smack, both thin and flabby.

**Darren Anderson,
Thornton Cleveleys**

Don't believe everything people tell you. A friend of mine told me that you don't have to iron

shirts if you hang them over a radiator whilst wet, so I followed his advice. Imagine my anger when they all got chewed up in the fan belt.

**Grant B Warner
New Maldon**

I think the best way for John Leslie to prove his innocence is for him to spend a week in the Big Brother house with All Saints whilst under the influence of viagra and powdered rhino horns. Whilst we are on the subject, I have recently compiled a list of the 5 women I would most like to attack. They are as follows:

1. Shania Twain
2. Winona Ryder
3. Scary Spice
4. Angelina Jolie
5. Carol Vorderman

**Hapag Lloyd
Runcorn**

Abdul

YOUR PROBLEMS ANSWERED BY THE LORD OF HARPOLE

Dear Abdul... My wife and I have been married for 20 years and we have three lovely | **LETTER OF THE DAY** |

children. Like all couples we have the usual ups and downs, but I always thought our marriage was strong enough to see us through. However, I recently met a younger woman at work. I don't know how it happened, but we fell in love and started an affair. I still love my wife, and sex with her is nice, but it is all very routine. This younger woman gives me such a thrill in bed. Now she's pregnant and I've told her I'm going to leave my wife and kids to move in with her.

I'm dreading telling my wife as I feel she will be distraught, but it is only fair that I tell her. I've decided to take her out for a curry to break the news, but I can't find anywhere in the centre of Newcastle offering a wide range of traditional indian meals in convivial surroundings and at reasonable prices.
Please help me, Abdul. This is tearing me apart.

Frank Jumpleads, Gateshead
(Name & address withheld by request)

Abdul says... Don't worry, Frank. Sometimes it must feel as if you're the only person in the world with this problem. But believe you me, the Rupali Restaurant, Bigg Market, Newcastle upon Tyne is full of men in your predicament.

You'll always find a warm welcome from me, a proper lord, and we boast the largest menu in the North East. Bring your wife along any evening and find a nice quiet corner. Buy her a delicious curry and tell her you're leaving her while she's eating it. With any luck, she'll be too upset to eat a pudding, making your evening even better value!

Dr. Abdul Latif, Lord of Harpole	**The Advice Lines you can trust**	
Irritable murg thaal kali syndrome **0000 666 787**	Premature bhindi bhaji with raita **0000 666 790**	*The Rupali ~ Where the curries sting your ring, not your pocket*
Tikka Bhuna with erectile problems **0000 666 788**	My son may be king prawn masala **0000 666 791**	
My aloo on puri fails to satisfy my man **0000 666 789**	Worried about size of my keema naan **0000 666 792**	

Calls cost from 60p per minute (naurath pullao 30p extra) & terminate at the Rupali Restaurant, Bigg Market, Newcastle upon Tyne.

TOP TIPS

A SERIES of copycat farts following someone else's admisssion of guilt can compound the misery of the perpetrator, whilst simultaneously giving your bowels the clean out you've always dreamed of.

**Dave Smith
Hartlepool**

PEOPLE called Steven. Save time by calling yourself Steve.

**Name lost
Sorry**

KEEP wives and girlfriends on their toes by telling them they are the fattest girl you have ever been out with.

**Hapag Lloyd
Runcorn**

SPECTACLE wearers. Rid yourself of cumbersome spectacles by getting a pair of contact lenses. To stop them falling out from time to time, take a length of brass wire, create a figure-8 shape and loop it around the outer rim of each contact lens. For added security, leave an extra length of wire protruding each side that can be used to hold the frame in place by hooking it round your ears.

**Stewart
Cowley**

TAX PAYERS. Beat the taxman by only ever doing a job for three months, then resigning and signing on for the next three months. That way, you get back the tax you paid while you were working.

**H.R.
e-mail**

DRUG dealers. Turn your users into fun aquariums by cutting your gear with sea monkeys.

**Pandeviant
e-mail**

RESIDENTS of Stevenage. Save money for Christmas by only buying enough fireworks for bonfire night, instead of enough to last from Halloween till November the fucking 10th.

**Brian
Stevenage**

FARMERS. Get up an hour later in winter, or buy a torch so the rest of us don't have to fart around adjusting clocks, watches and videos twice a year.

**Victorio Angel
e-mail**

GENTS. When coming out of a florists, always punch the first person that you see to ensure that no one thinks you are gay.

**Guy A Bell
Plymouth**

SHOE Express customers. Throw your purchases away and wear the boxes instead. They'll be harder-wearing, more stylish and better fitting.

**Steph Jackson
Newcastle**

PEOPLE called Steve. Save time by calling yourself Ste, (pronounced 'Stee').

**Name lost
Sorry**

CONTESTANTS on Bullseye. Give your address as the Moon, that way, if you lose, your 'bus fare home' will amount to several million pounds.

**Steve Chiltern
e-mail**

SIT on your cock till it goes numb. Hey presto! It's just like wanking off somebody else.

**Matt
e-mail**

AS THE GERMAN TOOK CONTROL OF THE DESPATCH RIDER'S BIKE, BARON VON RICHTHOFEN EXPLAINED THE PLOT.

HA! VEN ZE FAKE LETTERS ARE PUT UP ZE CHIMNEY, ZE BRITISH TROOPS VILL GET ZE SOCKS, ZE HANKIES, ZE AFTERSHAVE UNT ZE WH SCHMIDT TOKENS...

...ZEY VILL BE SO DISAPPOINTED, ZEY VILL LOSE ZE VILL TO VIN VORLD VOR VUN!

IN NO TIME AT ALL, THE DOPPELGANGER ARRIVED AT THE BRITISH HQ...

...AND HIS PERFECT ENGLISH AROUSED NO SUSPICIONS AT THE GATE.

WOTCHER, COCK! WOT 'AVE YOU GOT THERE THEN?

GAW! IT'S THE LETTERS FOR SANTA, OLD CHAP!

LAVERLY! BRING 'EM IN. THE FIELD MARSHALL IS WAITING, ME OLD CHINA PLATE.

LETTERS FOR SANTA, SIR

SPLENDID, SPLENDID! GOOD SHOW!

TOP HOLE, MY MAN. I'LL GET THESE BLIGHTERS UP THE CHIMNEY. YOU GET YOURSELF A NICE CUP OF TEA, WHAT?

YES, SIR.

SO...

I SAY!

WHAT THE?!...

GREAT SCOTT! HE PUSHED IN... HE PUSHED RIGHT TO THE FRONT!!

GET DOWN, EVERYONE! HE'S A BALLY BOSCH!!

TAKE THAT, YOU SQUAREHEAD!

AIIEEE!!

WHAT'S GOING ON?

LOOK AT THESE GIFT REQUESTS. SOAP ON A ROPE... BATH SALTS... NOVELTY TIES... AN ANDY CAPP OMNIBUS...

THESE LETTERS ARE FAKES!

...AND ME BACK BODY'S NOT BEEN RIGHT FOR YEARS. ME LAST SOLID STOOL WAS AT THE JUBILEE STREET PARTY.

HMM...

SILVER JUBILEE, THAT IS.

...SILVER, YES.

IT WAS DOLLY'S POTTED TONGUE SANDWICHES THAT DID IT. LEFT THEM ON THE FORMICA UNIT, SHE DID, AND I'VE BEEN DOING LOOSE DUTIES EVER SINCE.

...SINCE, YES.

AND EVEN IF I DO DO A SOLID ONE, IT'S JUST A HANDFUL OF RABBIT TODS.

AND THEY FLOAT AS WELL

FLOAT.

THEY DO. THEY FLOAT.

SEVEN O'CLOCK EVERY MORNING. SPASMS IN ME ANUS, IT IS. **SPASMS** LIKE A BIG HAND SQUEEZING ME RECTUM FROM THE INSIDE.

I SEE...

YOU DON'T KNOW WHAT IT'S LIKE.

NOW CISSIE'S THE OPPOSITE. SHE'S GOT THE BUGS IN HER BOWEL AND SHE'S BACKED UP TO THE MIDDLE OF NEXT WEEK.

...NEXT WEEK, YES.

HMMM.

IT'S LIKE CONCRETE.

I SPEND A LOT OF TIME TRYING, DON'T I ADA. BUT IF I DO BRING DOWN A FEESHUS, I ALWAYS BLEED.

AND SHE'S GOT TO BE CAREFUL...

...BECAUSE SHE HAD A PROLAPSE FOUR YEARS AGO AT THE BINGO.

SHE JUST NEEDED LEGS ELEVEN FOR ALL FOUR CORNERS AND IT WOULDN'T COME UP. WELL, THE STRESS WAS TOO MUCH, AND WHEN MAGGIE'S DEN COME UP THE WHOLE BOWEL BROKE AWAY AND COME OUT.

LIKE EIGHTEEN INCH OF INNER TUBE, IT WAS. THE MAN FROM THE TOP RANK HAD TO BURN ME CHAIR.

I MEAN, SHE SHOULDN'T HAVE GONE, SHOULD SHE. SHE'S HAD A WEEPING FISTULA AS LONG AS I'VE KNOWN HER, HAVEN'T YOU, CISSIE?

OOH, I'VE SUFFERED.

YES... WELL...

OOH, SHE'S SUFFERED WITH HER SPHINCTERS, SHE HAS. SHE'S A MARTYR TO HER BACK PASSAGE.

A MARTYR.

ERM... RIGHT...

STILL. AT LEAST IT TAKES ME MIND OFF ME SEPTIC VAGINA.

EEH. DON'T GET ME STARTED ON HER SEPTIC VAGINA. THE WHOLE WOMB'S COME ADRIFT FROM THE UTERUS.

ERM...

REMEMBER, CISSIE? IT ALL FELL OUT AT THAT JUMBLE SALE. YOU KNOW, THE ONE WHERE YOU GOT THAT FAWN BARATHEA OVERCOAT FOR TWENTY PEE.

...TWENTY PEE, YES.

RIGHT, RIGHT. WELL, IF I CAN JUST STOP YOU THERE FOR A SECOND, LADIES...

I'M PLEASED TO TELL YOU, YOU'VE BOTH GOT THE JOB...

...WELCOME TO B & Q!

NEXT DAY...

B&Q SUPERSTORE

DRILLS & TOOLS

...COME TO THINK OF IT, IT WERE TAUPE, NOT FAWN, CISSIE.

NO. IT WEREN'T TAUPE, ADA.

TAUPE'S MORE BEIGE THAN FAWN. THOUGH I HAVE GOT A TAUPE ONE, BUT IT'S MORE OF A NUDE BEIGE THAN A TAUPE. IT COULD PASS FOR CHAMPAGNE.

OOH, THAT SOUNDS NICE...

EXCUSE ME, DOES THIS DRILL HAVE VARIABLE SPEED, SO I CAN USE IT AS AN ELECTRIC SCREWDRIVER?

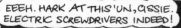

EEEH. HARK AT THIS 'UN, CISSIE. ELECTRIC SCREWDRIVERS INDEED!

...INDEED! YES!

THERE WAS NO ELECTRIC SCREWDRIVERS IN OUR DAY.

NO, YES.

...AND NO BANANAS, NEITHER.

...BANANAS, YES, NEITHER, NO.

OR BROWN EGGS.

...OOH, EGGS, YES.

YOU HAD A HAMMER AND YOU WERE GRATEFUL.

YOU DID, AND YOU WERE, YES.

AND THERE WAS NO STOCKINGS NEITHER. YOU COULDN'T GET 'EM. YOU HAD TO DRAW 'EM ON YOUR LEGS WITH BISTO...

DRAW 'EM, YES.

WITH BISTO

...OR SUCK OFF A YANK.

THAT'S RIGHT, YES...

...**AND** SWALLOW.

EEH. HAPPY TIMES...

...DO YOU REMEMBER **DIPHTHERIA**, CISSIE?

EEH. THEM WERE THE DAYS. I LOST EIGHT SISTERS AND ALL OF ME BROTHERS WITH IT.

EEH. FANCY.

DEAD IN THE BED NEXT TO ME, THEY WERE.

WHAT DID YOU DO?

I JUST GOT ON WITH IT.

WELL, YOU HAD TO IN THEM DAYS, DIDN'T YOU.

YOU DID. YOU HAD TO.

TIMBER

EEH. HAPPY TIMES.

...TIMES, YES.

I REMEMBER WHEN ALL THIS WAS TREES.

2 HOURS LATER... ...WOULD ADA AND CISSIE MAKE THEIR WAY TO THE CUSTOMER SERVICE POINT, PLEASE. CUSTOMER WAITING.

WILL TO LIVE

CRASH!

ARE WE THERE YET, ADA?

NEXT DAY... I THINK YOU KNOW WHY I'VE CALLED YOU IN, LADIES. TO BE FRANK, IT IS CLEAR TO ME NOW THAT YOU ARE A PAIR OF UTTER INCOMPETENTS WHO DON'T KNOW YOUR ARSES FROM YOUR ELBOWS.

IN SHORT, TWO PEOPLE LESS SUITED THAN YOURSELVES TO HOLDING DOWN JOBS DEALING WITH THE PUBLIC IN A LARGE RETAIL OUTLET WOULD BE HARD TO IMAGINE.

YOU LEAVE ME WITH NO OPTION...

B&Q EMPLOYEES OF THE MONTH

A. BRADY

un-faithful SHEP

WINK

Paul Palmer

ER...

YOU'RE HOME EARLY, AREN'T YOU?

YES! I THOUGHT WE COULD GO WALKIES!!

OH...ER... NOT TODAY, THANKS! I'M...ER...THAT IS... I'VE GOT A SORE LEG!

AGAIN!?!

HANG-ON-A-MINUTE!

ALRIGHT! WHERE IS HE?

WHAT!?!

C'MON! I KNOW YOU'RE UP TO SOMETHING!!

A-HA!

COME ON OUT! I KNOW YOU'RE HIDING SOMEWHERE!

HOW-COULD-YOU!?!

SHAME!

BLUSH!

IT WAS JUST TO THE PARK AND BACK! IT DIDN'T MEAN ANYTHING!

I JUST DID MY BUSINESS AND CAME STRAIGHT HOME!

MAN'S BEST FRIEND! PAH!!

It's STAR-M

IT'S THE END of the world as we know it. So sang REM in their 1991 pop hit. But little did they know that on February 12 2060, that song will *come true* when meteorite *NT7 crashes to earth.*

The lump of space rock, the size of a *Nationwide League Division 2 football stadium*, is on a collision course with earth traveling at speeds up to and in excess of **25,000 mph** - that's as fast as *200 Formula 1 cars*. When it hits the earth, it will leave a crater the size of *several Wembley Stadiums*, and devastate an area half the size of Wales *many times over.*

The initial impact will create a tidal wave the height of the *post office tower* with *two double decker buses on top*, which will wash over the earth at the speed of *three Concordes* and with the destructive power of *enough Hiroshima bombs to fill the Centre Court at Wimbledon.*

rain

Lumps of white hot molten rock, some the the size of a cricket ball, others the size of a *fridge,* will rain down causing death and destruction. And all this will happen in less time from now than the age of a plumber taking early retirement - *that's less than three Gareth Gates's lives laid end to end.*

Predictions say 99% of life on earth will be destroyed, and it's a conclusion which has sent the showbusiness world into shock. For if the boffins' worst fears prove correct, the impact of NT7 will kill off many of our favourite stars.

heart

"The impact of a huge meteor could spell disaster for celebrities from light entertainment, the soaps and the pop world," warned astrophysicist Professor Les Kellett of Great Yarmouth University.

loans

"Even in the unlikely event that a star survived the initial asteroid strike and global firestorm, the subsequent 10-year nuclear winter and worldwide ice age would devastate the lucrative summer season circuit on which so many of our stars depend.

helmet

"Acts such as the Chuckle Brothers, Joe Pasquale and Stu 'I could crush a grape' Francis, could be hit particularly hard by such an apocalypse, especially if the end of the world also leads to a downturn in pantomime bookings."

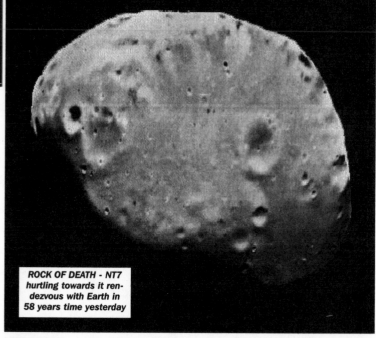

ROCK OF DEATH - NT7 hurtling towards it rendezvous with Earth in 58 years time yesterday

One celebrity who isn't worried about surviving the impact of NT7 is roly poly outdoors expert Ray Mears.

The 35-year-old machete enthusiast has survived some of the most extreme conditions on earth, from the Arctic to the Sahara desert. He told us: "After the end of the world, my survival skills will be more valuable than ever." And he had these tips for any stars wishing to join him in the post-apocalyptic wilderness.

- *Stock up on tinned food now while you have the chance. Make sure you have enough meat, vegetables and fruit to last you for the rest of your life.*

- *Don't forget a tin-opener. Without it, you're dead.*

- *So you've eaten your food. How are you going to wash the pans? There won't be any washing-up liquid after the end of the world, so you'll have to make your own out of shampoo - but remember to rinse thoroughly.*

- *After the holocaust there'll be no scouring pads, so removing dried-on foods such as scrambled eggs from those pans could prove tricky. If leaving them to soak overnight doesn't work, try rubbing them with a hedgehog.*

- *So you've washed your pans - how are you going to dry them? You can't leave them in the sun, the atmosphere is choked with billions of tons of radio-active dust, and all your tea-towels were swept away in the tsunami which followed the initial impact. No problem. A bed sheet can provide several perfectly serviceable tea-towels if it is cut into oblongs and hemmed on an overlocking sewing machine.*

20 MINUTES....to DOOM!

NT7 WILL STRIKE our planet at 7.44pm on February 12th 2060. However, there will only be 20 minutes warning before it lands. We asked the stars what *they* would be getting up to during their last 1200 seconds on earth.

"I'm not worried about the end of the world," said slightly sinister former Swap Shop presenter **Noel Edmonds**. *"I'm building a huge diamond dome over my enormous private estate at Crinkley Bottom. Diamond is the hardest substance in the universe, so me and my money and helicopters will be all safe.*

I'll spend the world's last 20 minutes just watching everybody panic outside my dome."

"I know exactly what I'll do," said zany ex-famous person **H** who used to be out of Steps. *"I'll write, record and release an upbeat pop single that's* all about Armageddon and how people shouldn't worry about it. Then I'd give a percentage of the money to children's charities."*

Staggeringly bad film director **Michael Winner** wasn't worrying either. *"I'll sit down and have a glass of wine,"* he told us. *"Then I'll watch all the good bits from all the films I've made over the last 40 years. Then I'll watch them again. Then I'll make a cup of tea. Then I'll hard boil an ostrich egg. Then I'll just wait,"* the fat cunt added.

Seaside town ready for Tsunami
-"Bring it on!"
says Lord Mayor

Blackpool is prepared for anything the universe can throw at it, said Lord Mayor councillor Ivan Taylor yesterday. And he had this message for doomsday meteor NT7: "We're ready for you. Come and have a go if you think you're hard enough!"

With two thirds of the planet covered by water, the chances are high that the errant asteroid will hit the sea. And if it does, scientists fear it could trigger a **tsunami** - a *two thousand foot tidal wave* which will travel round the world at supersonic speeds, destroying everything in its path.

civic

But at a meeting of Blackpool council last week, civic dignitaries drew up a six-point plan to ensure that even after the end of the world it will be business as usual for the popular Lancashire resort. "Our town has always been known as the north-west's premiere fun capital," said councillor Taylor. "We're certainly not going to let this bit of Blackpool rock disrupt anybody's holiday," he quipped.

goldwing

And he went on to outline the six-point plan which aims to prevent the half mile high wall of water dampening anybody's holiday spirits.

• *The illuminations and flower clock will be turned off at the mains to prevent short-circuiting when the tsunami engulfs the Golden Mile.*

• *People living along the seafront will be evacuated to nearby Lytham St Annes on a fleet of trams and buses until the danger has passed.*

• *Rubbish collections will be suspended on the day of the tsunami. Binmen will work the following Sunday to catch up. In the event of the day after the tsunami striking being a Bank Holiday, refuse collections may take two weeks to get back on schedule. Residents are asked to be patient during this period.*

• *The Piers will be closed to everyone except essential personnel for reasons of public safety while the tsunami strikes.*

• *The times for the the penguin parade and chimps' tea party may be subject to late change. Visitors are asked to contact Blackpool zoo before noon on the day of the meteor impact for up to date details.*

• *Ladies from the Blackpool, Fleetwood and Lytham Women's Institute will distribute cups of hot tea and coffee during the mopping-up operation.*

Councillor Taylor, his wife the lady Mayoress, and various other local dignitaries intend to co-ordinate emergency proceedings from the top of Blackpool tower. He said: "Make no mistake, This town is ready for Armageddon. We have even been to Tandy and bought some walkie talkies."

Glass Sales to Break Records in 2060 ~ report

The catastrophic impact of meteor NT7 will be bad news for all life on earth, but good news for Britain's glaziers, according to Glass & Glaziers Monthly, the glazing industry's leading trade magazine.

"We're looking forward to smashing profits, and it's all thanks to the end of the world," laughed Paul Frasier, boss of the Professional Glaziers' Association.

giant

"I doubt there'll be a window in the country that won't get put through when this giant flaming ball of doom hits the earth, and they're all going to need replacing. The public will be putty in our hands." But glass watchdog organisation OffGlaze sounded a note of caution.

kendo

"We'll be watching out for overcharging in the immediate aftermath of the apocalypse, and coming down hard on any profiteering glaziers," warned Glazing Tsar Keith Hellawell. "The public can rest assured that whatever other worries they have regarding Armageddon, I'll be working to keep glass prices pegged at a sensible level."

"Don't worry ~ It's not the end of the world," says Sting

❝ I used to sing about walking on the moon, so I know more than most people about meteorites. I also know a bit about saving the planet. You may remember me doing it a few years ago, when I took that plate lipped man onto the Wogan show.

To know how to stop a meteorite, you first have to know a bit about what they're made of. Here's a cutaway section, showing all the different layers.

The outside of a meteorite is called the **surface**. It is made of **craters**. Beneath the surface lies the inside of the meteorite, like an onion it is made of several different layers: **rock**, **stone**, **meteorite**, and the central **core**.

Now we know everything about a meteorite, but how are we going to prevent one ending the world? I've thought of *three* plans to stop NT7 in its tracks.

1 *Explode it.* The Americans could send an atom bomb which would blow it into billions of sand-sized pieces of rock. These would rain harmlessly down onto our atmosphere as shooting stars, creating the world's most spectacular firework display. We could sell tickets to watch, and send the money to the people of the Amazonian rain forests, so they could buy new trees and more plates for their bottom lips.

2 *Move the earth* out its path. It may sound ridiculous, but with 60 years' notice, I reckon there's plenty of time for scientists to build an enormous fan on the moon which could blow the earth out of harm's way like a giant balloon, allowing NT7 to cruise safely by.

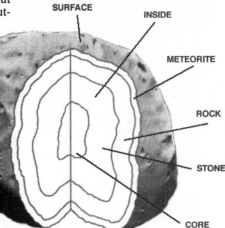

Top Pop Star and ex-school teacher Sting outlines his plans to save the planet.

3 *Deflect the meteorite* into a different orbit. An enormous cricket bat 200 miles long could be sent into space along with West Indian cricket ace Brian Lara. In the zero gravity vacuum of outer space, it would weigh the same as a normal earthbound cricket bat. Space-suited Brian could effortlessly hit NT7 for six, right out of the Milky Way, or even skillfully nick it to Jupiter or Saturn. Making such a huge bat would, however, seriously deplete the world's willow forests, but it would be a price well worth paying to save the planet.

Having now saved the world twice, I don't want any thanks. Just something simple would do, like renaming Earth 'The planet Sting' in my honour. **❞**

THE ADVENTURES OF BEN ELTON

I'VE GOT MY OLD MATE LENNY HENRY ROUND FOR TEA

WE'LL HAVE A NICE CHINWAG ABOUT THE OLD COMIC RELIEF DAYS

SO HOW'S YOUR DIFFERENTLY-PROPORTIONED WIFE, LENNY? NOT THAT SHE'S "YOURS" IN THE POSSESSIVE SENSE, OF COURSE

WOMEN AREN'T CHATTELS TO BE OWNED BY MEN, YES INDEED, MY NAME'S BEN ELTON LADIES AND GENTLEMEN.

DING-DONG

HUNH?

WHO'S AT THE DOOR?

NICK-NICK! EVENIN' ALL!

CRIKEY!

I FORGOT I'D INVITED MY NEW MATE JIM DAVIDSON FOR TEA, AS WELL

JIM WON'T BE HAPPY HAVING TEA WITH A BLACK LEFTIE

IT'LL OFFEND HIS TRADITIONAL PATRIOTIC SENSIBILITIES

QUICK LENNY — WE'LL DISGUISE YOU WITH SOME FLOUR, A CROWN AND A PAIR OF BIG FALSE EARS

RIGHTO BEN

COME IN, JIM — I WAS JUST HAVING TEA WITH PRINCE CHARLES HERE

NICK-NICK. RULE BRITANNIA

YIKES — THE FLOUR IS TICKLING MY NOSE..

AA-A-ACHOO!

GULP!

ERM... HERE, JIM

SOME LOVELY UNION JACK PANTS FOR YOU TO LOOK AT

NICK-NICK! BOO-HOO! THESE PANTS MAKE ME SO PROUD TO BE BRITISH

THAT'LL KEEP HIM OCCUPIED FOR A MOMENT

THIS LARGE STUFFED FISH'S HEAD AND AN OLD MOP WILL DISGUISE YOUR BLACKNESS, LENNY

SNIVEL, WHIMPER, LAND OF HOPE AND GLORY, NICK-NICK

>AHEM< LOOK, JIM — ANDREW LLOYD WEBBER, THE POSH RIGHT-WING TUNE-SCRUMPER HAS POPPED IN FOR TEA, NOW

HE'S A LORD, Y'KNOW

YOWP!

?

A CAT IS AFTER THE FISH'S HEAD

WHY NOT TAKE A CLOSER LOOK AT THE UNION JACK PANTS, JIM?

CRUMBS — WHAT'LL I DO NOW?

BIOLOGICAL GERM RESEARCH LAB

OHO!

CAREFUL WITH THAT JAR OF "MICHAEL-JACKSON-TURNING-WHITE-DISEASE" GERMS WHICH I'VE ISOLATED

A COUPLE OF DROPS OF THIS'LL TURN LENNY WHITE ENOUGH TO PASS FOR STAN BOARDMAN

NAB

WOW!

I'VE TRIPPED!

PING

OH GOSH!

THE "MICHAEL-JACKSON-TURNING-WHITE-DISEASE" GERMS HAVE ACTED ON JIM IN REVERSE!

NICK-NICK! GRR! UNDERMINE MY SENSE OF IDENTITY, WOULD YOU?

POOR OLD BEN! LOOKS LIKE HE'S GOT INTO JIM DAVIDSON'S BLACK BOOKS!